IMAGES
of America

BUTLER COUNTY

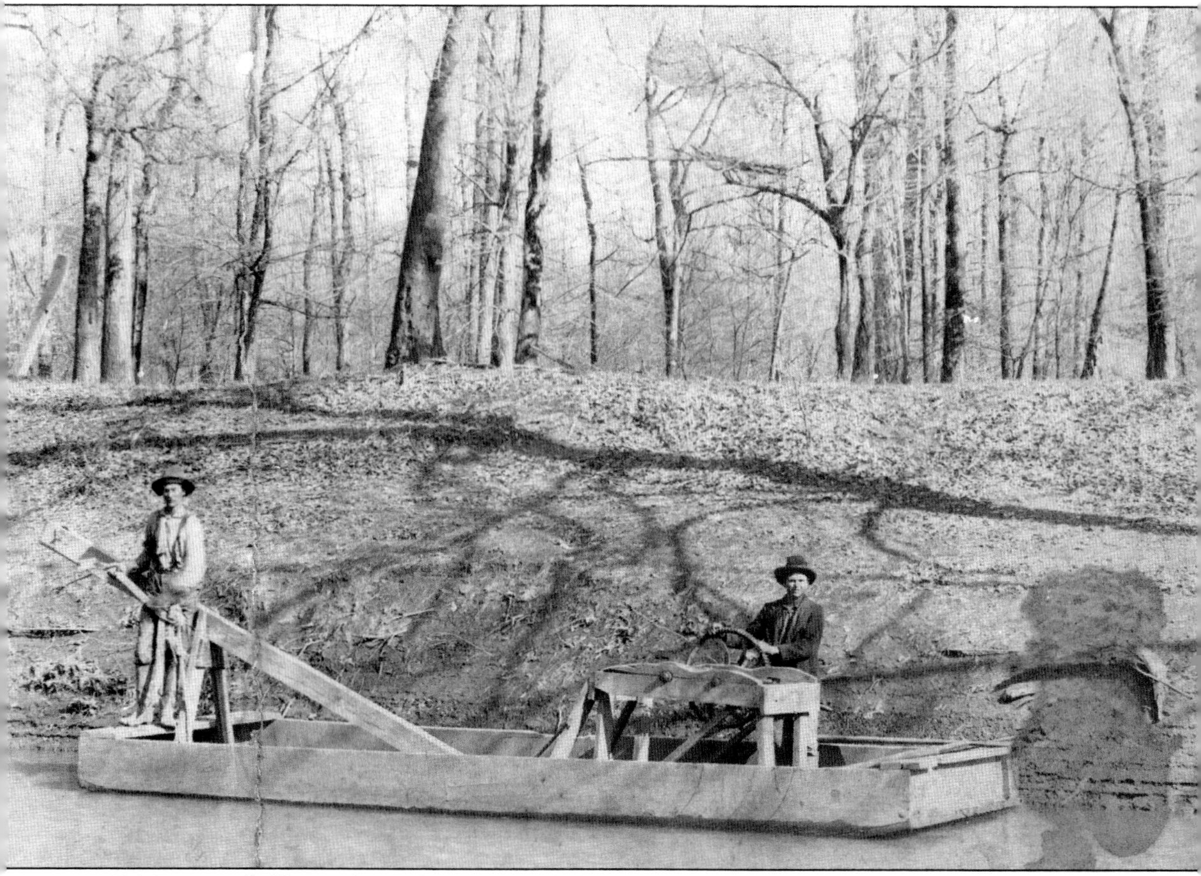

Ed Sumner (left) stands on the bow of a skiff (as this type of craft was called in the early days of river life). Sumner ran one of the three groceries in the Huntsville community in the 1940s and 1950s. Sumner, considered a local character, once had a stranger stop by his store to inquire about the location of Huntsville; Sumner replied, in a commanding tone: "Stand real still—if you take one step in any direction you will be out of it." The reason this skiff was built is unknown, and the man at right is unidentified. (Courtesy of Dickie McKinney.)

On the Cover: This rare photograph shows the *J.C. Kerr* tied up at the mouth of the Barren River. Around 1892, this packet boat was in regular service, making twice-weekly trips from Evansville, Indiana, to Bowling Green, Kentucky, for about a year. The steamer was later rebuilt, with a texas deck added as sleeping quarters for the crew. She returned to service as the *Chaperon*, making runs from Bowling Green to Mammoth Cave. She was sold to a Mississippi company and sank on the Yazoo River in 1922 while operating under the name *Chocktaw*. (Courtesy of the Kentucky Library and Roger Givens.)

IMAGES
of America

BUTLER COUNTY

Roger G. Givens and Nancy Richey

ARCADIA
PUBLISHING

ISBN 978-0-7385-9381-4

Published by Arcadia Publishing
Charleston, South Carolina

Printed in the United States of America

Library of Congress Control Number: 2011946065

For all general information, please contact Arcadia Publishing:
Telephone 843-853-2070
Fax 843-853-0044
E-mail sales@arcadiapublishing.com
For customer service and orders:
Toll-Free 1-888-313-2665

Visit us on the Internet at www.arcadiapublishing.com

For Jeanette Wilson Farley and Elizabeth Herron Bruner, who pushed until they opened doors.

—Nancy

I dedicate this book to my wife, Deborah, for her persistence in reminding me that I should put my local historical knowledge into a publication.

—Roger

Contents

Acknowledgments

A pictorial history of Butler County would not be complete without the inclusion of some of the significant works of George Dabbs; special thanks to his grandchildren—Jo Ann Dove, David and Gene Dabbs, and Susan Hampton—for sharing them with the world in this publication. It is truly appreciated. Also, to David G. Miller, we extend our gratitude for the use of his father's photograph. To Joe Forsythe, we extend a thank you for his support. Lastly and by no means least, thank you to Tommy Hines for allowing the use of his personal pictures and granting access to the collections of the Green River Museum. Nancy wants to thank her coauthor for sharing his amazing knowledge and love of Butler County with everyone through this book. Unless otherwise noted, all images appear courtesy of the Kentucky Library and Roger Givens.

Introduction

When the first settlers moved into the area that would become Butler County, Kentucky, they found a land of plenty. Settlers noted flocks of turkey so numerous they blackened the sky, deer in herds of 50 or more, canebrakes so thick pioneers had to chop through them, and a virgin forest with trees as tall as 100 feet. In 1810, Butler County was officially formed from parts of Logan and Ohio Counties, and residents established a local government and built roads to other county seats. They also quickly constructed a courthouse and a jail and established ferries across the Green and Mud Rivers. As in other areas, many of these efforts were completed using slave labor.

The Green River severed the county into three distinct parts, which proved an impediment to growth due to unaffordable ferriage fees and the winter and spring rains that prevented access to the county seat and its trading days. The pioneers realized that the Green River could be a major asset in getting products in and out of the valley and cleared it of navigational obstacles by 1811.

The county grew slowly at first. In 1836, the state of Kentucky began construction of a slackwater navigation system on the Green and Barren Rivers, with one lock and dam in Butler County and another in Muhlenberg and Ohio Counties. The Butler County lock and dam was within a few hundred feet of the Butler County settlement of Rochester. The system—which provided year-round navigation from Evansville, Indiana, to Bowling Green—spurred growth in the county and the development of the towns of Rochester and Woodbury and offered a needed incentive for the expansion of Morgantown.

After a few years of peaceful and productive growth in Butler County, the county developed two ideologically distinct factions regarding slavery. However, Kentucky's efforts to remain neutral kept the state out of the Civil War until September 1861. In Butler County, a staged show of support for the Union took place in August 1861, when Col. Pierce Hawkins provided tactical training and drills for three of four companies of potential Union troops. Not to be outdone, 40 or 50 potential Confederate cavalrymen drilled on the same field with them.

On September 17, 1861, Confederate forces occupied Bowling Green, and Confederate captain Thomas Lewers set up an outpost of about 150 cavalrymen at Woodbury to observe enemy activity. Around the same time, Colonel Hawkins set up Camp Underwood along the Green River above Rochester to recruit the 11th Kentucky Infantry to fight for the Union. Additionally, after hearing of the Confederate camp at Woodbury, Col. John H. McHenry, of the 17th Kentucky Infantry at Camp Galloway (near Hartford), believed the rebels were going to attack his men; he sent for reinforcements from Col. Stephen Burbridge, of the 26th Kentucky Infantry at Camp Silas Miller (in Owensboro). They joined forces at Cromwell, and the following morning—October 27, 1861—they set out for Woodbury. Splitting forces, they began their offensive with Colonel McHenry traveling up the south side of the Green River and Colonel Burbridge moving up the north side. At Big Hill, near Morgantown, Pvt. Granville Allen, of the 17th Kentucky Infantry, was killed after encountering a scouting party of 14 Confederate cavalrymen from Woodbury.

Two days later, on October 29, Colonel Burbridge drove the Confederate forces out of Woodbury in a rout, and the Confederates retreated to Little Muddy Church, where they met reinforcements. After a two-hour rest, they headed back to Woodbury to find that Union troops had already left for Morgantown. They caught the Union forces as the last group was crossing the Green River at Borah's Ferry in Logansport, where a small skirmish took place and four or five men were wounded.

Other local action occurred when Confederate general John Hunt Morgan moved his brigade through Butler County in October 1862. He crossed the Green River at Aberdeen, originally heading toward Russellville. Upon being informed of a formidable force of Union troops nearby, in the direction of Bowling Green, close to the Russellville Road, Morgan turned his troops in a perpendicular direction—toward Rochester. In Morgantown, 16 of Morgan's stragglers were captured by Union troops; this supposedly happened at the Leach house on Roberts Street, as it is reported to this day that there are Civil War–era bullet holes in the older part of the house, and no other known actions in which bullets could have been fired occurred in the vicinity.

The occupation of Kentucky by Union troops during the war was detrimental to the state and Butler County, causing considerable political and emotional damage. Several of Butler County's Confederate sympathizers were arrested and incarcerated in Bowling Green, including county judge Thomas P. Wand. Dr. Francis Porter died while he was jailed in Bowling Green.

The two most famous prison breaks of the Civil War were both led by men from Woodbury. Maj. Andrew G. Hamilton, along with Col. Thomas E. Rose, engineered the escape of 109 Union officers—57 of whom safely reached Union lines—from Libby Prison in Virginia, and Confederate captain Thomas Hines led the escape of General Morgan and five fellow officers from the Ohio state penitentiary. In 1864, Hines was the military commander of the covert "Northwest Conspiracy" operating out of Canada; he eventually gained a reputation, according to various sources, as "the most dangerous man in the Confederacy."

The ideological differences of residents and the actions of Union occupational forces created partisan factions in the local population. The area north of Green River, with hilly terrain and small farms, had little need for slaves. However, slaves were widely used south of the river, where the land was flatter and contained larger farms—of the 792 slaves in Butler County in 1860, fewer than 50 resided on the north side of the river. Many of the original county leaders and their families were slaveholders and Southern sympathizers.

However, the period after the Civil War provided a boom for Butler County's economy and population growth. The river bottomland was still mostly virgin forest, providing an abundant supply of timber desperately needed for the railroads. These raw materials were used for the building and repair of tracks throughout the nation, and the Green River provided ways to get the timber to markets.

The federal government obtained ownership of the Green and Barren Rivers navigation system from the state and established a maintenance headquarters in Woodbury, which included a district office and a superintendent's home in 1912. From Woodbury, the government operated a fleet of dredge boats to keep the river clear and the locks operable. During the second half of the 19th century, both Rochester and Woodbury surpassed Morgantown in population, maintaining that lead until 1880. In 1900, Butler County's population peaked at 15,896, including an African American population of 726.

The economic boom produced a thriving, culturally enriched community centered on the river port towns of Morgantown, Rochester, and Woodbury. In the early 1900s, the county supported four banks, six hotels, five drugstores, three milling companies, two axe-handle factories, one outdoor and two indoor theaters, four high schools, and more than 80 one-room elementary schools, including six African American schools.

For a county with such a small population, Butler County has produced a number of notable people, including Oklahoma senator John W. Harreld; three members of the US House of Representatives, Everette B. Howard (Oklahoma) and Maurice H. Thatcher and John W. Moore (Kentucky); two chief justices of the Kentucky Court of Appeals (which served as Kentucky's supreme court until

1975), Bayless L.D. Guffy and Thomas H. Hines; Navy admiral Claude Bloch; Methodist bishop John Monroe Moore; and Congressional Medal of Honor recipient Don J. Jenkins.

Sadly, the saying "all good things must come to an end," proved true for Butler County. Railroads and other forms of transportation began to dominate the freight industry in the early 1900s, driving riverboats out of business. The last packet boat, the *Evansville*, burned at the dock in Bowling Green on July 25, 1931, and was never replaced, thus ending regularly scheduled river transportation. The US Army Corps of Engineers shifted operations from Woodbury to Paducah in 1927, and from there to the district office in Louisville in 1947. In May 1965, the dam at Woodbury washed out, ceasing all river traffic to Bowling Green. Rochester experienced three major fires in its business district and has never rebounded from the destruction—in 2010, the town's population was 186.

The entire county experienced a steady decline in population after the turn of the 20th century. The Great Depression brought about a significant decrease, particularly in the African American population, as no jobs were available. Seeking employment, people migrated to larger cities like Louisville, Indianapolis, Chicago, and Detroit. The decrease continued until 1960, when the county population bottomed out at 9,586, including only 70 African American inhabitants.

In the mid-1970s, a coal boom boosted the county's economy and brought about a slight population increase, and in the mid-1980s, Morgantown secured three plants that manufactured automobile parts, giving a significant boost to the economy and spurring population growth to 13,010 (in 2000). By the early 2000s, however, the operations had ceased, resulting in a small population decrease. The 2010 US Census listed Butler County's population at 12,690.

Images of America: *Butler County* includes photographs reflecting the riverboat era—Butler County in its heyday—and the area's leaders, schools, churches, and the activities of its people, all painting a memorable picture of the great heritage of Butler County.

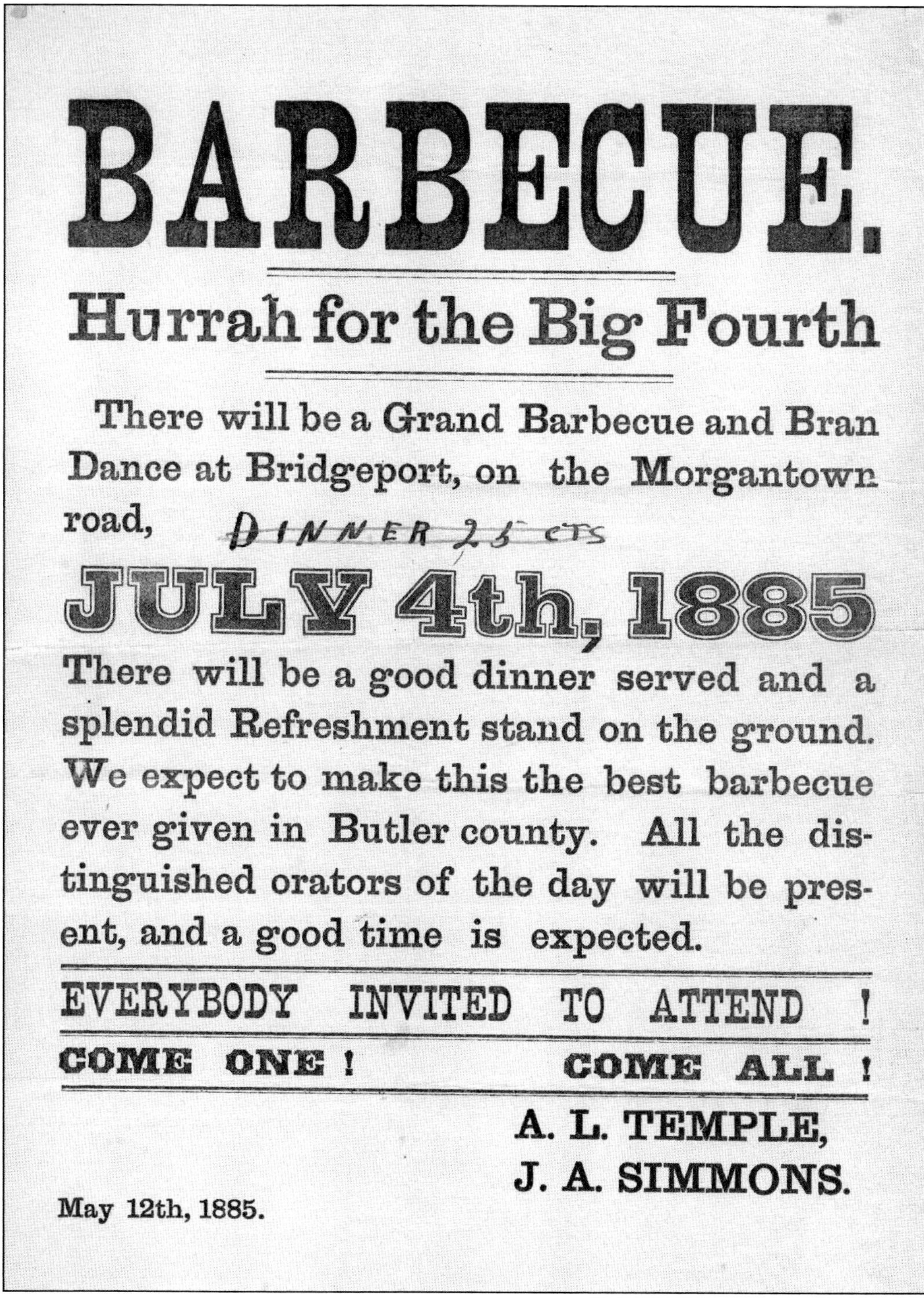

BARBECUE.

Hurrah for the Big Fourth

There will be a Grand Barbecue and Bran Dance at Bridgeport, on the Morgantown road, DINNER 25 CTS

JULY 4th, 1885

There will be a good dinner served and a splendid Refreshment stand on the ground. We expect to make this the best barbecue ever given in Butler county. All the distinguished orators of the day will be present, and a good time is expected.

EVERYBODY INVITED TO ATTEND !

COME ONE ! COME ALL !

A. L. TEMPLE,
J. A. SIMMONS.

May 12th, 1885.

This flyer advertises a July 4, 1885, barbecue and barn dance and boasts of "the best barbecue ever given in Butler County." The celebration also included distinguished orators of the day. The event is believed to have been in the Reedyville community. The celebration of the Fourth of July is still a big event for Butler County, but now the focus is on catfish instead of barbecue.

One

People and Places

In the 1790s, settlers began moving into the areas of Logan and Ohio Counties that would become Butler County. In January 1810, Butler County was formed by an act of the Kentucky legislature and named in honor of Gen. Richard Butler, a Revolutionary War hero. By the time of the county's founding, it had a total population of 2,181 settlers, including eight freemen and 274 slaves. Suffolk, which overlapped with part of present-day Rochester, was the only platted and organized town in 1810, but it failed to grow and fell into financial difficulties. The county was almost equally divided by Green River. Of the 322 households recorded in 1810, 69 were slaveholders, mostly on the south side of the river, while two families on the north side owned one slave each. By the time of the Civil War, Butler County had grown to a total population of 7,927, including 792 slaves.

In 1900, the county's population peaked at 15,896. The development of the navigation system on the Green River provided a spark of growth that proudly brought the county into the 20th century. In the midst of the riverboat era, three thriving river port towns developed—Morgantown, Rochester, and Woodbury. Butler County's river bottomland trees were cut and shipped out via the Green River to make railroad ties. Ironically, the growth of the railroads was a significant factor in the disappearance of the riverboat industry, causing a downward spiral in the county's population.

Going into the mid-20th century, Butler County was primarily an agrarian society consisting of small, self-sustaining family farms. The area's first significant land-based industries were garment factories that opened in the 1950s and early 1960s. In the 1980s and 1990s, Butler County's population experienced more fluctuations with the openings and subsequent closings of plants that manufactured car parts.

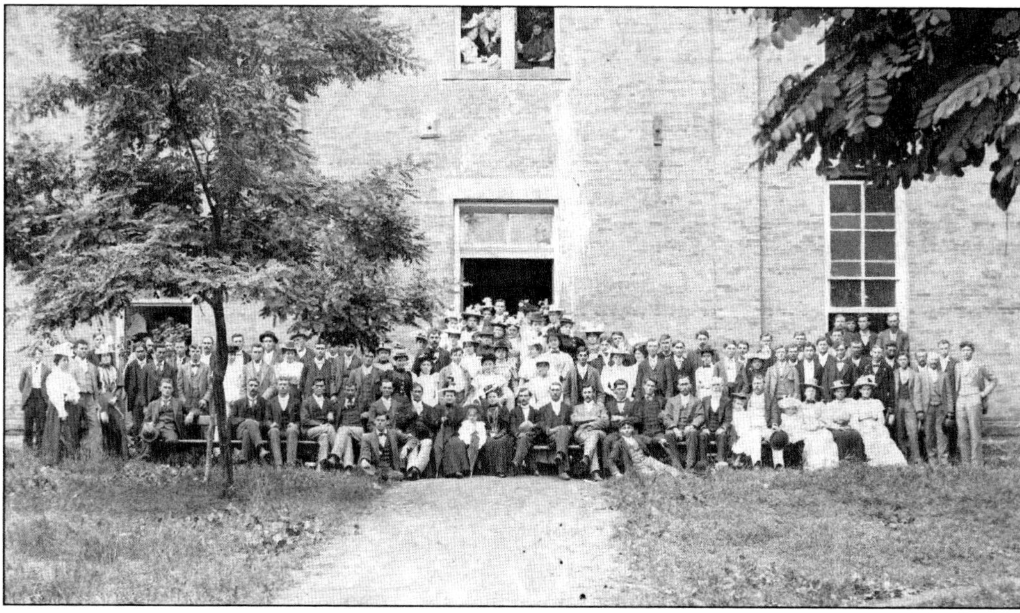

This Robert B. Morehead Jr. photograph is one of the earliest images of the 1872 county courthouse. The occasion is believed to have been a political gathering. Morehead, the son of a Morgantown physician, opened a studio in Morgantown in the 1890s and operated there until about 1904, when he sold his studio to George Dabbs and moved to Nashville.

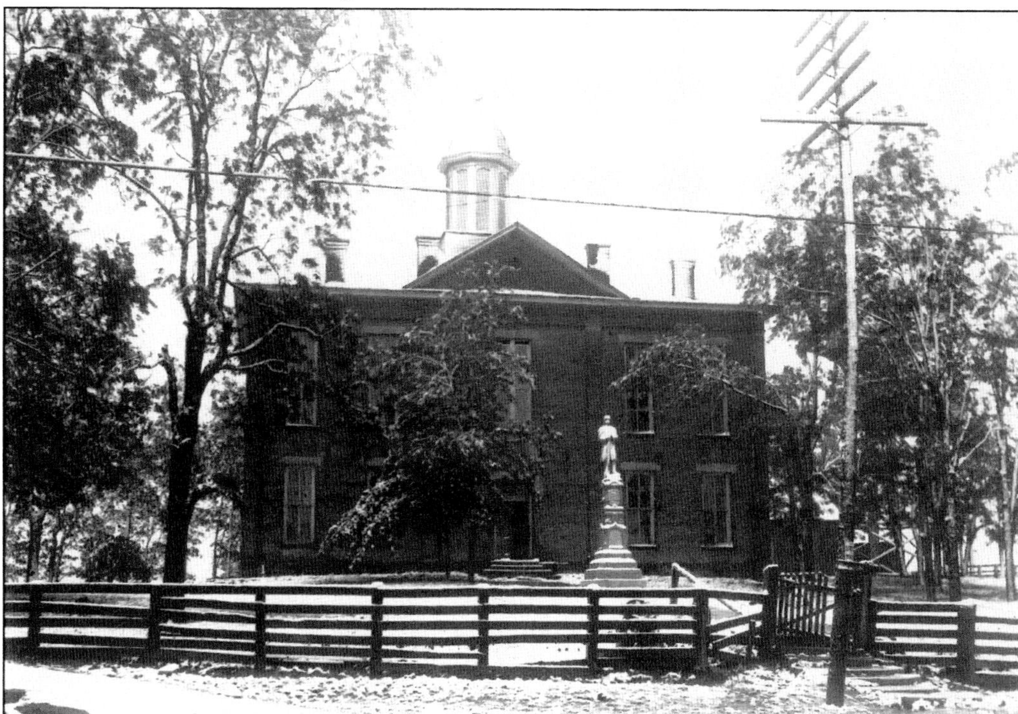

This winter scene showcases the second county courthouse, built in 1872. The date of the photograph is unknown, but it was taken after the Confederate-Union Veterans' Monument was dedicated in May 1907. This courthouse was replaced with the current structure in 1974.

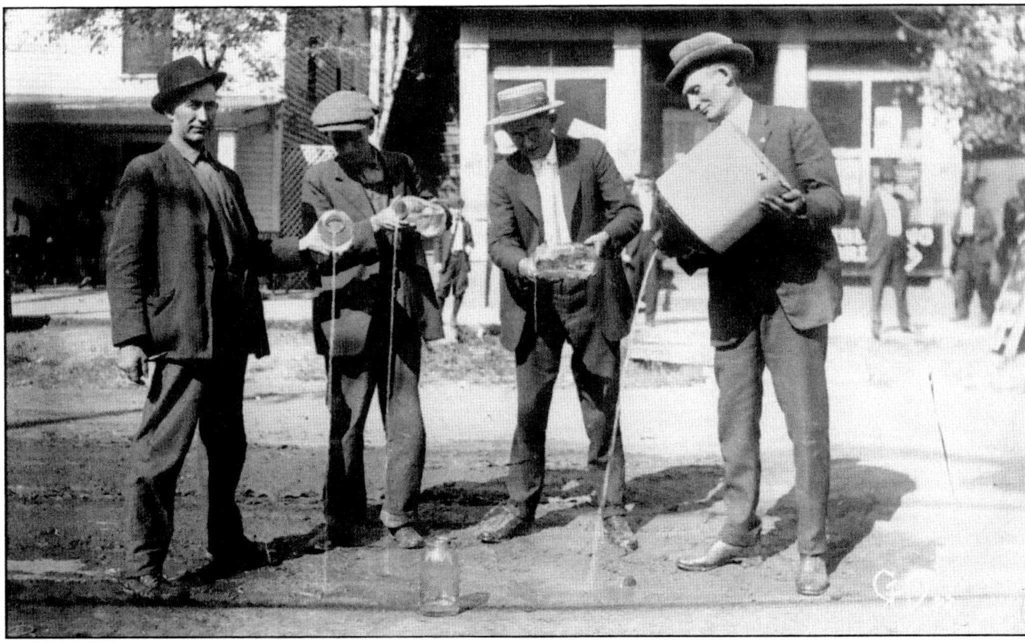

Prohibition did not stop the flow of whiskey, as evidenced by this 1922 photograph. Deputy Sheriff Herman Jackson (right) and Sheriff Herman Hammers (second from right) raided a still and are pouring out the moonshine in front of the courthouse. The Richmond Hotel is in the background at left.

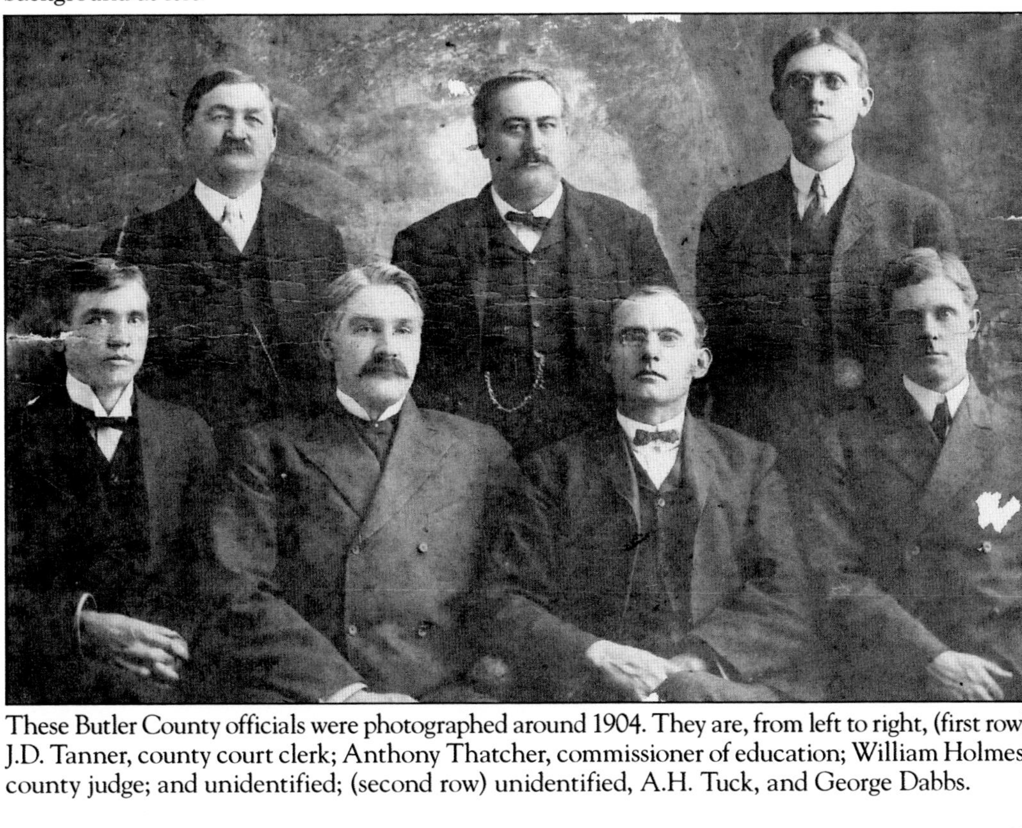

These Butler County officials were photographed around 1904. They are, from left to right, (first row) J.D. Tanner, county court clerk; Anthony Thatcher, commissioner of education; William Holmes, county judge; and unidentified; (second row) unidentified, A.H. Tuck, and George Dabbs.

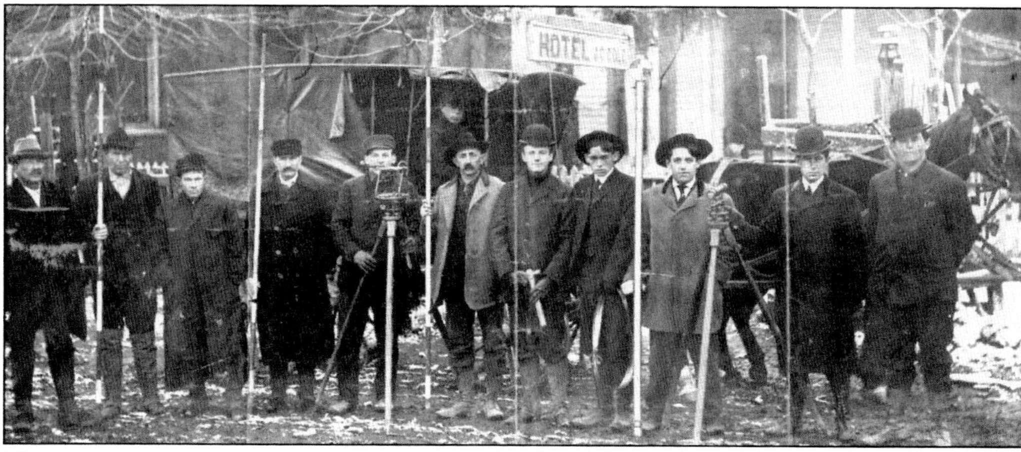

This surveying crew was mapping a proposed railroad from Bowling Green to Horse Branch, in Ohio County, to connect the Illinois Central lines. The members of the crew are, from left to right, W.A. Jones, Jess McGinnis, James Hobson, Willie Smith, unidentified, John Sublett, unidentified, John H. Jones, Walter Smith, ? Wyatt, and ? Wiesenberger. Seated in the wagon behind the men is Mr. Dent. Morgantown's J.C. Cole Hotel is visible in the background.

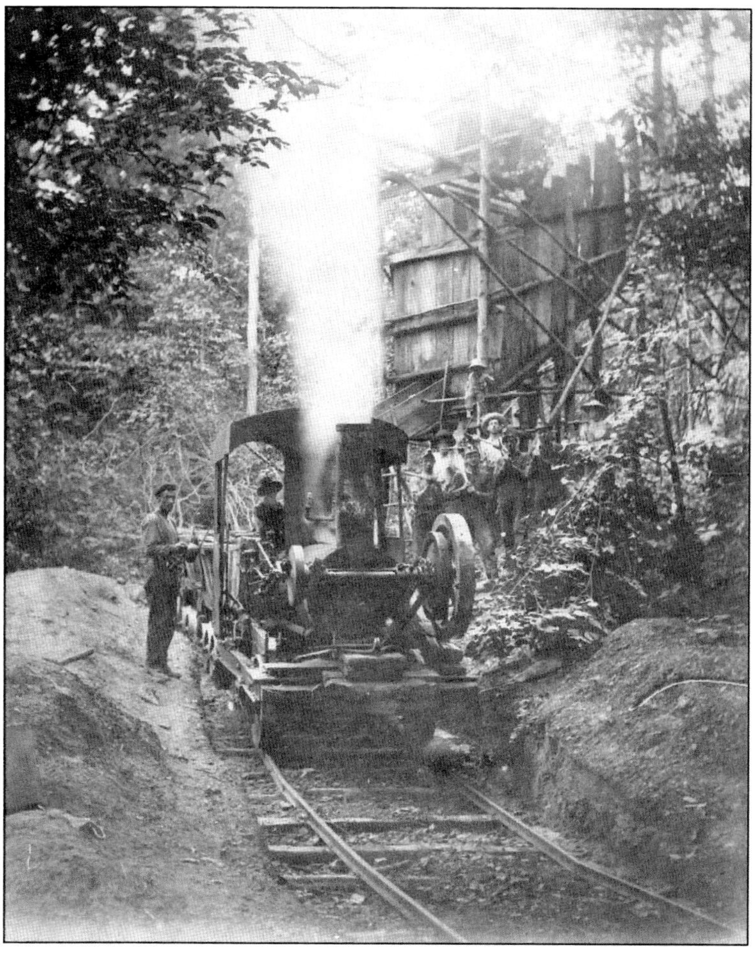

The *Topmiller* train was a privately owned miniature train that ran from a coal mine in the Leonard Oak area to the Green River, where the coal was loaded onto barges for shipment. It was the only train ever to operate in Butler County. A crudely constructed tipple is visible in the background.

This limestone rock formation, known as Pivot Rock, is located on private property about a quarter-mile from the Green River and one mile below the Morgantown boat ramp. The man in the photograph is George Dabbs, who took this self-portrait in the early 1900s. This formation has been described as a top balanced on its pointed end.

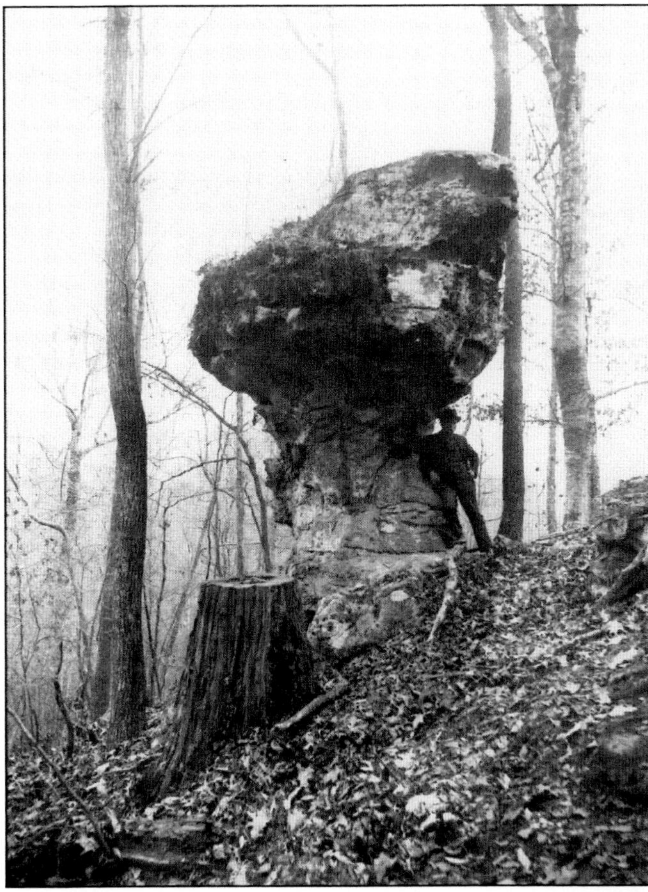

A large crowd gathered for the opening of Little Muddy Bridge, the first modern concrete bridge in the county. It opened in November 1929 as part of the improved roadway between Morgantown and Bowling Green on what was then State Highway 71. In the mid-1950s, the road's name was changed to US Route 231.

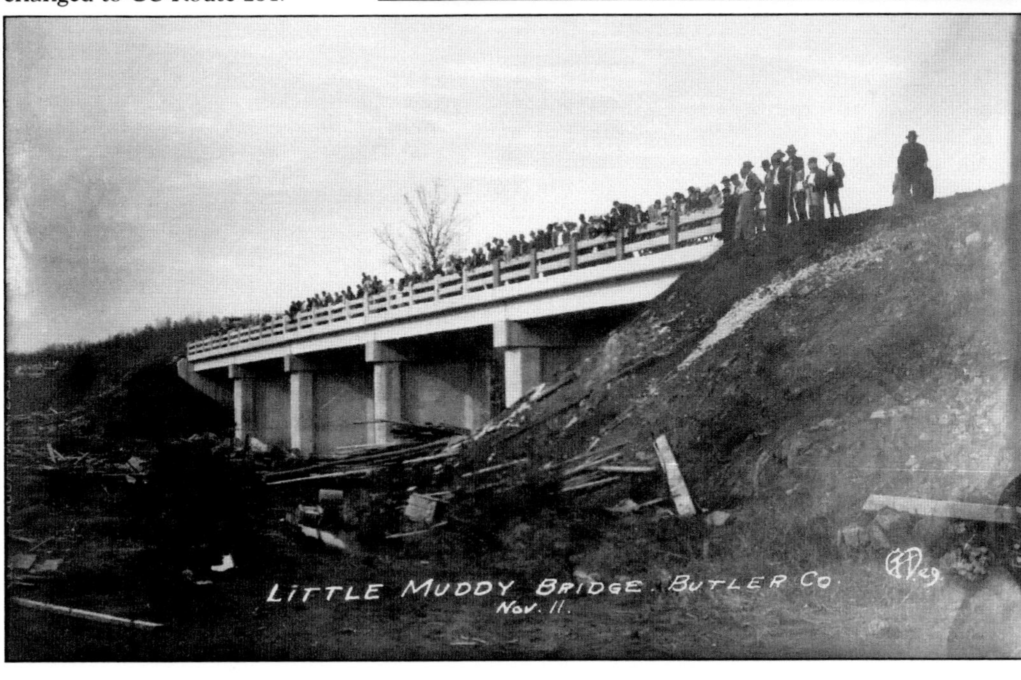

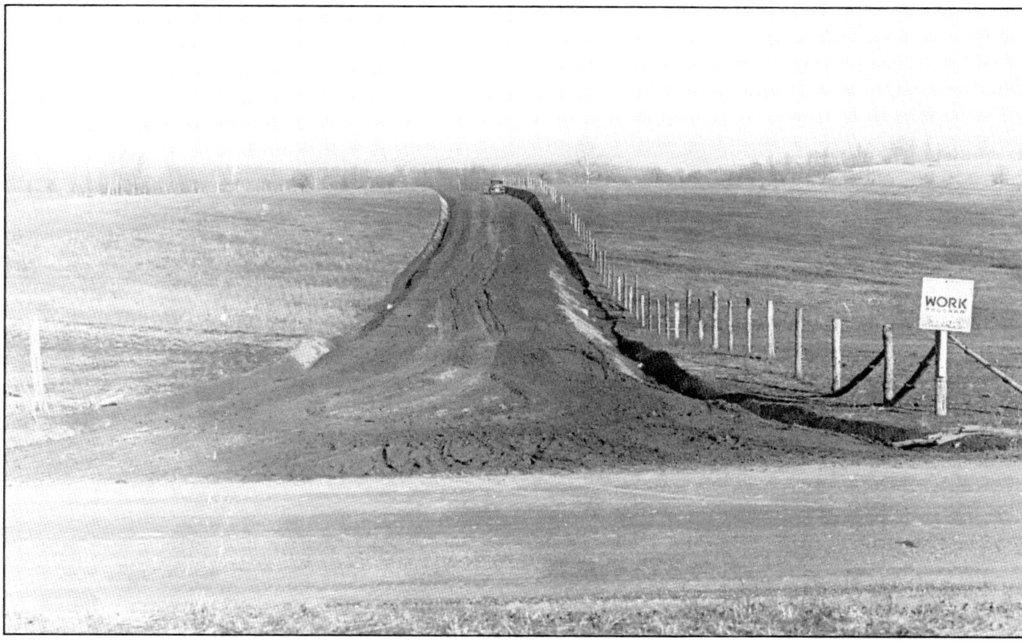

Pres. Franklin D. Roosevelt's Works Progress Administration (WPA) completed road projects in Butler County during the Depression, including this farm-to-market road sponsored by the Fiscal Court. The total estimated cost for the project was $181,707—the federal government paid $165,987 and the local court paid $15,720.

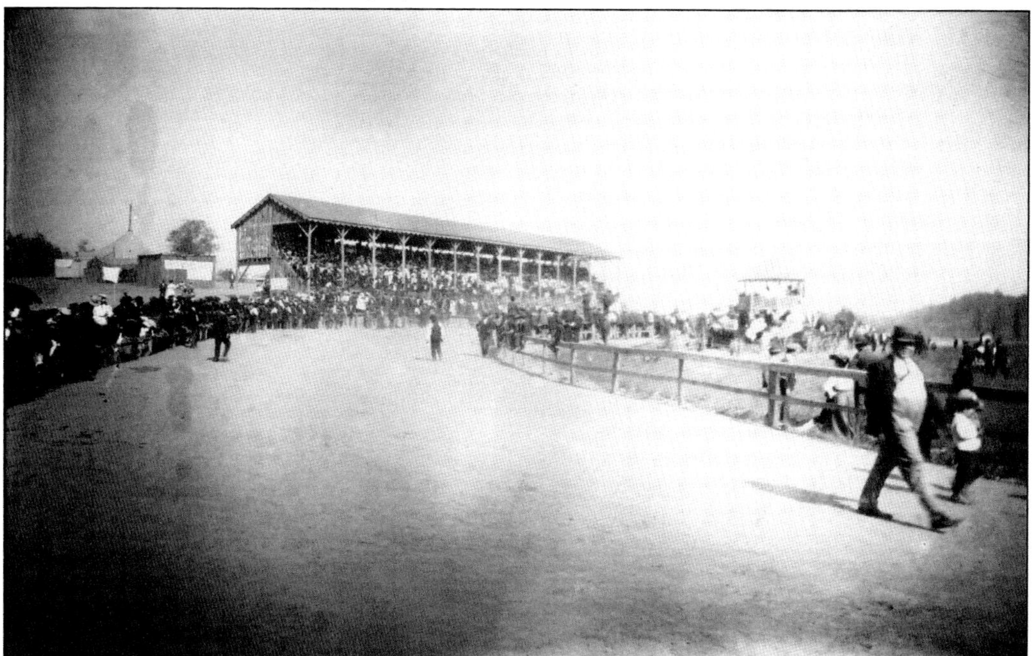

The Butler County fairgrounds, located on 17 acres south of Morgantown, opened in 1907 after being developed by 50 stockholders with a desire to provide the county with cultural and social advantages enjoyed in other areas. Harness racing was a primary attraction, although competitions centered on quilts, garden produce, and livestock were very popular.

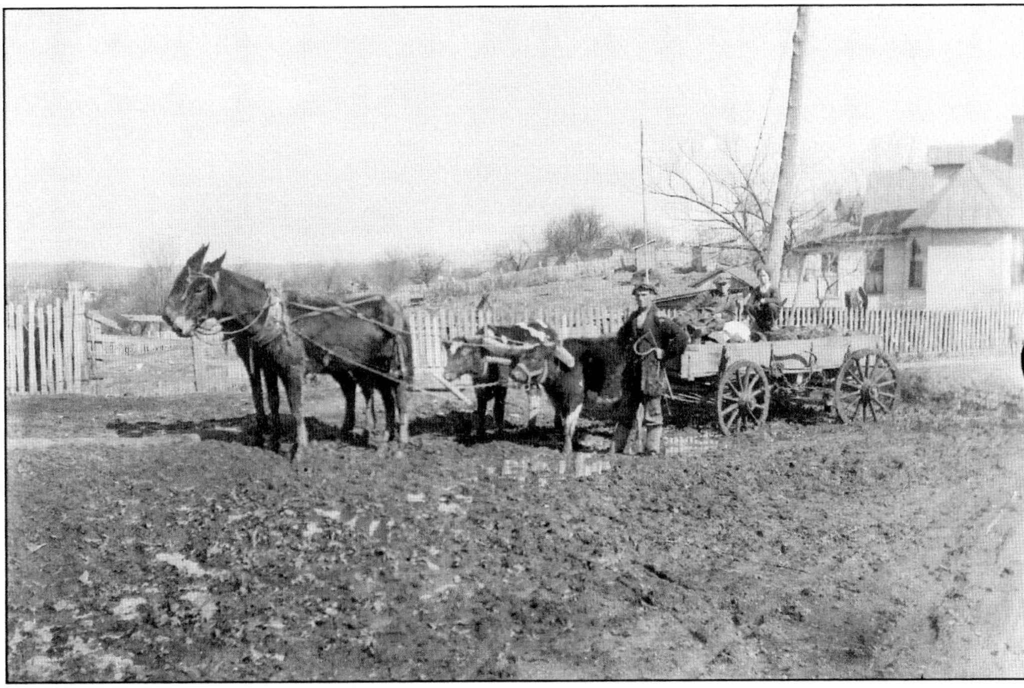

Traveling was often difficult in the days before the automobile, as shown in this winter scene in which mud covers the tops of the driver's shoes. This is an unusual wagon-pulling arrangement, with a pair of mules and a pair of oxen hooked together to the same wagon.

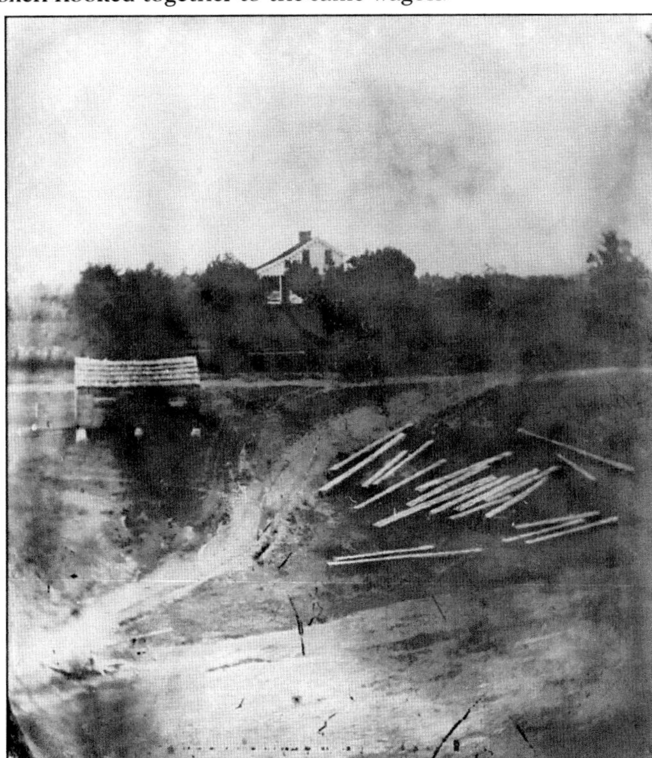

At right, railroad ties that are cut and ready for shipment rest on the riverbank. Ties were commonly loaded onto barges through a chute down the riverbank. Marketing railroad ties was a large part of Butler County's economy around 1900.

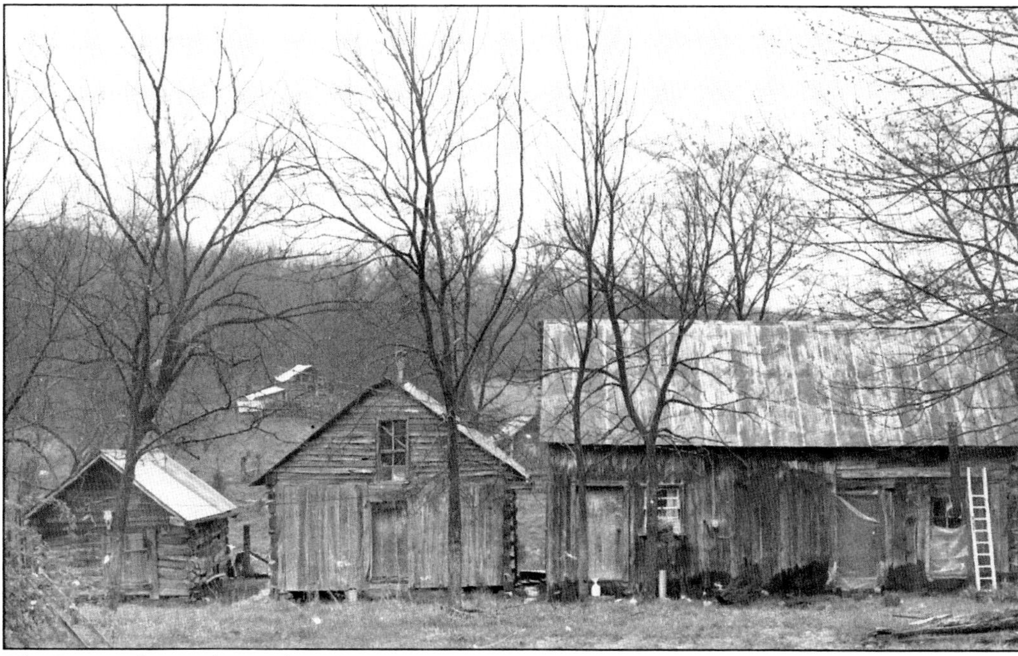

The Beason home, located in the Boston community, was designated a Kentucky Landmark in 1985. Henry Beason, a former slave, bought the 100-acre farm in 1877. Two more generations of Beasons operated the almost completely self-sustaining farm until 1973, when it was sold. These buildings were constructed by "raisings" around 1905.

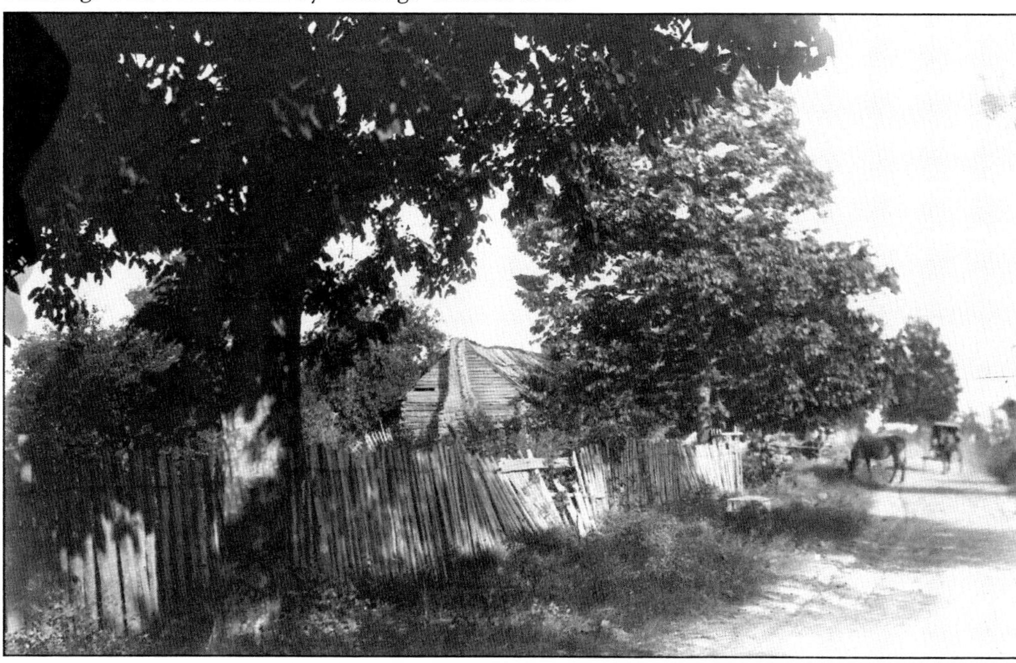

The photographer titled this "Negro housing near Morgantown, 1890." The 1890s were the beginning of a decline in the African American population in Butler County as economic conditions led to a lack of employment opportunities. This image shows the side of a log cabin with a chimney and a tilting stockade fence beside a dirt road.

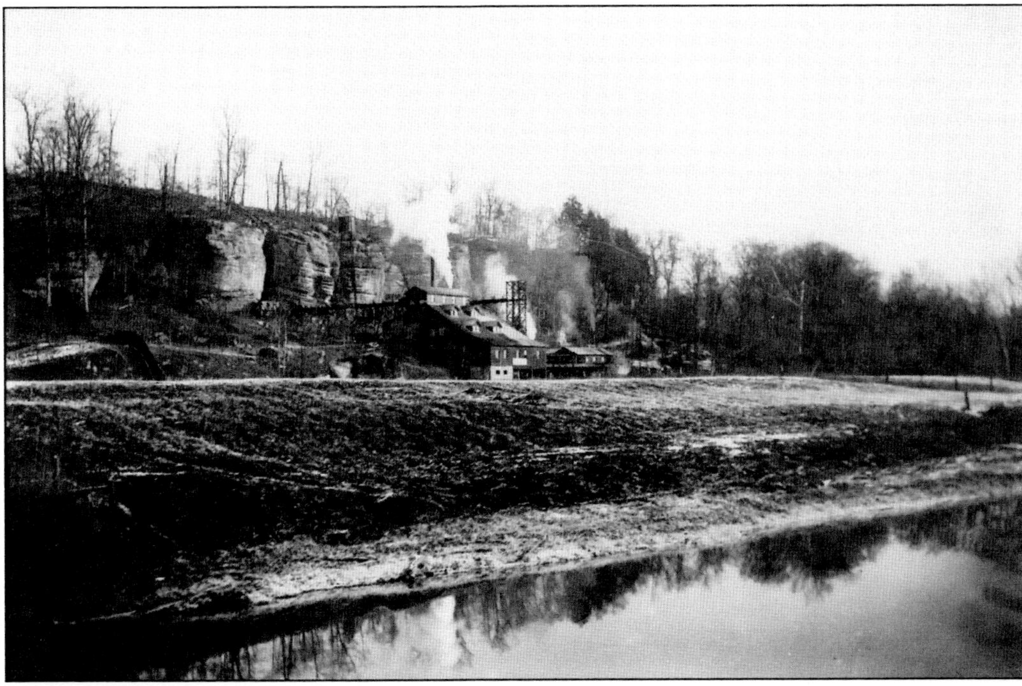

This view from aboard a boat on the Green River shows the Aberdeen Mining Company's main tipple. In 1900, this was Butler County's largest mining operation. The company also had an office in Morgantown. The Aberdeen Hotel is just past the mining company buildings.

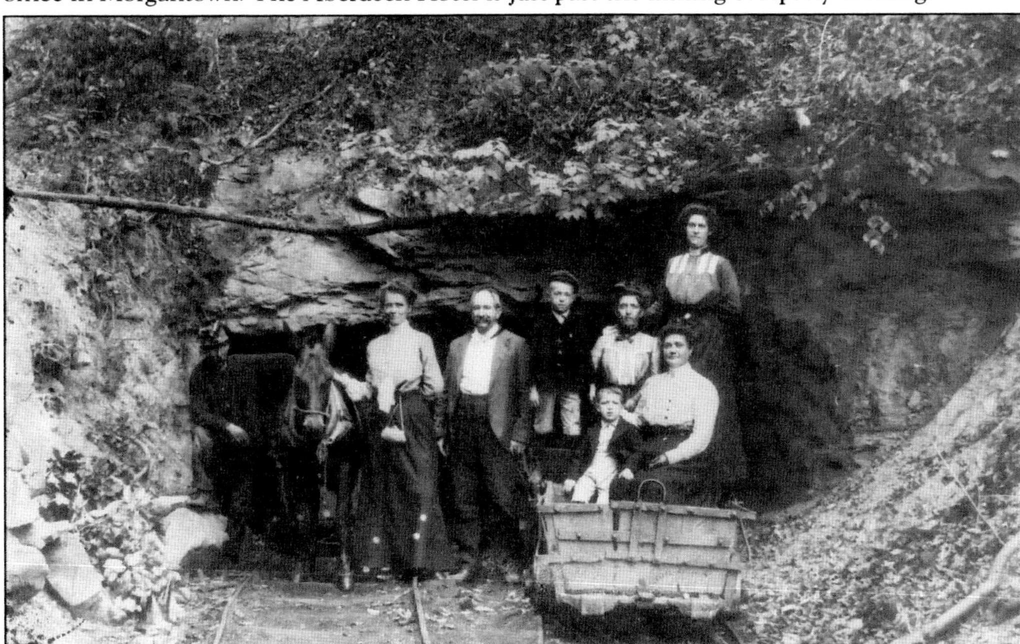

Coal mining has been an important factor of Butler County's economy through the years. This photograph shows the entrance to one of the Aberdeen Mining Company operations. Lucy Render, the wife of Aberdeen Mining owner J.D. Render, and her son, Clarron, are sitting in the coal buggy. Around 1900, Aberdeen Mining was one of the county's largest employers.

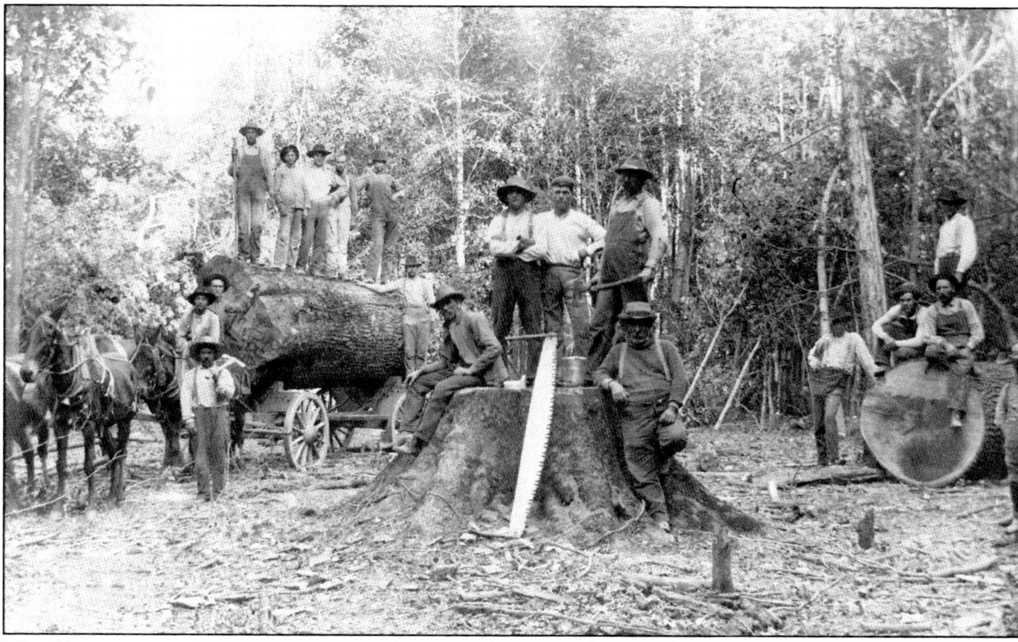

The 19 men posing for this c. 1900 photograph are justly proud of cutting down this tree, which had a diameter of more than six feet. A part of it is already loaded onto a log wagon for shipping down the river. The men show off their large crosscut saw by placing it in the center of the tree stump. (Courtesy of Special Collections: Ekstrom Library, University of Louisville.)

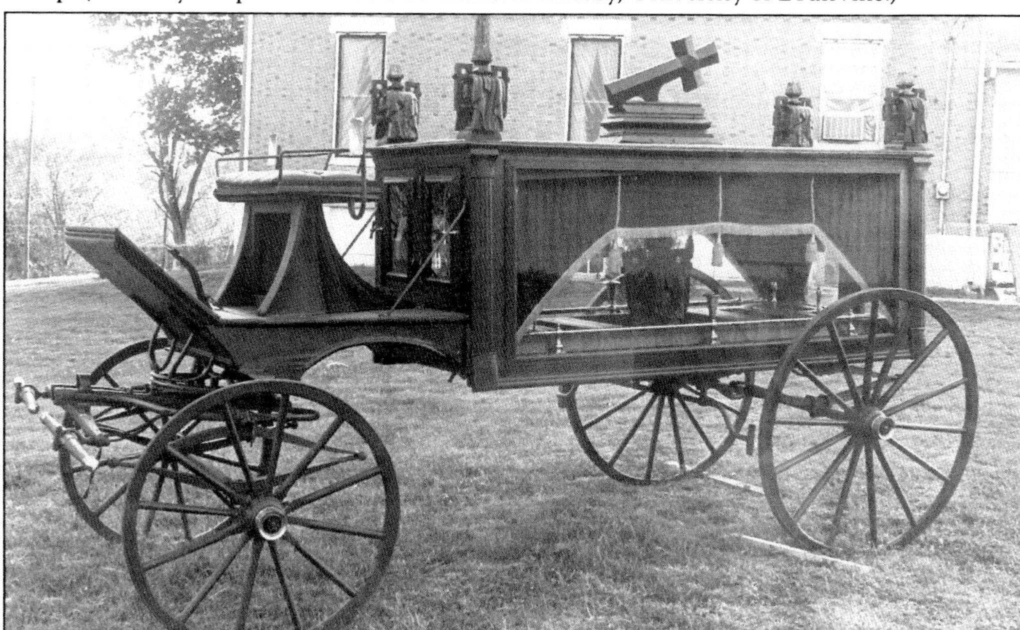

Smith Funeral Home was at the forefront of memorial services in Butler County. Benjamin F. Smith originally purchased this Cunningham hearse in 1886. It was shipped by rail from New York to Bowling Green and then by riverboat to Morgantown. It was last used in 1987 for the funeral of Dwight Smith, the last of the Smith family to own the hearse.

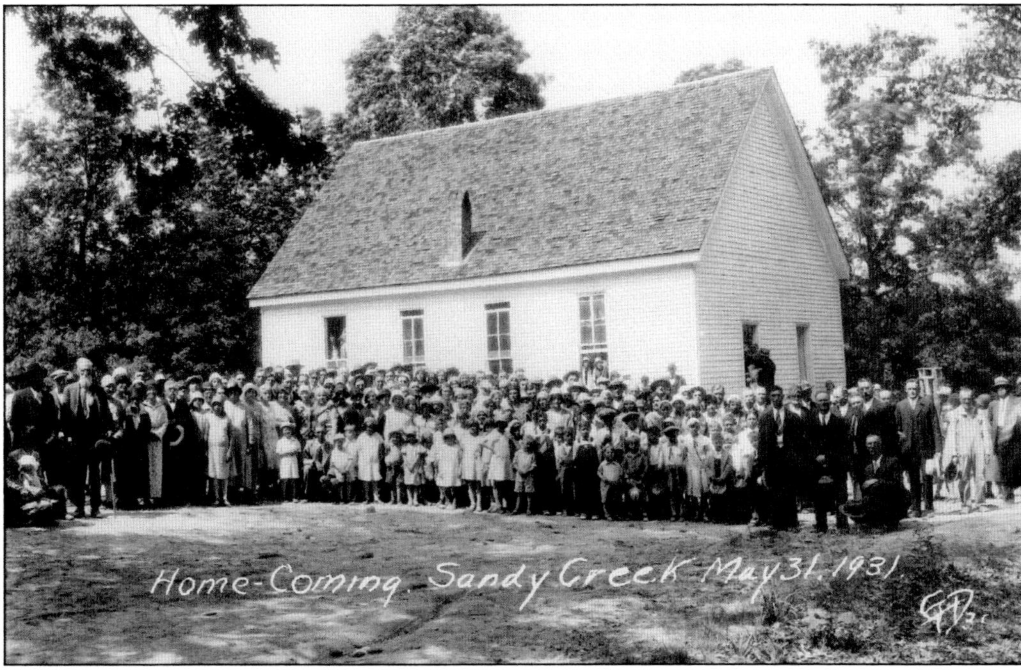

On May 31, 1931, a large crowd gathered for homecoming at Sandy Creek Baptist Church, Butler County's oldest church. The church was established in 1805 with 37 white and three African American members. This building was replaced in the mid-1950s with a modern brick structure. Church members still enjoy the annual homecoming.

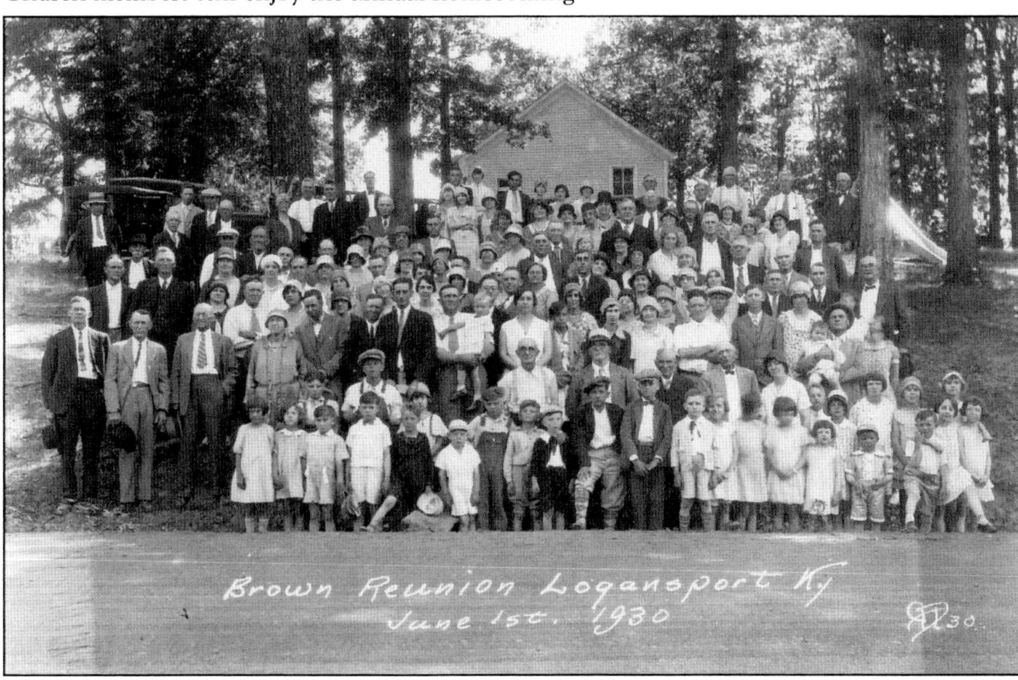

Family reunions, such as this Brown family reunion held in 1930 in Logansport, are a long-standing tradition in Butler County. Note that most of the men are wearing suits and ties, which would be almost unheard of today. The old Salem School is in the background.

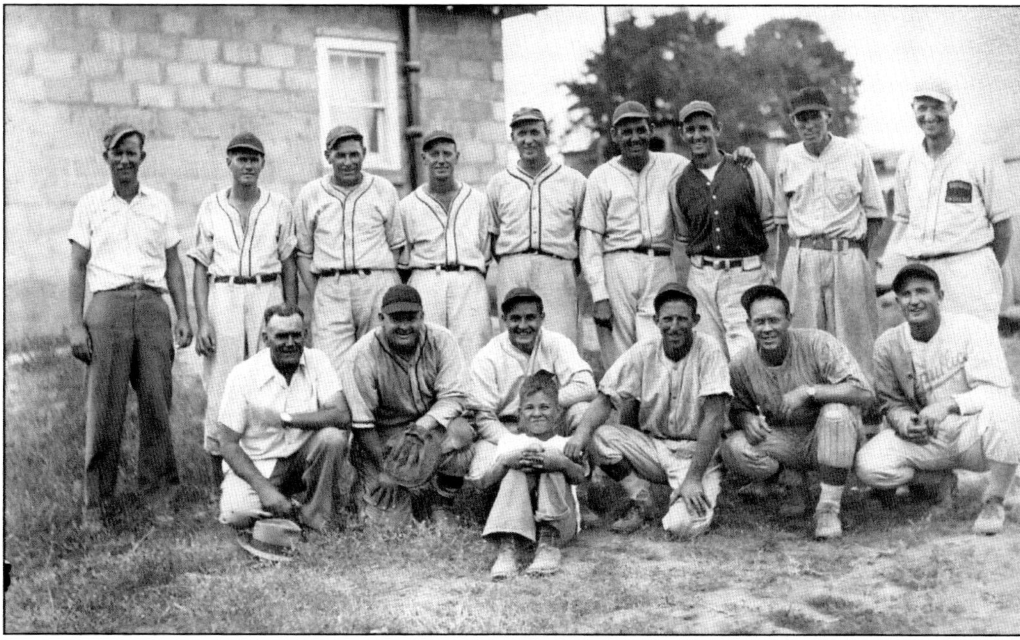

This late-1940s Morgantown baseball team included, from left to right, (seated in front) Bobby Green; (kneeling) unidentified, James Waddle, ? Green, Rex Taylor, "Buster" Rone, and Junior Green; (standing) J.R. Taylor, Elwyn Annis, unidentified, Courtland Annis, Troy Tuck, James Drake, unidentified, Woodrow Read, and Forest West.

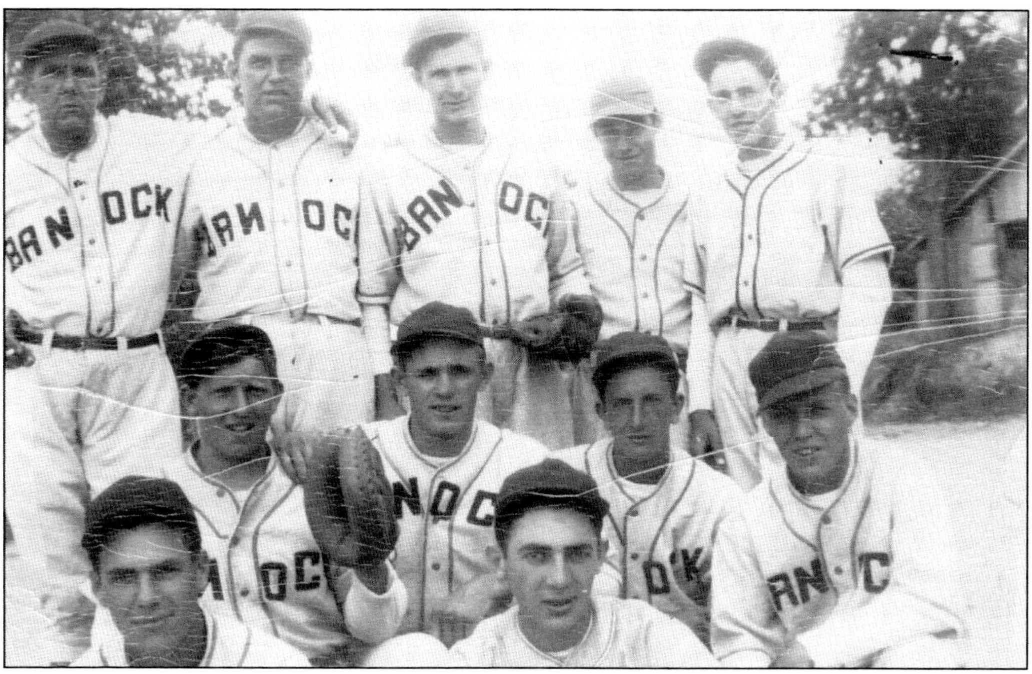

Baseball was a favorite sport in all areas of the county; this Banock team was from the north side. From left to right are (first row) Glen Daugherty and Forest Taylor; (second row) David Coleman, Lewis Evans, Glendal Coleman, and Clifford Daugherty; (third row) Jess Snodgrass, Lex Smith, Stanley Evans, Otha Snodgrass, and Harvey Taylor.

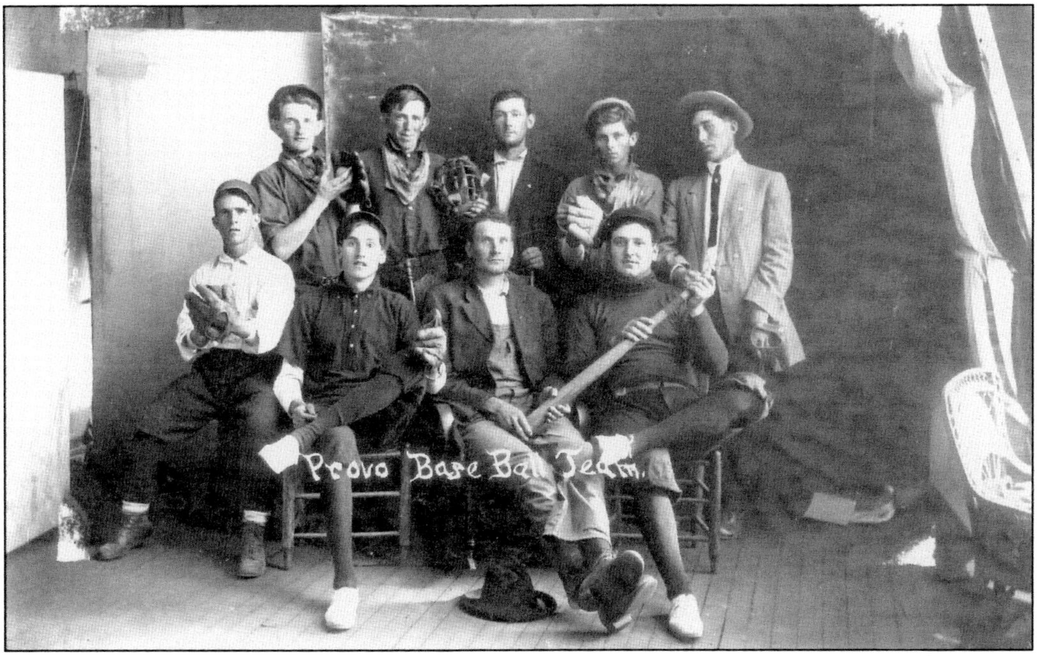

This Provo baseball team from around 1916 included, from left to right, (first row) Joe Cuba Moore (who was adopted from Cuba after the Spanish-American War), Osie Pendley, El Holman, and Bryce Pendley; (second row) Ivan Wilson, Rob Taylor, Ernest Holman, Exie McKinney, and Jess Lee.

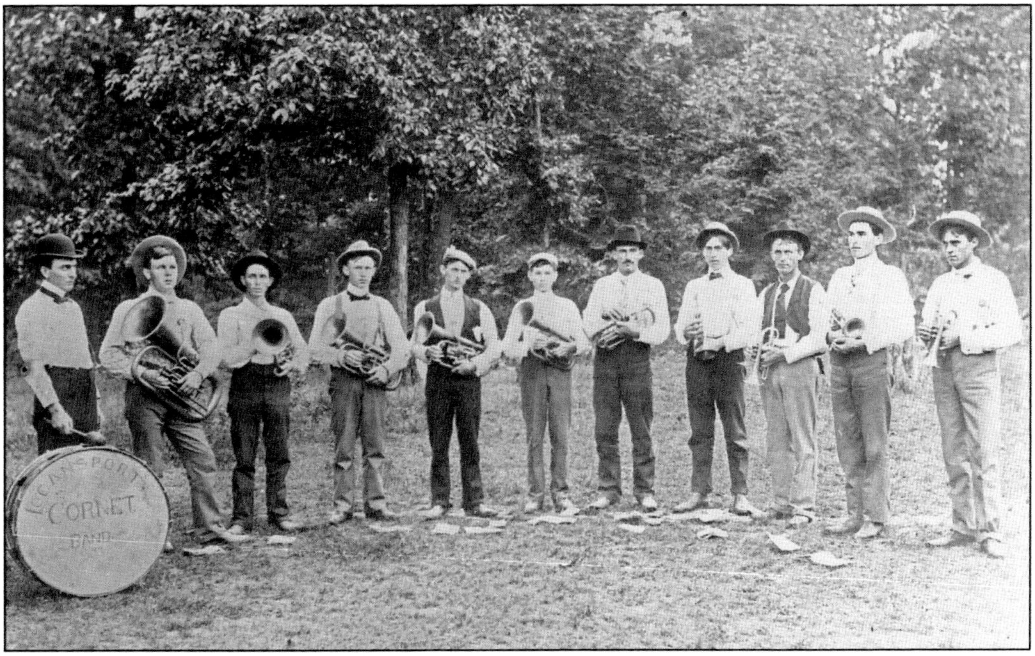

Music was a large part of Butler County culture around 1900. Besides the Logansport Cornet Band (shown here), there were three other known area bands: the Rochester Band, the Morgantown Band, and the Ney Cook Band, which played commercially at nightclubs and festivals in other counties.

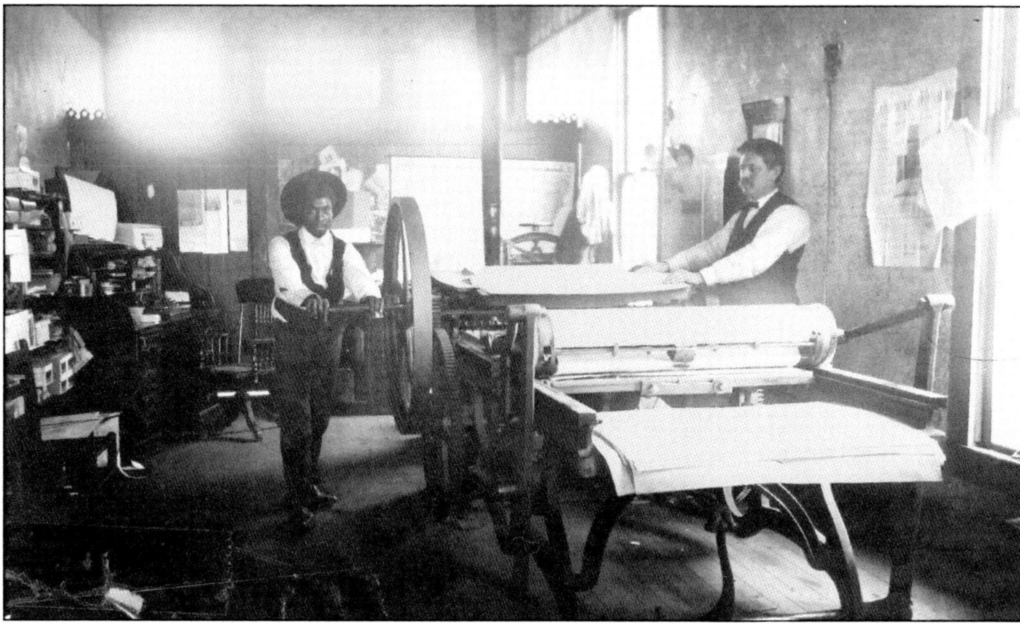

The *Green River Republican*, Butler County's third newspaper, was established in 1885. Henry B. Morehead, the paper's first editor and eventual owner, is at right, "feeding" the Prouty printing press as Mote Helm turns the crank. The publication continued operation under different editors and owners until June 1992, when it was purchased and merged with the *Butler County Banner*, the county's eighth newspaper.

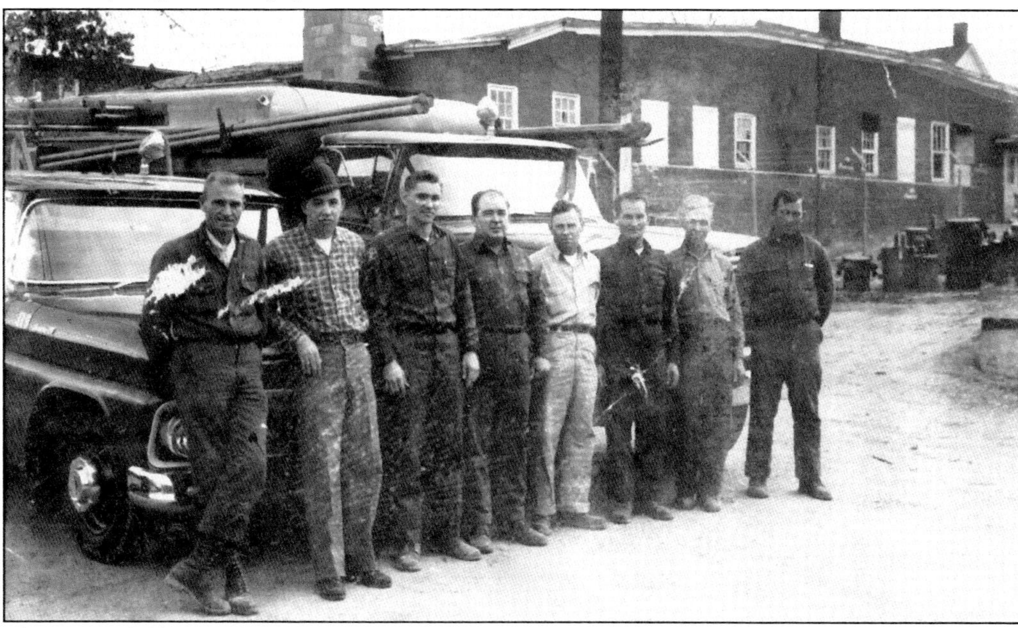

The c. 1962 field crew of the Butler County office of the Warren Rural Electric Cooperative (WRECC) included, from left to right, Jeff Gray, Virgil Mitchell, Glendal DeWeese, Joe Forsythe, Carlton Drake, Edgar Romans, Leroy Boyd, and Hayward Coleman. As part of the Rural Electrification Administration program, WRECC began supplying Butler County residents with electricity in September 1939. The old Morgantown skating rink is visible in the background.

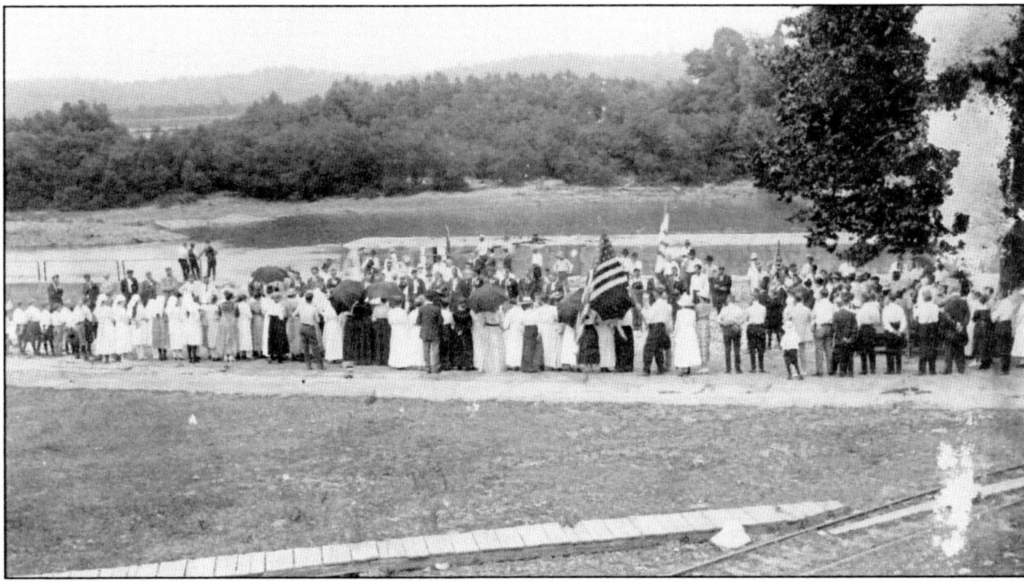

The United States' entry into World War I inspired the development of American Red Cross chapters across the country, creating service opportunities through chapters in every county. Volunteers served their neighborhoods by collecting canned food items and clothing. In the above image, the community came together in support of the departing soldiers, with the Green River in the background. Below, a group sporting the American flag and the Red Cross flag posed in front of Brown's Cash Store. The only identified individual is Thomas Phelps Wand, the young boy third from the right (on the step), who wears a cap and baggy pants. Note the large poster at right advertising the Butler County Fair. (Above, courtesy of Tommy Hines; below, courtesy of Barbara Drake Bresler.)

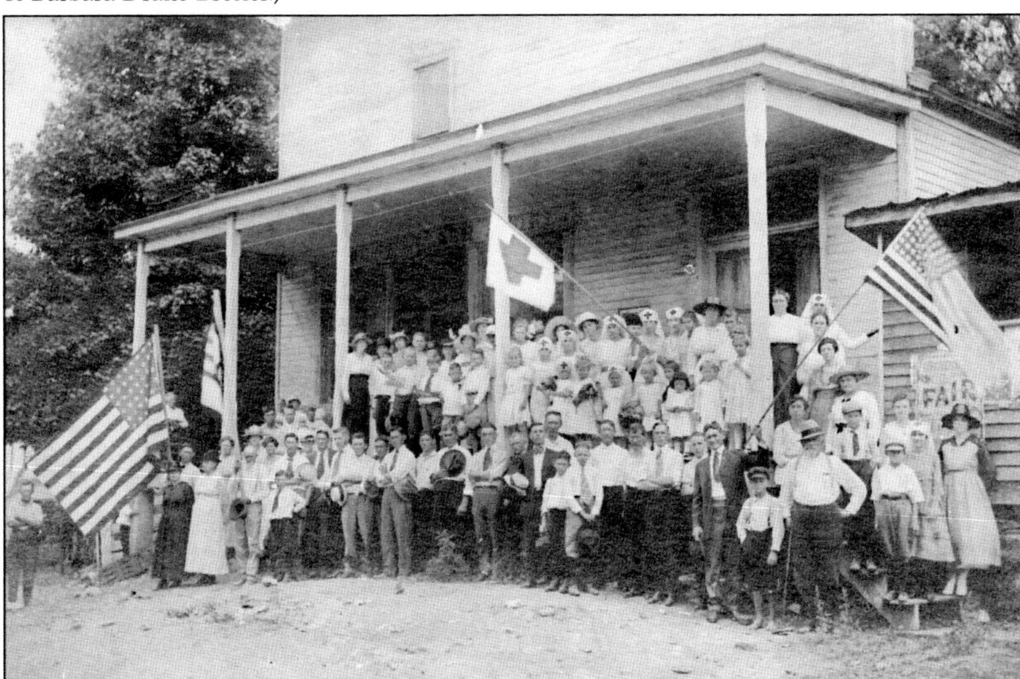

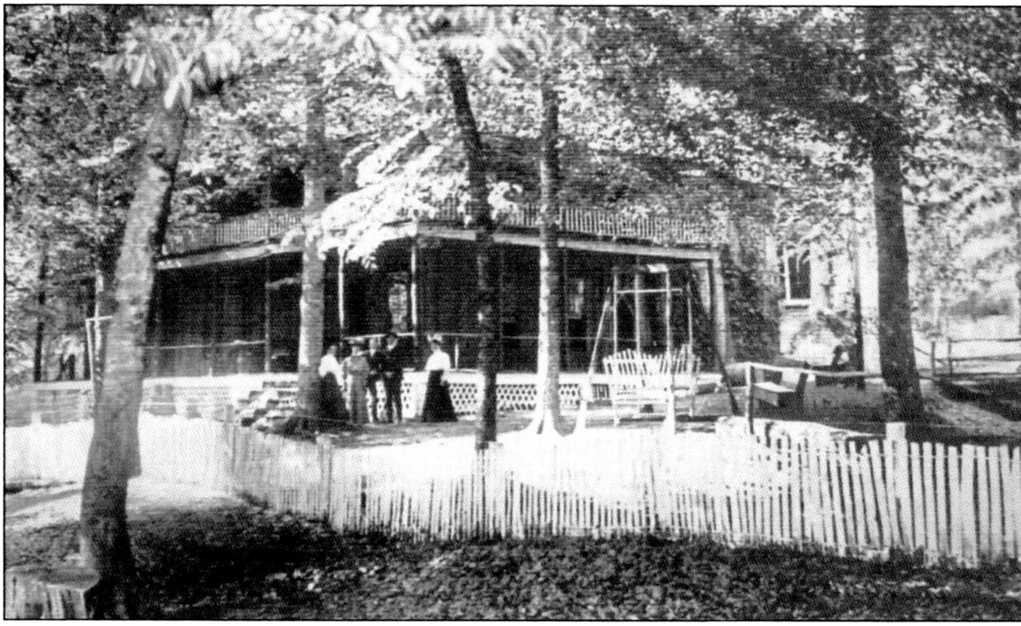

The Pipe Springs Hotel was located about a mile outside of Morgantown, near Doolin's Lake, and operated by Henry Morehead, editor of the *Green River Republican*. Pictured here are, from left to right, Nell Thurman, Edna Smith, Otis Travis, John Thurman, and Sallie Dabbs. The hotel burned down in the 1910s.

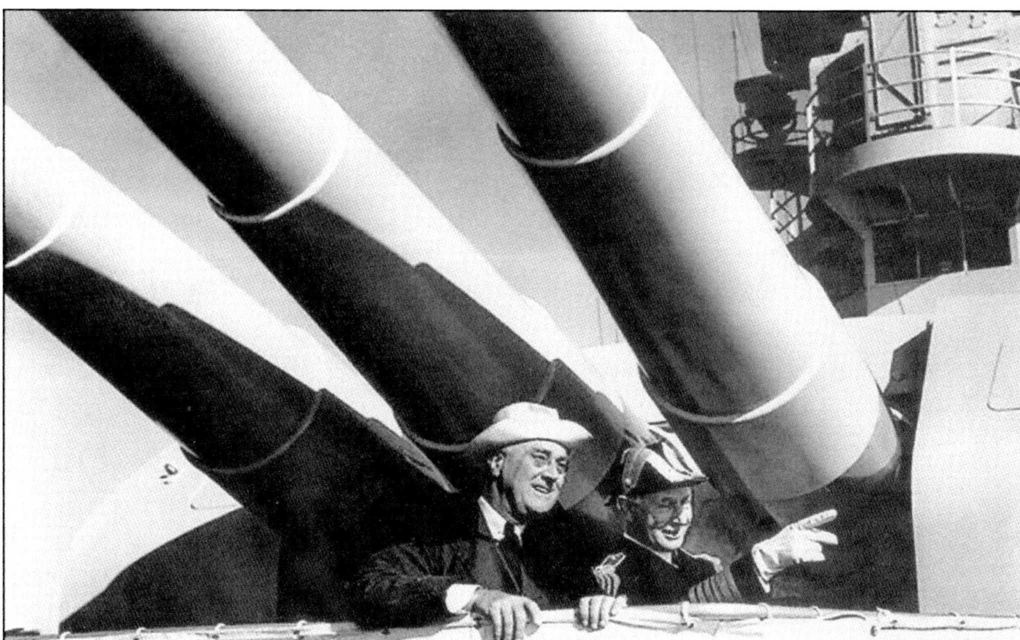

Admiral Claude Bloch (right), pictured with Pres. Franklin D. Roosevelt, was one of two men born in Woodbury—and one of nine from Kentucky—to achieve the rank of admiral. Bloch graduated from the US Naval Academy and served in the Spanish-American War and World Wars I and II. He was commander-in-chief of the US fleet from 1938 to 1940 and commandant of the naval district at Pearl Harbor from 1940 to 1942.

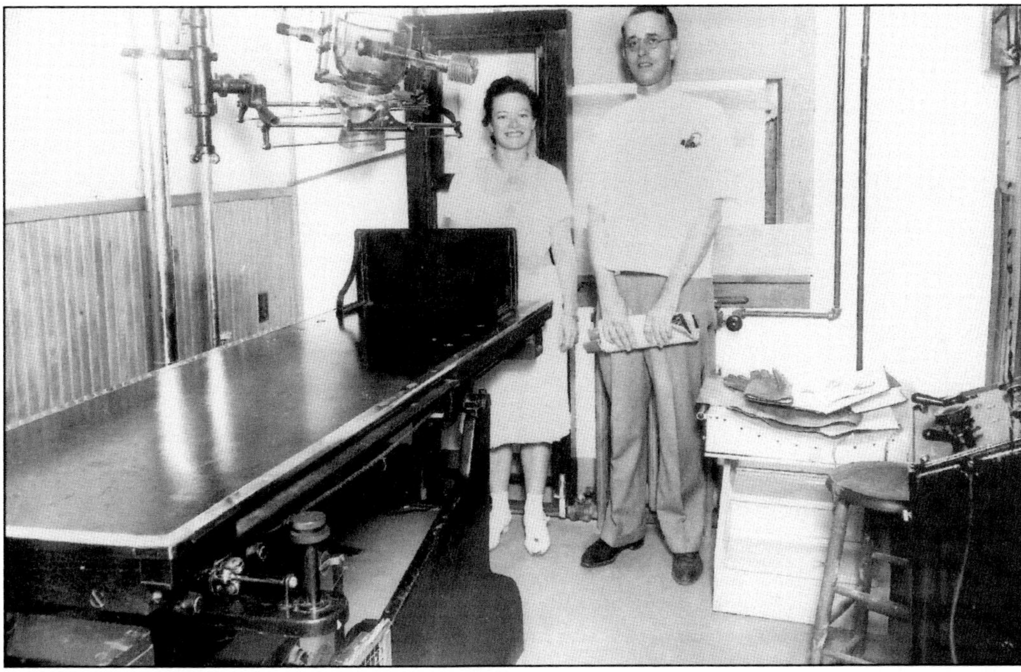

Dr. David G. Miller and nurse Polly Kelly display the x-ray machine Miller installed in his Morgantown clinic. A graduate of Vanderbilt, Dr. Miller established his practice in 1936. A pioneer in the medical field, he brought a complete clinic, including surgical facilities and a laboratory, to the rural community. Dr. Miller and his accomplishments were featured in the *Saturday Evening Post* and *Time* magazine. (Courtesy of David G. and Sarah Miller.)

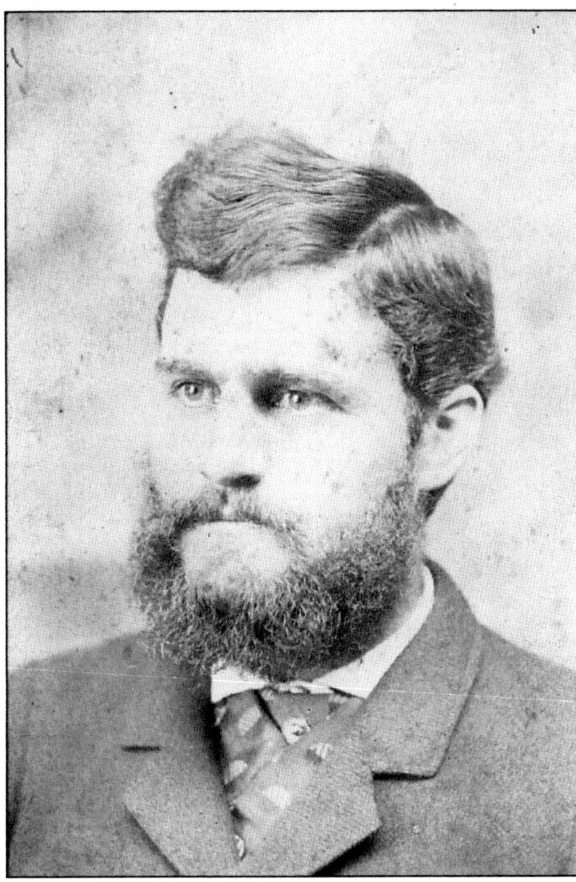

Dr. J. French Duncan was 30 years old when he moved to Butler County in 1889 after earning a medical degree from the University of Louisville. He was born in Warren County and eventually moved back to Bowling Green to practice medicine.

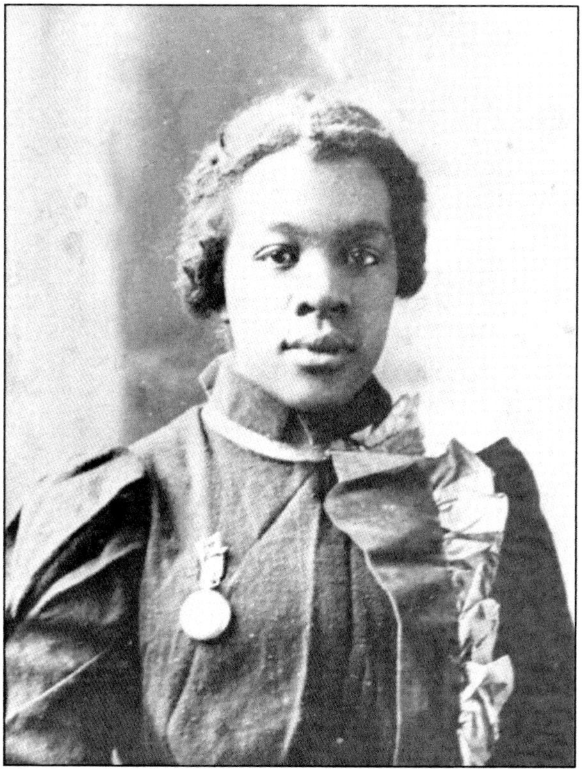

Ora Porter, the first African American Butler County native to earn a college degree, was Bowling Green's first registered nurse. Born in 1880, she attended Tuskegee Institute School of Nursing, graduated in 1904, and worked for the privately owned St. Joseph's Hospital.

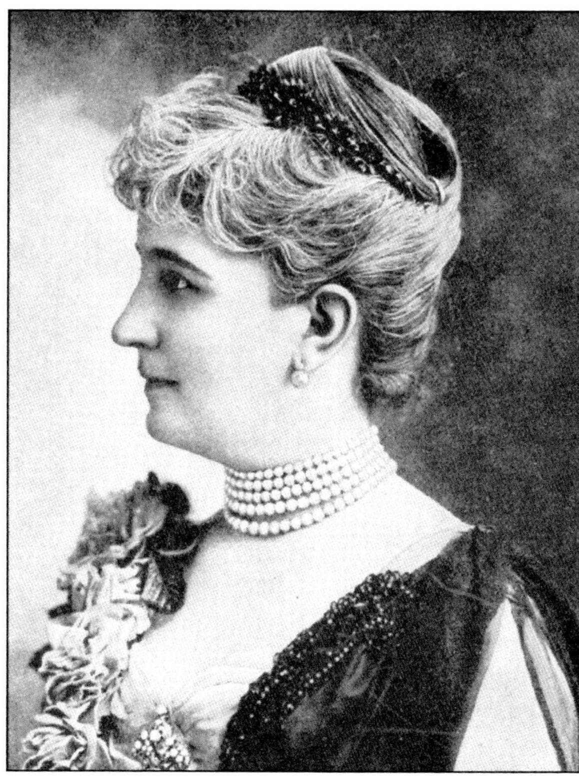

Bertha "Cissie" Honoré was born in May 1849 on her father's 4,000-acre plantation near Woodbury. She married Potter Palmer in Chicago in 1871, and he built the famous Palmer House Hotel as a wedding gift to her. The luxurious hotel still operates today as the Palmer House (a Hilton hotel). Palmer also built the Palmer Mansion in Chicago. (Courtesy of Chicago History Museum, ICH12053.)

Samuel Austin, elected judge of Butler County in 1850, was its first county judge following the adoption of the 1850 Kentucky Constitution. He later served as a county magistrate. He married Nancy Wand James on August 9, 1831, and died on December 3, 1884. He is buried in Salem Cemetery.

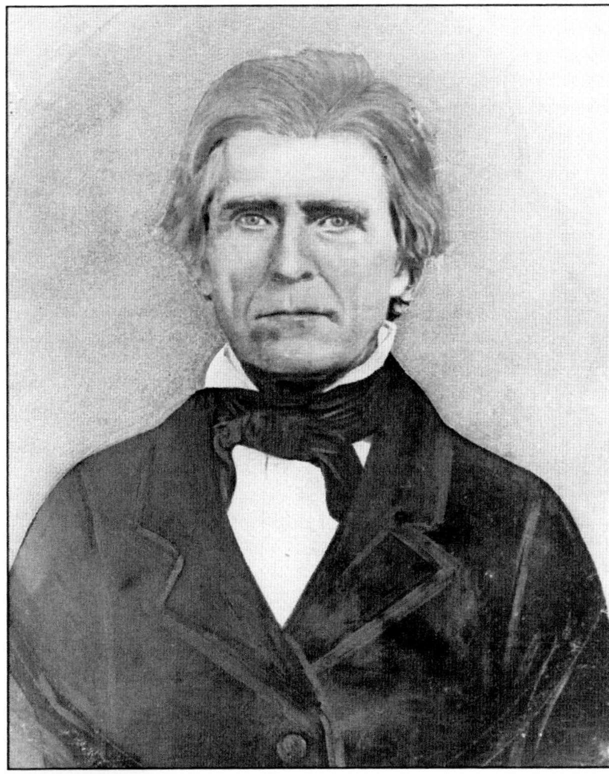

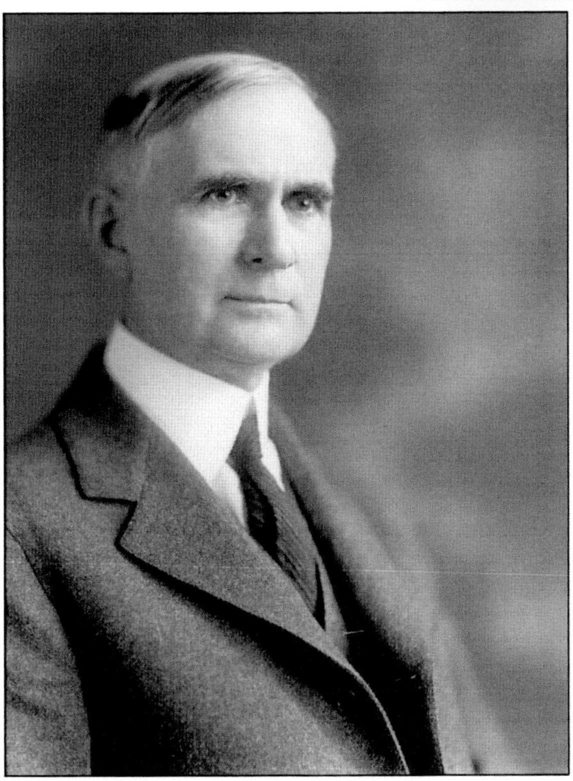

At the age of three, Maurice Hudson Thatcher moved with his parents from Chicago to Morgantown. He served as circuit clerk from 1893 to 1896, as Western Kentucky's assistant US attorney from 1901 to 1908, and as governor of the Panama Canal Zone from 1910 to 1913. He was elected to congress in 1922 and was instrumental in passing legislation to create national parks at Mammoth Cave and Abraham Lincoln's birthplace. The Thatcher Ferry Bridge over Panama Canal (now called the "Bridge of the Americas") was named for him.

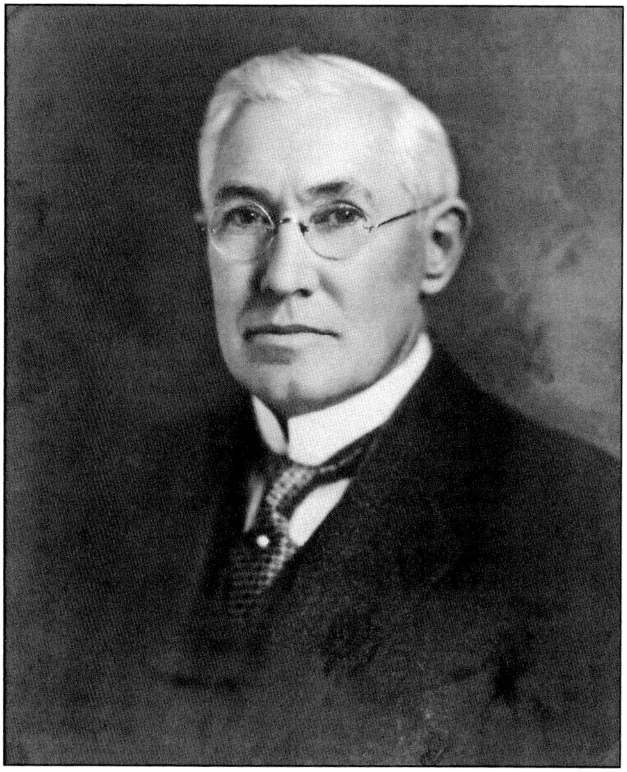

Bishop John Monroe Moore received a PhD from Yale, entered the ministry of the Methodist Episcopal Church, South, in 1898, and was elected bishop in 1918. He was a founder of Southern Methodist University and the presiding bishop at the Kansas City, Missouri, reunification conference of the Methodist churches. (Courtesy of Bridwell Library, Perkins School of Theology, Southern Methodist University, Dallas, Texas.)

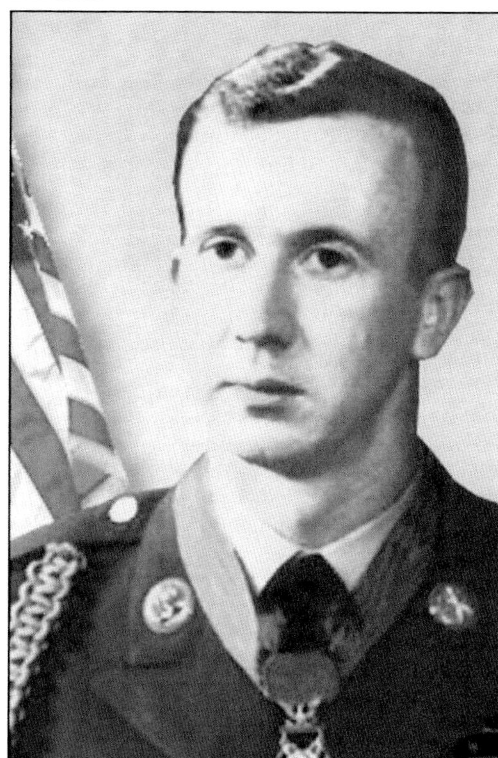

Sgt. Don J. Jenkins was awarded the Congressional Medal of Honor in 1969 after serving as a machine-gunner in Vietnam. During his service, he maneuvered to an exposed position to fire on the enemy and was seriously wounded. Without regard for his own life and wounds, he made three trips under fire to pull injured comrades back to safety.

Samuel Barnett was editor of one of the county's first newspapers, the *Butler County News*, founded in 1882. Owned by the Morgantown Publishing company, it boasted a circulation of 528 in 1886. The four-page weekly came out on Thursdays and supported Democratic policies.

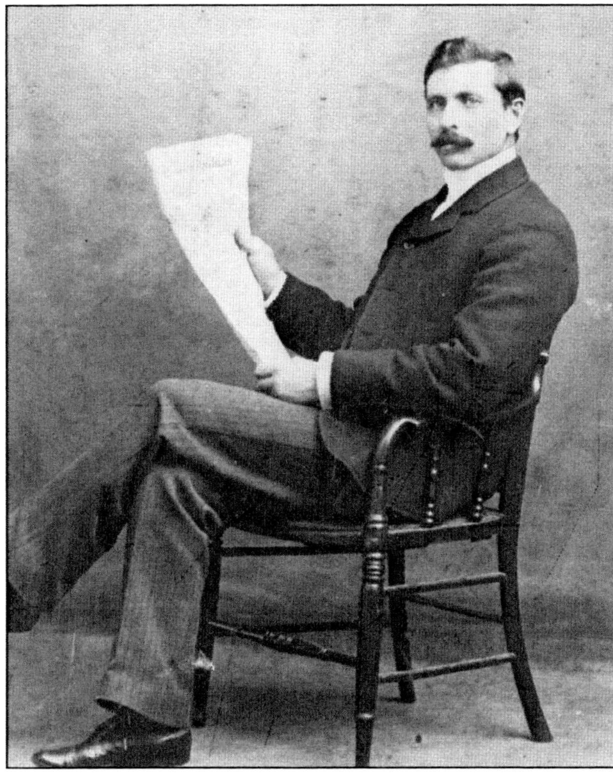

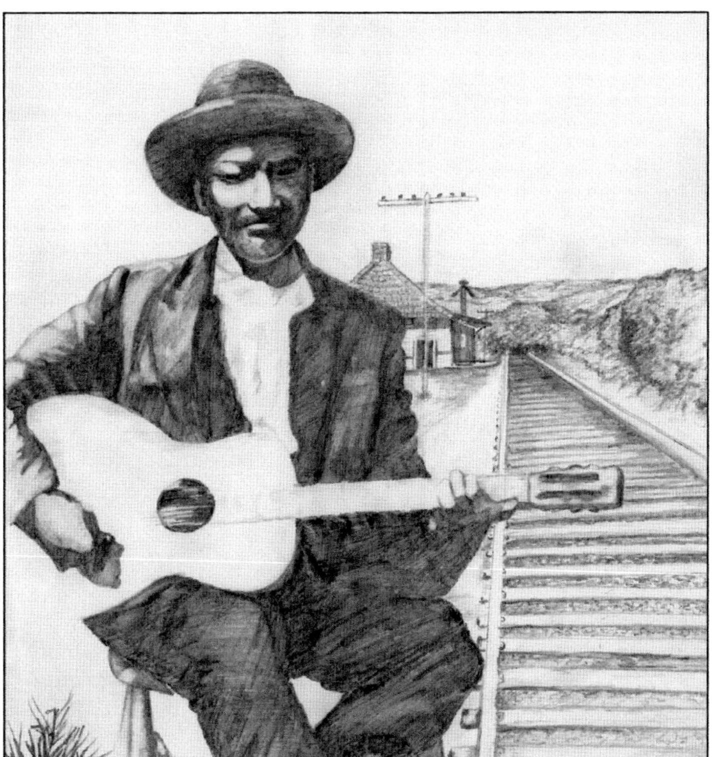

This likeness is of Arnold Shultz, an African American musician whose influence on guitar and bluegrass music is renowned. Directly or indirectly, he influenced legends such as Bill Monroe, Kennedy Jones, Ike Everly, Mose Rager, Merle Travis, and Chet Atkins. Shultz popularized an unusual style of playing lead and bass notes simultaneously, known as thumbpicking. He died in Morgantown in April 1931. (Illustration by Gary Bewley.)

To the Democrats

—OF THE—

5th Judicial District!

In view of the unfair and extraordinary efforts made in certain quarters to prejudice public sentiment against the officials of the democratic party in Butler county, and to create the impression that an attempt was made to defeat a fair expression of democratic sentiment at the convention held in Morgantown on the 24th day of October, 1885, we beg leave to make the following statement:

1. The democratic committee ot Butler county is composed of thirteen members, of whom four are for Mr. Rodes and nine for Mr. Reeves

2. The friends of Mr Reeves on said committee, without the aid of any of the friends of Mr. Rodes, passed a resolution that no one should vote in the convention to be held on the 24th, except those who had been heretofore recognized democrats.

3. In spite of said resolution, duly passed by the county committee of Butler county, efforts were continually made to vote republicans in said convention.

4 A few days before the meeting of the convention of the 24th, Mr. W A. Helm, chairman of the Butler county committee, proposed to Mr. Henry T. Clark, a citizen of Bowling Green who was staying in Butler county in the interest of Mr. Rodes, to join him in an open letter saying that no one who had not been theretofore a recognized democrat would be allowed to participate in the convention on the 24th, which proposition Mr. Clark declined.

5 At the presidential election held in November, 1884, which is the basis of the pending judicial convention, 761 votes in all were cast for Cleveland and Hendricks, of which at least two-thirds were south of the river in Butler county.

6 There are in Butler county not exceeding 900 democratic voters.

7 Of these we will be able to *name* two-thirds or more who voted for Mr. Reeves in the convention held in Morgantown on the 24th inst.

8 We will be able to *name* every democratic voter in Butler county, and to show by proof how many of them participated in the convention of the 24th, and who each one was for, for judge, and we will be able to demonstrate that at least two-thirds of them were for Mr. Reeves.

9 We will be able to show that there is no truth in the statement that W. A. Helm, chairman of the committee of Butler county, refused to take a vote on the nomination of Moses H. Fuqua for chairman of said convention, or that he refused to allow or grant a division or count of the vote for each nominee for chairman of said convention.

10 The convention of the 24th, in Morgantown was honestly and fairly organized in strict accord with Democratic usages; no effort was made to defeat the will of the majority, but every effort was made to take the sense of the majority in electing said chairman, and T. J. Bunch was fairly and honestly elected chairman of said convention by an overwhelming majority.

October 28th, 1885.

11 Up to the hour of the convention Mr. Rodes' friends were begging for a prorata of the county.

W. A. Helm, chrm'n county com.
T. J. Bunch, chairman of convention.
A. T. Dockery,
R. B. Kuykendall,
Jno. M. Carson,
T. D Fuller,
D. Y. Fostsr,
W. H. Kitchens.
P. G. Whitaker,
G. M. Doolin,
W. A. Dockins,
T. W. Burgher,
James Phillips,
J. A. Kuykendall,
G. B. Phelps,
B. F. Phelps,
J. F. Hays,
J. W. West,
E A. Taylor,
Henry Vaughn,
Henry T. England,
P. W. Thomasson,
E. Bery,
J. B. Dockin,
John Dortch,
W. C. Green,
C. C. Shultz,
J. R. Read,
W. M. Barks,
J. W. Newton,
M M. Hinant,
Charles Hudnall,
L. Mendel,
O. P. Butler,
A. L. Forsythe,
M. F. Brown.

Today, Butler County is a predominantly Republican county, but that was not always the case. This list of leading county Democrats includes W.A. Helm, a delegate to the Democratic National Convention in 1892, and T.J. Bunch, the county court clerk from 1874 to 1881. Willis L. Reeves won this controversial race for circuit judge.

Two

Green River Heritage

The Green River has been both a major factor and a serious obstacle to the growth of Butler County. The river snakes its way through the county, separating it into three large, separate sections. In the early years, the center of government and political power was located on the south side of the river in Morgantown. This county seat area ultimately grew but left the people north of the river isolated from the center of economic activity. Several ferries were established, granting access to the county seat and its businesses. However, the swollen river still isolated the north side of the county for much of the winter and rainy spring seasons. Even when the river was at normal stages, a steep toll was charged for crossings that were not related to official county business, making it more affordable for those on the north side to trade with neighboring counties. The problems associated with the river were a tremendous hindrance to the cohesiveness needed for regional growth.

Conversely, the river brought tremendous economic opportunities to the county. The river routes were a means of getting valley products to major markets such as the port of New Orleans, where a flatboat was recorded entering from Greensburg in 1805. The state saw the opportunities and, in 1808, required residents along the river to clean obstacles to navigation from the watercourse. In the 1820s and 1830s, the growing use of steamboats to get products to market encouraged the development of a slackwater navigation system that provided year-round transportation in and out of the valley. With the opening of the county to the steamboat trade, the population decline was reversed, resulting in the development of two new towns—Rochester and Woodbury. The steamboat era brought about a productive, pleasurable, nearly 100-year-long growth period across the entire area.

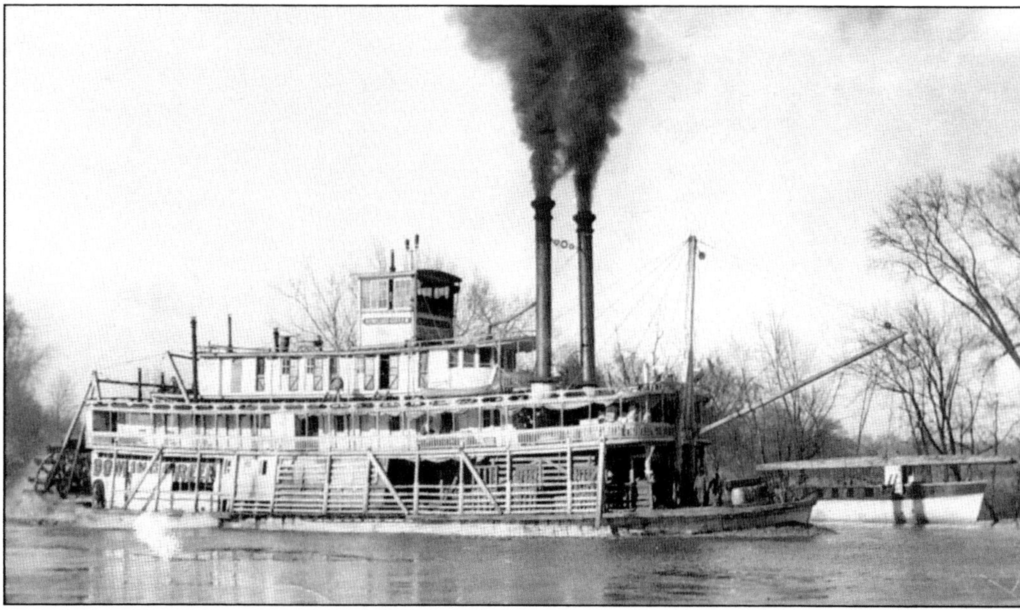

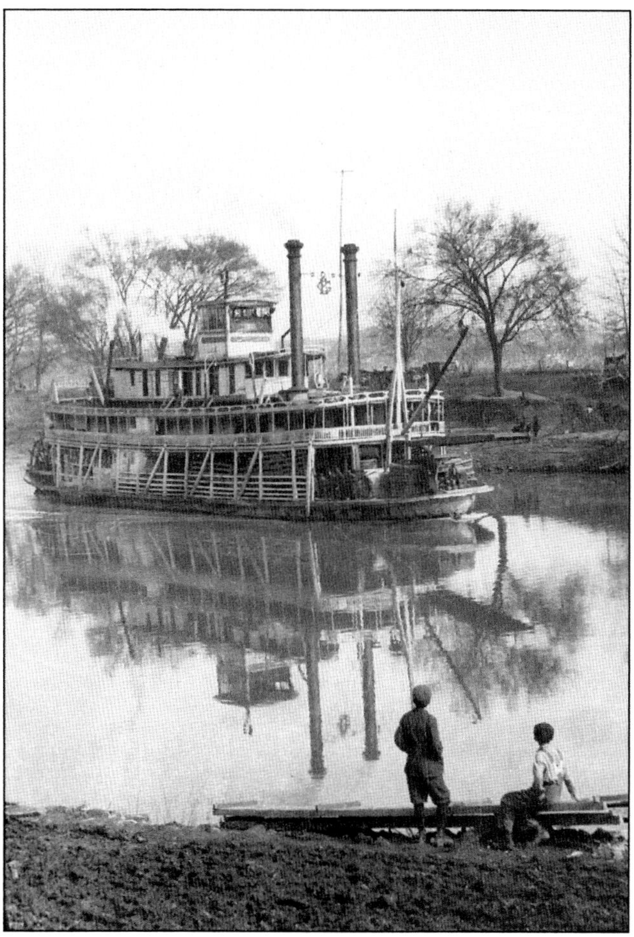

The *Bowling Green* rounds the bend at Morgantown at full speed, heading upstream toward Woodbury. The river is high, as the houseboat on the far bank rides near the top of the riverbank. At this elevation, boats would require full throttle to run against the swift current.

This photograph of the *Bowling Green* was taken by George Dabbs, who had a particularly keen sense of what was historically important in his photography. His photographs have been featured in books and magazines about riverboats, such as *Steamboats on the Green*, by Agnes S. Harralson, and *The Waterways Journal*.

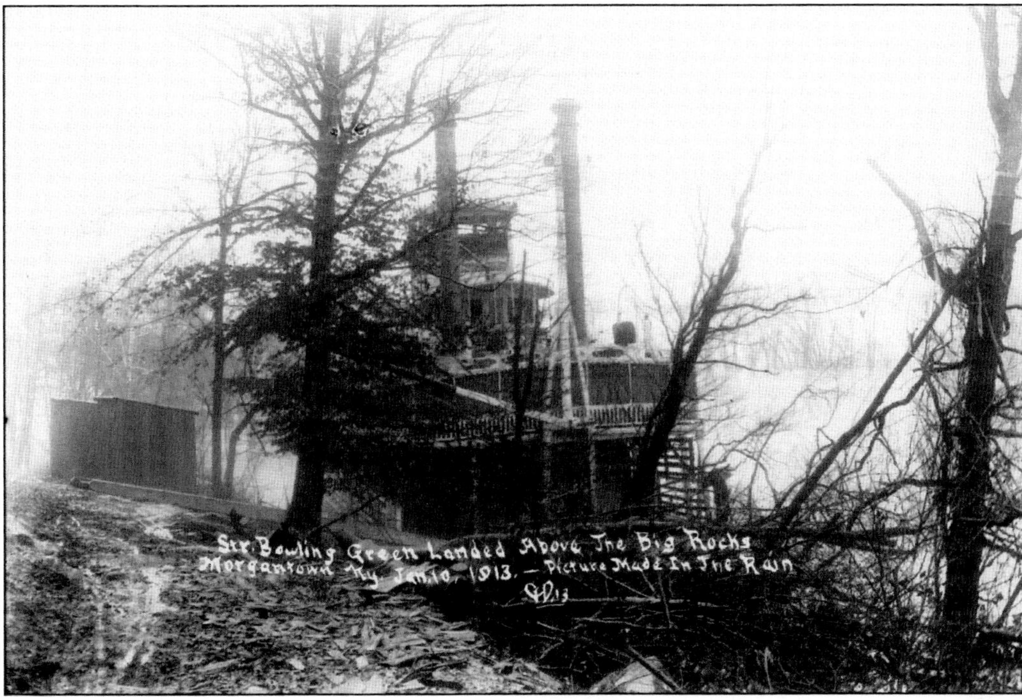

The steamer *Bowling Green* is pictured tied up above the rocks at Morgantown on January 10, 1913. The packet boat made regularly scheduled, twice-weekly runs from Evansville, Indiana, to Bowling Green. This was the third and last *Bowling Green*, and it sank on May 31, 1920, at South Carrollton, Kentucky. All passengers got off the boat safely.

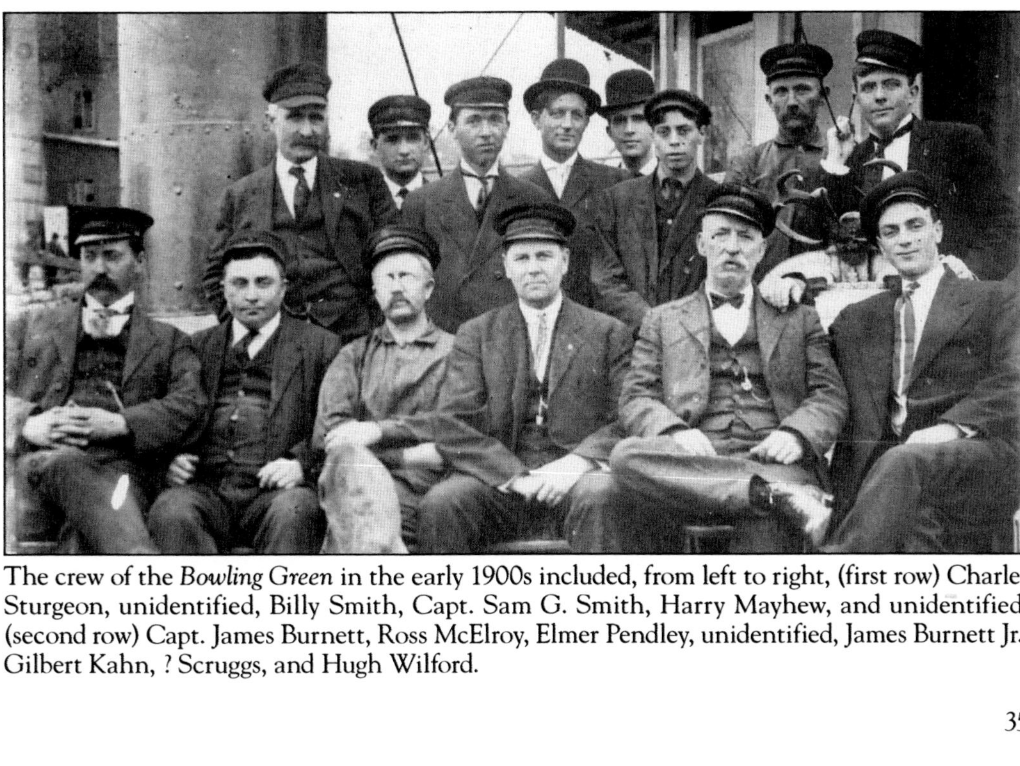

The crew of the *Bowling Green* in the early 1900s included, from left to right, (first row) Charles Sturgeon, unidentified, Billy Smith, Capt. Sam G. Smith, Harry Mayhew, and unidentified; (second row) Capt. James Burnett, Ross McElroy, Elmer Pendley, unidentified, James Burnett Jr., Gilbert Kahn, ? Scruggs, and Hugh Wilford.

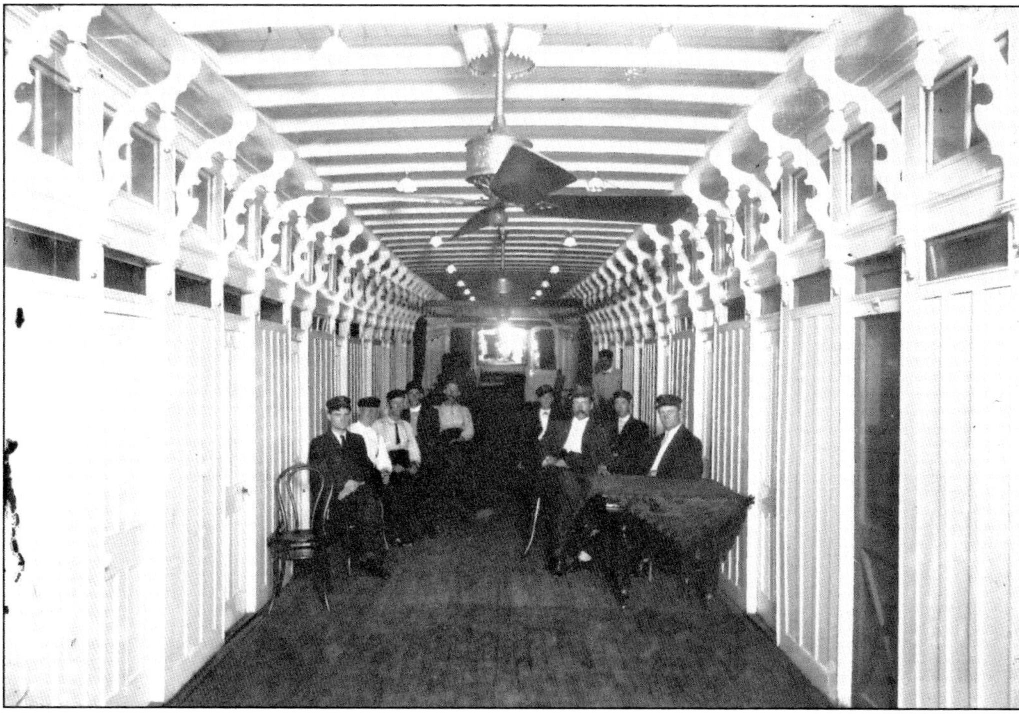

The interior of the *Bowling Green* offered a cool place to rest. The crew members pictured here are, from left to right, Ross McElroy, Harry Mayhew, L.A. McMurty, Kim Thompson, unidentified, Capt. Charles Sturgeon, Elmer Pendley, unidentified, and Sam Smith. The man standing in the back is unidentified.

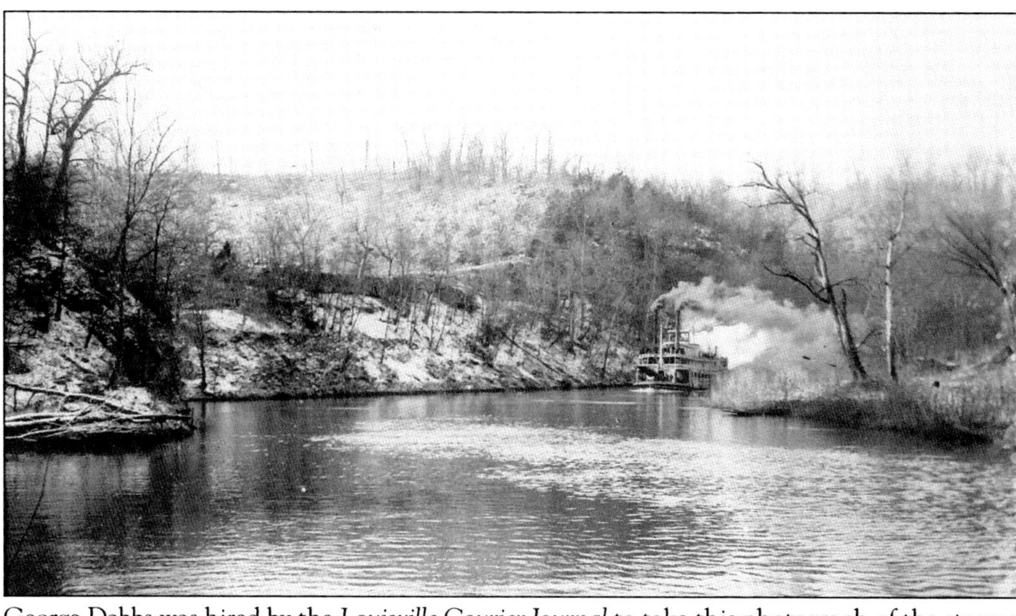

George Dabbs was hired by the *Louisville Courier-Journal* to take this photograph of the steamer *Chaperon* on its maiden voyage to Mammoth Cave on the upper Green River. The pilot let Dabbs off onto the bank then backed upstream for the photograph. In the 1960s, Dabbs painted the photograph and had prints made; it became one of his most popular works.

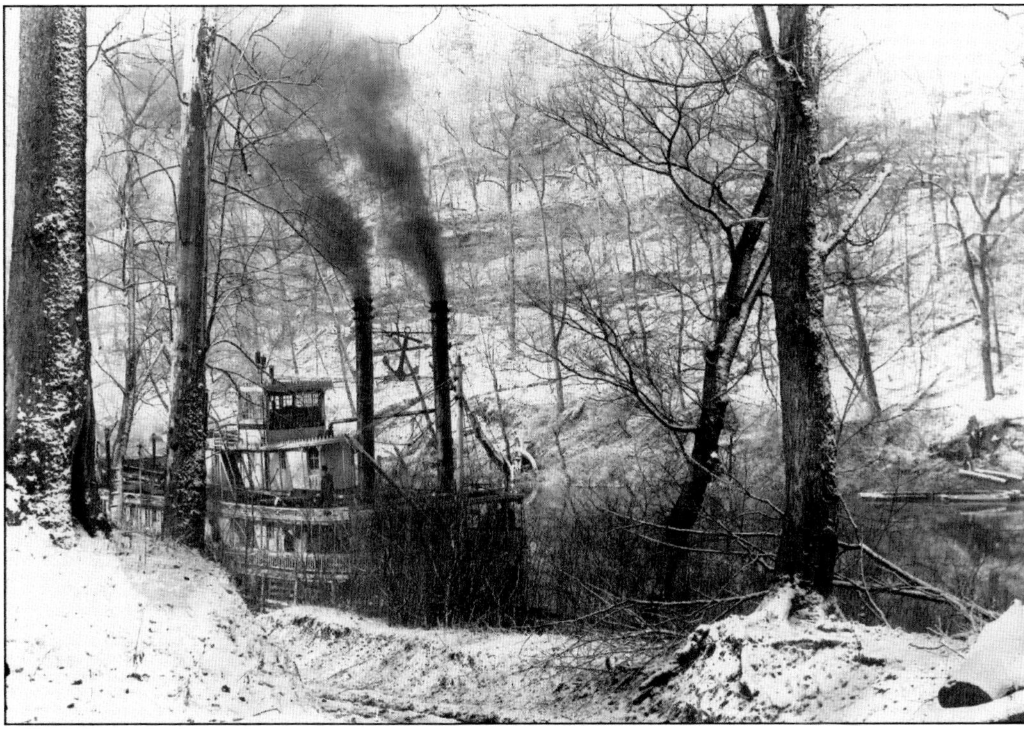

A snowy winter scene shows the *Chaperon* with owner and captain Jeff Williams standing on the second deck. The steamer picked up passengers in Woodbury on her way to Mammoth Cave. The *Chaperon* was named the *J.C. Kerr* until 1904, when it was placed on the Barren and upper Green River run from Bowling Green to Mammoth Cave, a route it continued to travel until 1917.

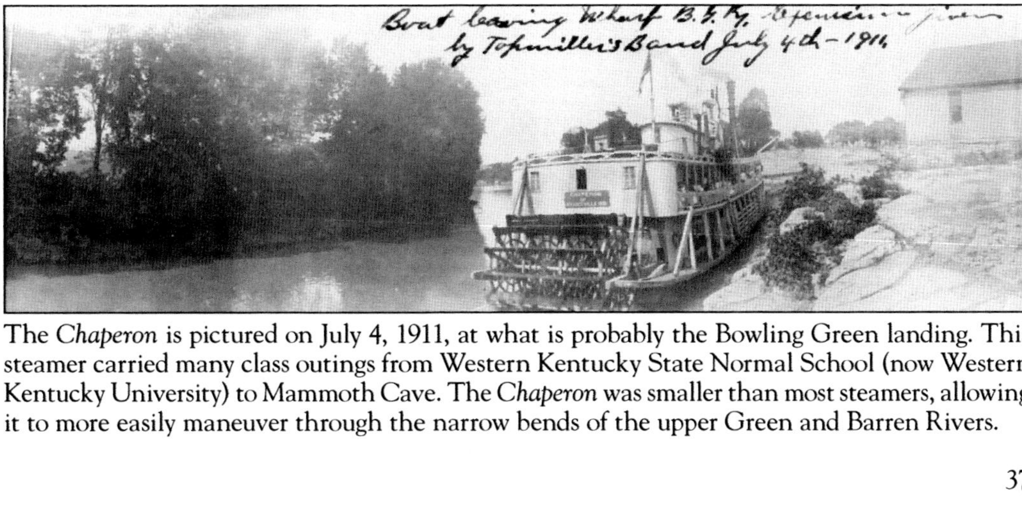

The *Chaperon* is pictured on July 4, 1911, at what is probably the Bowling Green landing. This steamer carried many class outings from Western Kentucky State Normal School (now Western Kentucky University) to Mammoth Cave. The *Chaperon* was smaller than most steamers, allowing it to more easily maneuver through the narrow bends of the upper Green and Barren Rivers.

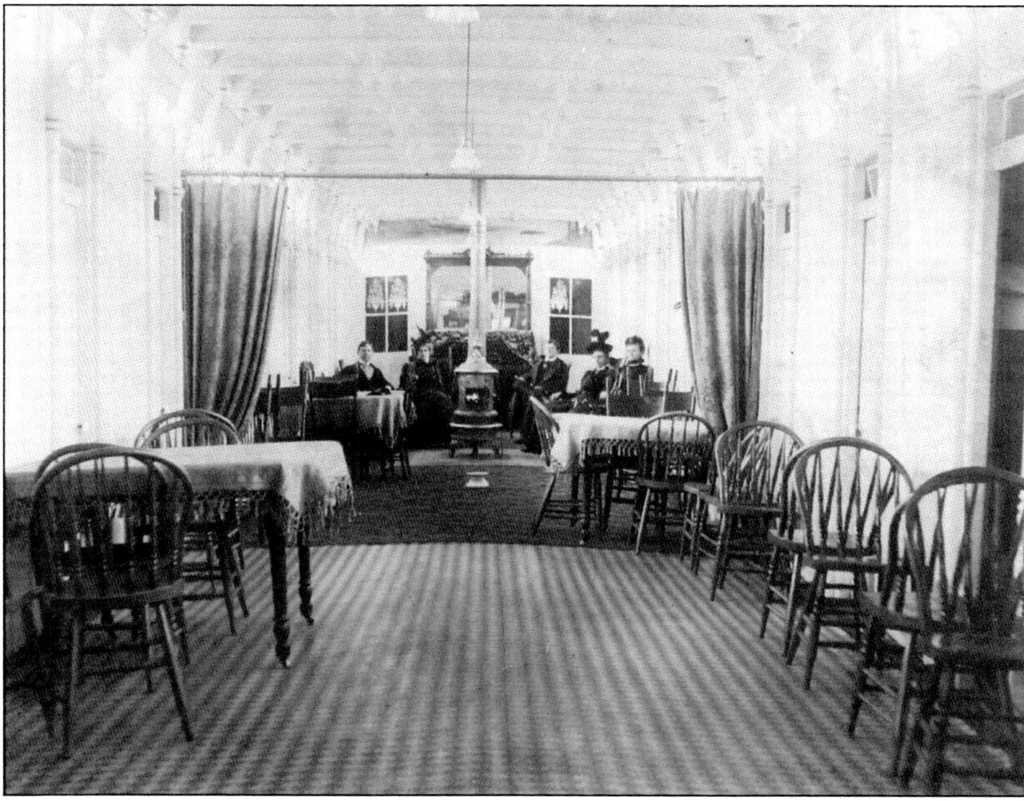

The interior of the *Chaperon* was not as luxurious as those of the *Evansville* and others, possibly because of the type of service it ran from Bowling Green to Mammoth Cave—it was in the "short trade," as it was known in the riverboat business. The *Chaperon* made the maiden voyage to Mammoth Cave in 1906 after Lock No. 6 was opened at Brownsville.

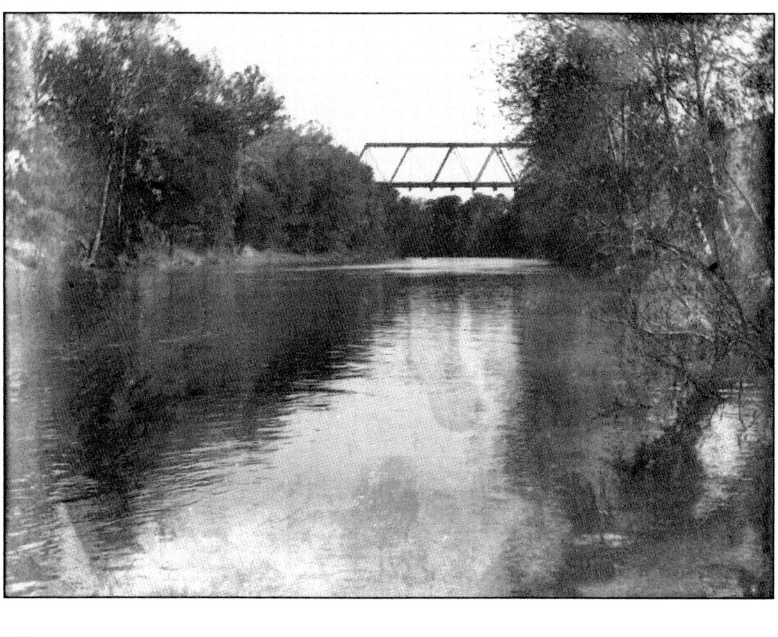

This c. 1900 photograph captures a view from the Mud River looking downstream at the old Mud River Bridge. The bridge, which connected Butler and Muhlenberg Counties at Rochester, was torn down in the early 1950s and replaced with a concrete structure.

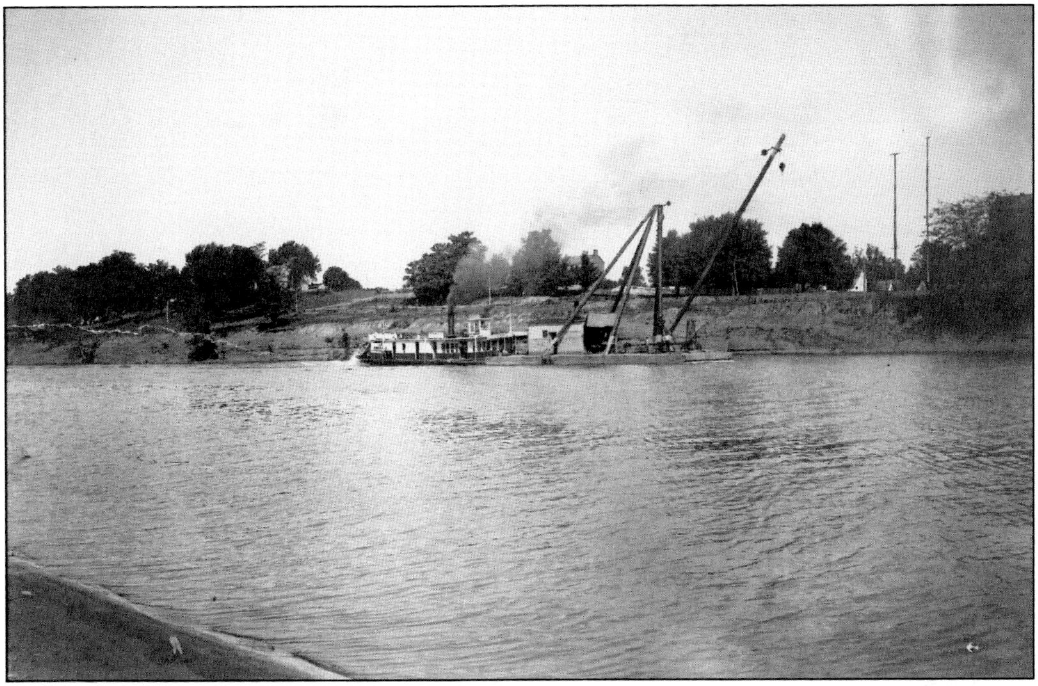

The US Army Corps of Engineers' *Emerald* was part of their fleet of five dredges headquartered at the district office at Woodbury. *Emerald* mostly operated on the Barren River. One of the boat's pilots was Capt. J. Porter Hines. Note the derrick and swing boom on the front of the boat; they were used to lift snags out of the river and onto the riverbank.

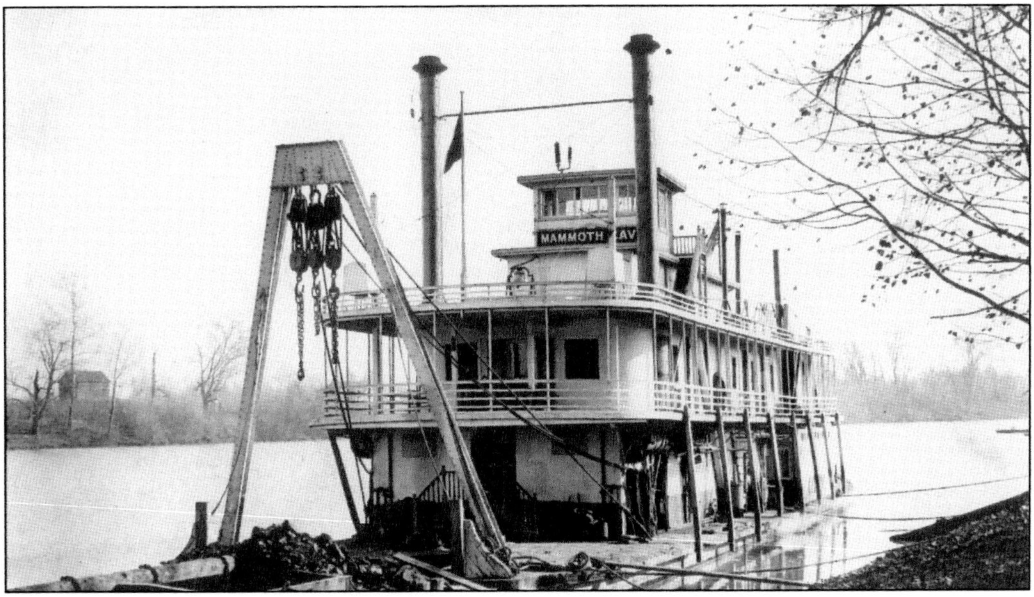

The *Mammoth Cave* was another dredge boat operated by the US Army Corps of Engineers out of its district maintenance headquarters for the Green and Barren Rivers at Woodbury. The last Butler County resident known to have worked on this boat was Johnny Decker. Decker's daughter, Faye Milan, remembers staying on the docked boat with her father and having ice cream from its kitchen.

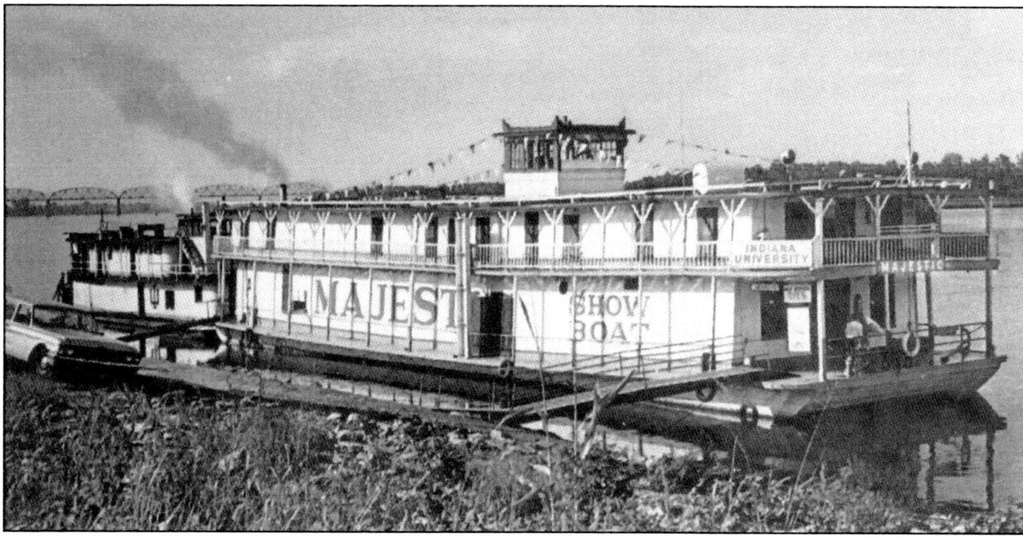

The showboat *Majestic* and her tow, the *Atta Boy*, brought theatrical entertainment to the Green River valley in the early 1900s. She made her final trip on the Green River in 1930, and was the last showboat to do so. The *Majestic*, which was sold to the city of Cincinnati in 1967 and is now home to a professional summer stock theater, became a national historic landmark in 1989.

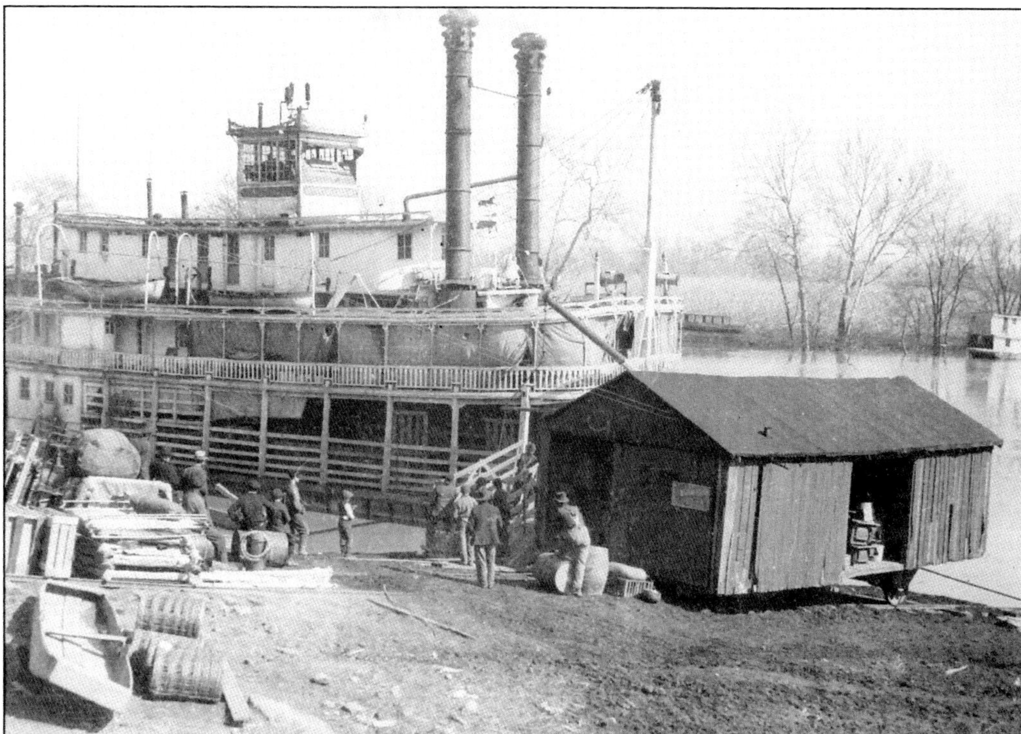

The Morgantown landing was a busy place when packet boats like the *Evansville*, seen here, made their stops. The river is almost at flood stage, as evidenced by the boats on the opposite bank. This c. 1906 photograph was taken by George H. Dabbs and later recreated in a painting and made into prints.

The packet companies gave discounts to passengers going to the Butler County Fair. Here, the *Evansville* picks up passengers as it locks through at Woodbury. The fair was promoted throughout the lower Green River Valley, as shown by the banner on the railing advertising the Butler County Fair of 1908.

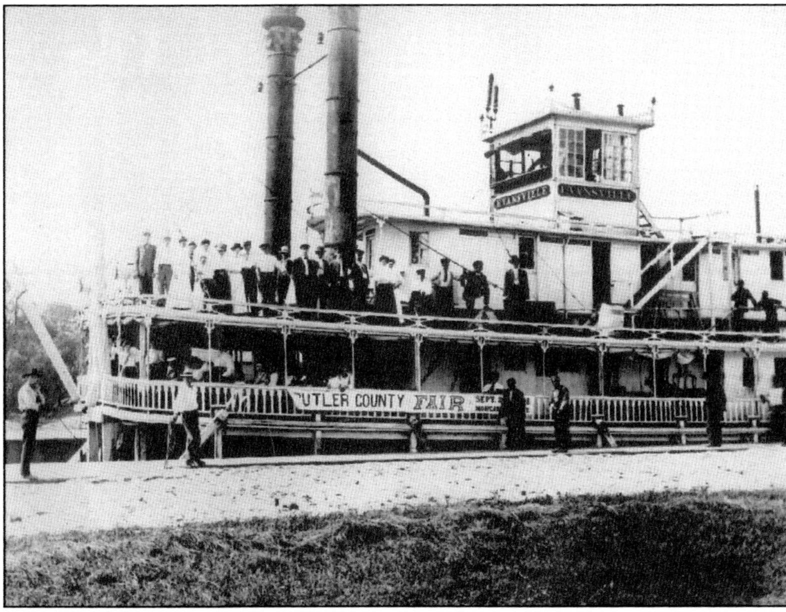

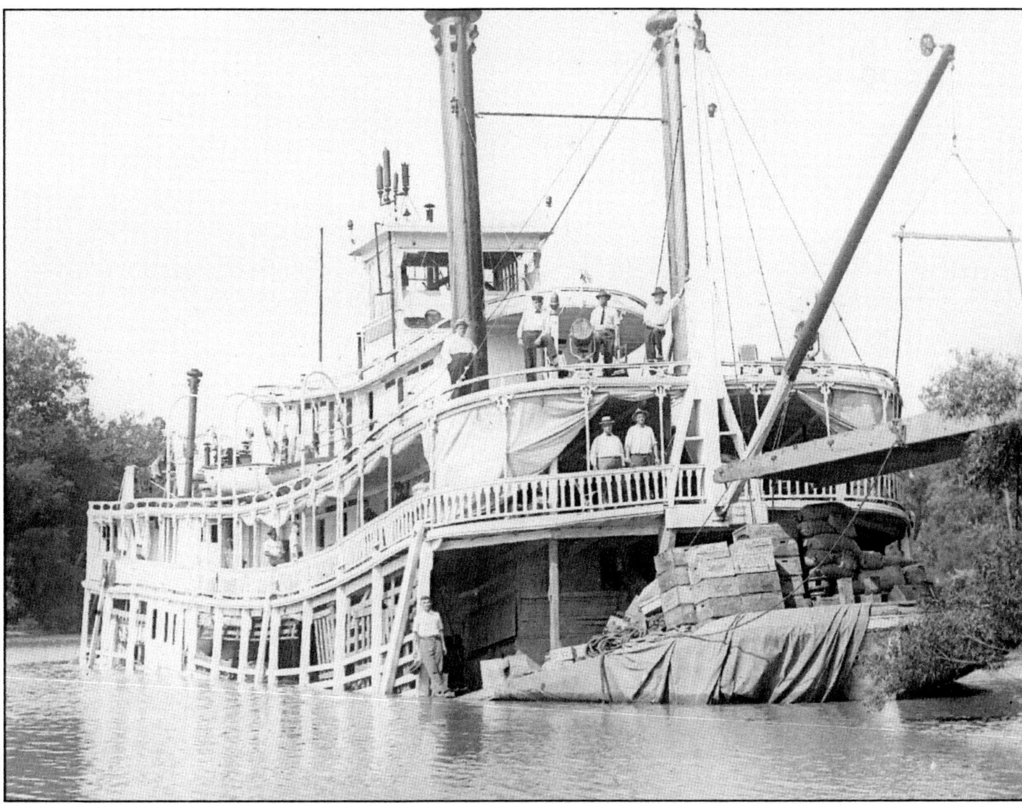

The *Evansville* rests on the river's bottom at Aberdeen. The "wildcat whistle" can be seen atop the pilothouse—Capt. Genie Lunn learned to play tunes on the whistle and could make sounds like a wild animal screaming, hence the name. Captain Lunn was from Morgantown, and before his mother died, he always played her a tune when passing.

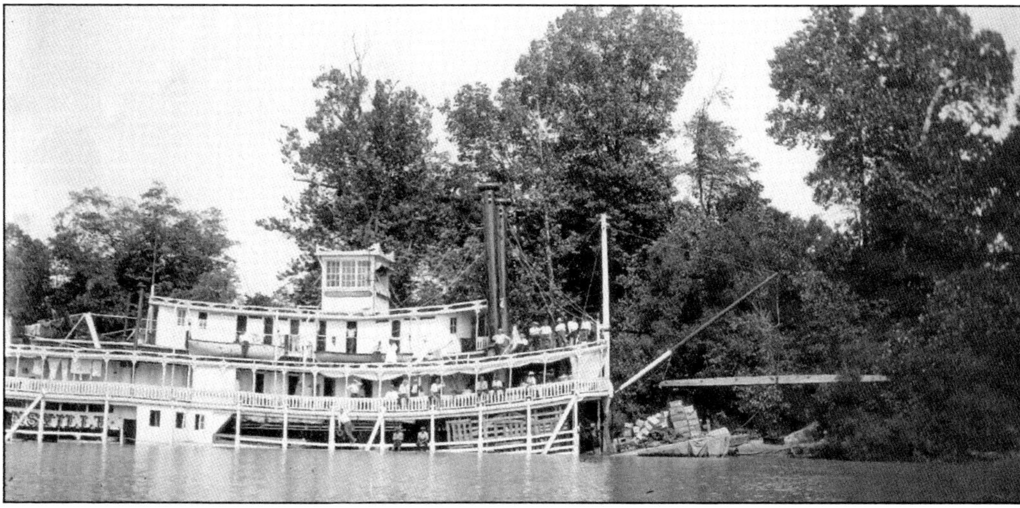

In this 1919 photograph taken at Aberdeen, the *Evansville* experiences some difficulty approximately where the Aberdeen Bridge now crosses the Green River. The passengers have moved to the upper decks and some of the cargo has been moved to the bow of the boat. No one was injured in the accident and, assisted by the *Speed*, she was raised and returned to service.

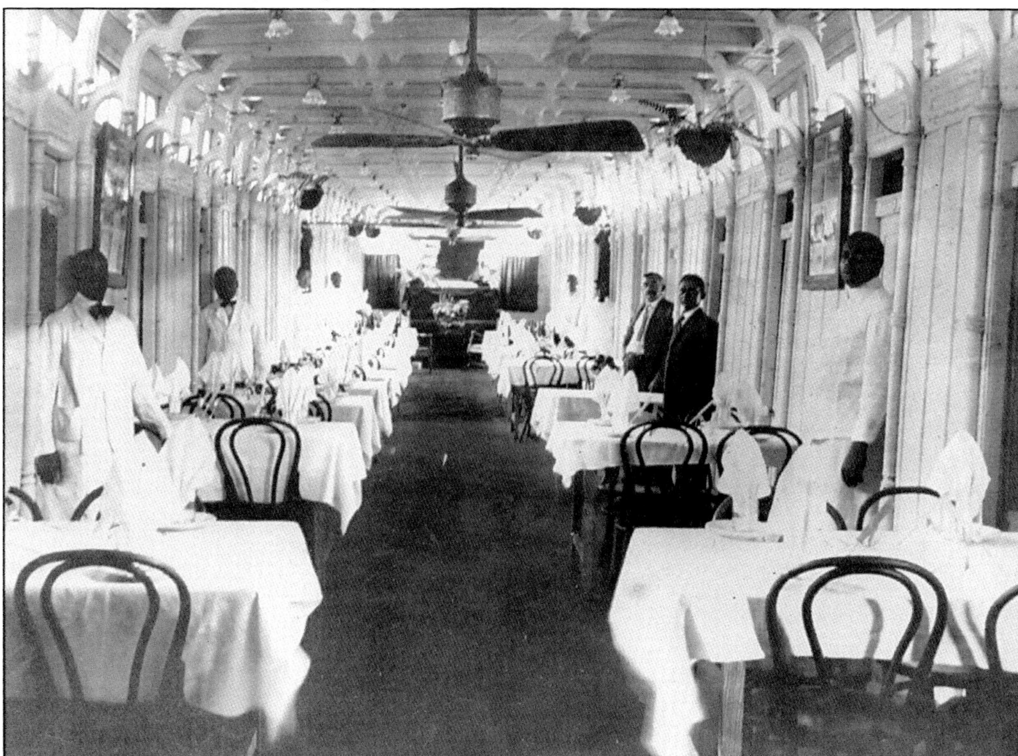

The interior cabin of the *Evansville* offered luxurious comfort for packet boat travelers on the Green and Barren Rivers. Riverboats also offered employment to many African American residents of Butler County, including Sam Radcliff of Morgantown, who was a cook on this boat. For many steamboat passengers, dining was the centerpiece of their time aboard, and they expected excellent food and service.

The charred, tangled remains of the *Evansville* are seen at the Bowling Green landing where she burned on July 25, 1931, after serving the Evansville-to-Bowling Green trade for many years. The *Evansville* was the last regularly scheduled packet boat in weekly service on the Green and Barren Rivers, and its burning brought the packet era to a close.

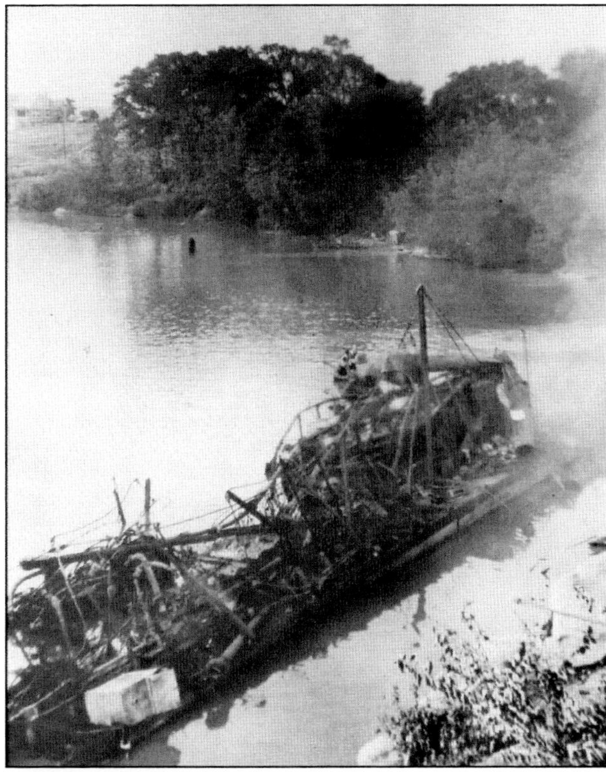

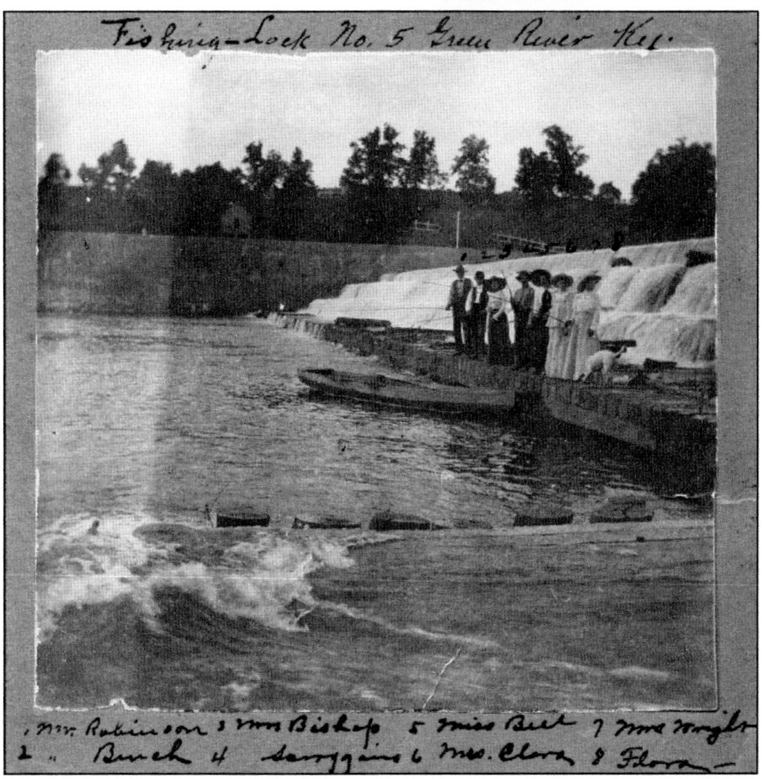

This well-dressed group tries to catch something for supper in August 1901. They are standing on Lock No. 5 near the junction of Edmonson, Butler, and Warren Counties. The group included (identified only by last names) Robinson, Bishop, Bell, Wright, Bunch, and Scuggins, as well as two girls—Clara and Flora—identified only by their first names.

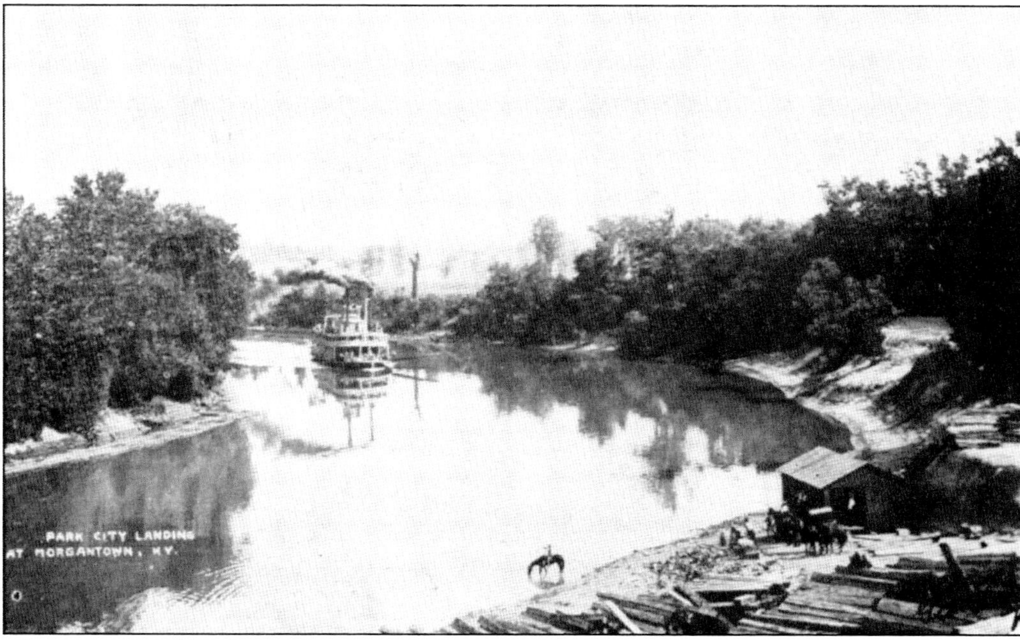

This George Dabbs photograph shows the steamer *Park City*—formerly *Gayoso*—rounding the bend at the Morgantown landing. A load of railroad ties is on the banks, ready for shipment. This image was first sold as a postcard by Butler County Drug Company.

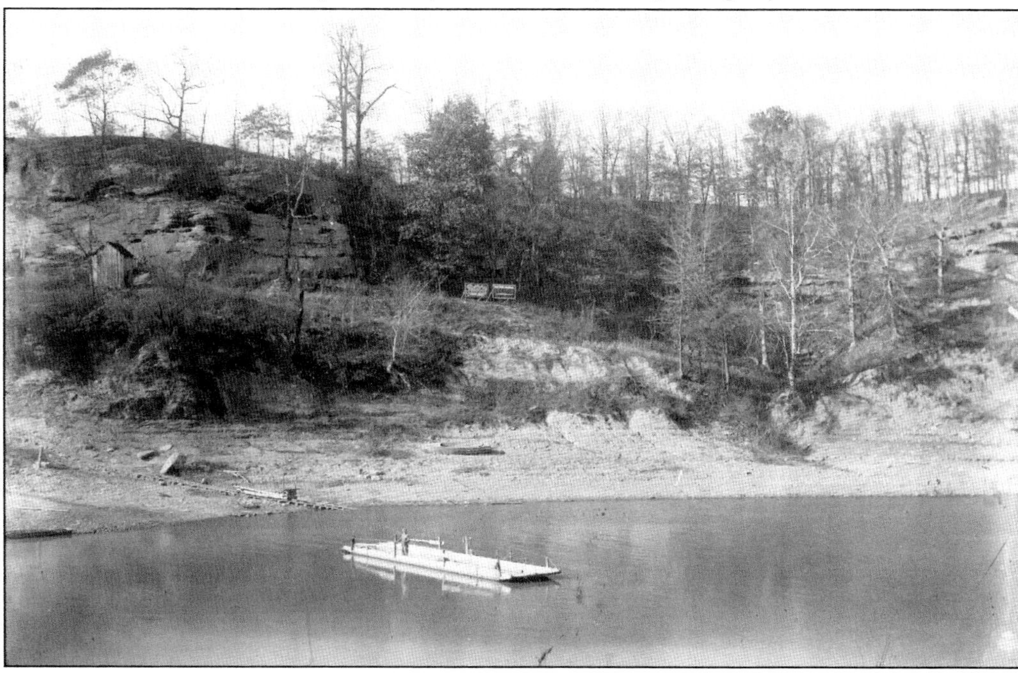

This photograph shows the bluffs above the Morgantown landing—approximately 200 feet above the water's edge at the river's normal summer elevation. Morgantown, located on a high hill overlooking the Green River, is surrounded by bluffs on three sides. The ferry was established here in 1810 and continued operation until 1954; the ferry-house is about halfway up the bluff on the left.

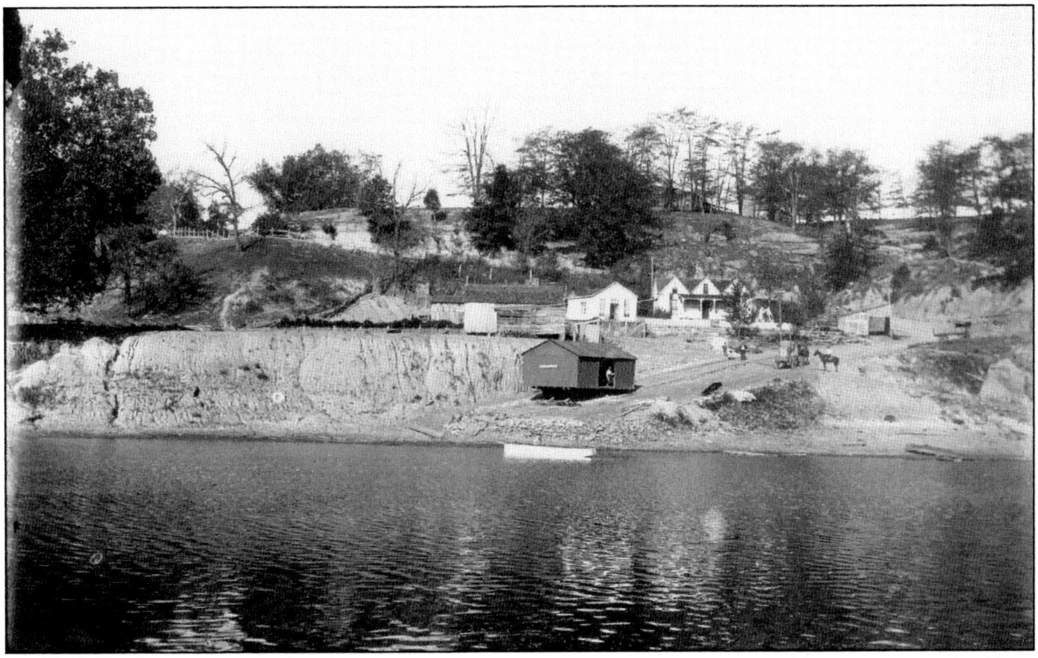

The Morgantown landing offers a good view of wharfmaster Charles Hill's home and office, known as Hillhouse. This photograph was taken before 1906, when the Morgantown Water and Electric plant buildings were constructed on top of the bluffs behind Hillhouse.

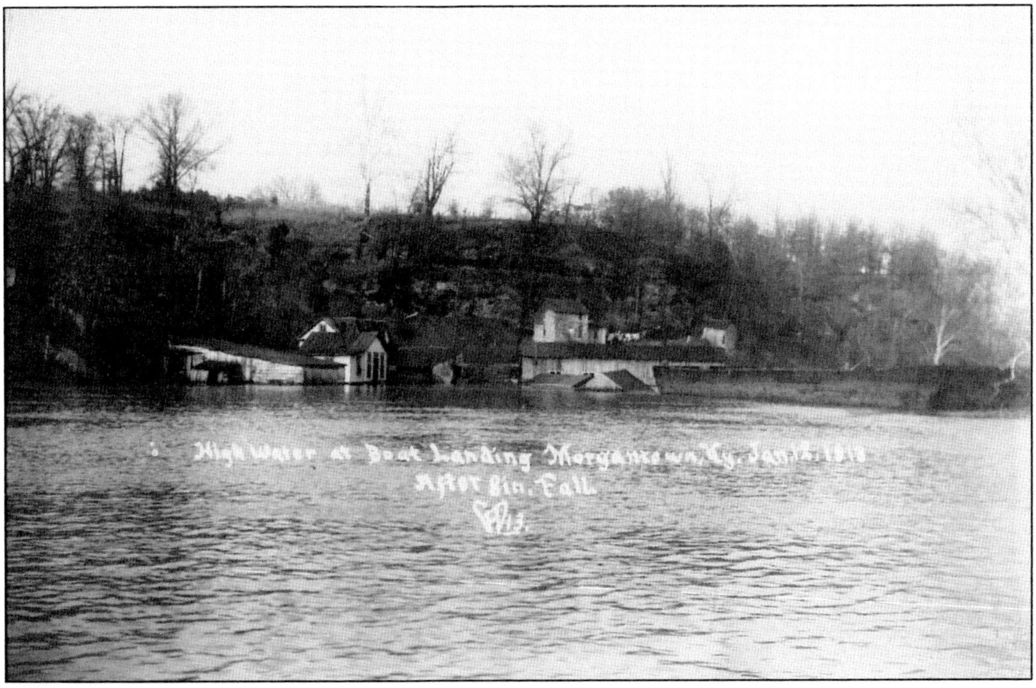

The caption on this photograph reads: "High water at boat landing, Morgantown, Ky. Jan. 12, 1913, after 8 in. fall." It is not clear if this meant after an eight-inch rainfall or after the river level had fallen eight inches, but judging by the markings on the buildings, it is thought to be the latter. The 1913 flood was the second-highest in Green River's recorded history.

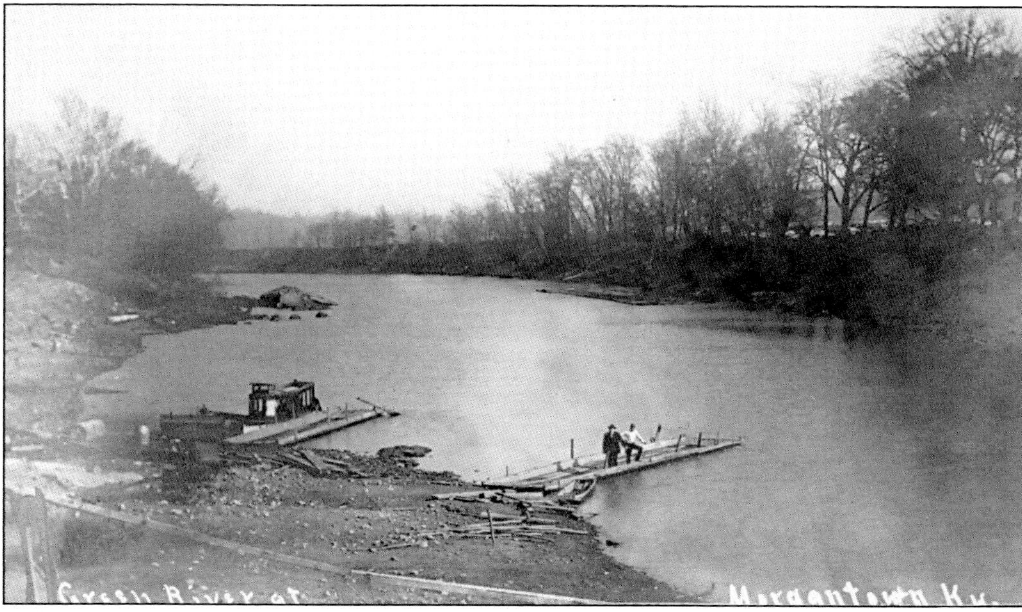

A downstream view of the Morgantown ferry and "way" shows the large rocks near the river's left bank. The "way," or slipway, was where boats were dry-docked for repairs. The rocks were later removed by the US Army Corps of Engineers. Roughly one mile downstream, the bend turns the river back around to the other side of Morgantown.

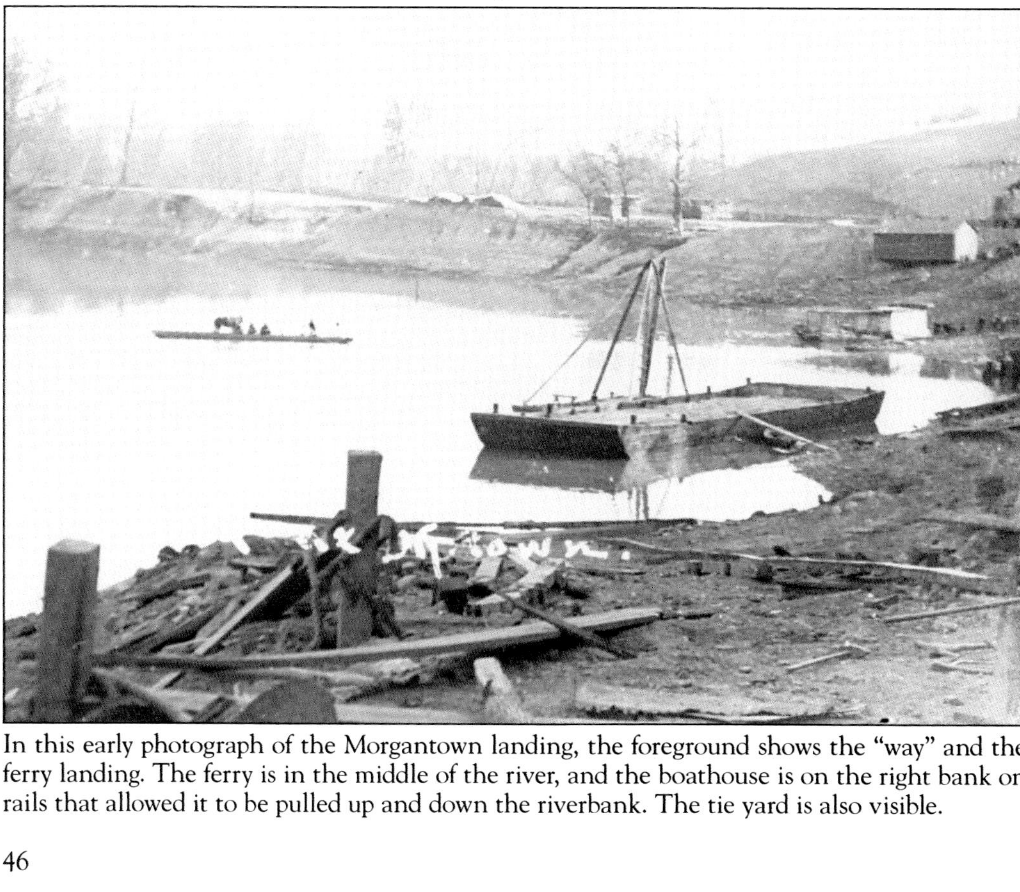

In this early photograph of the Morgantown landing, the foreground shows the "way" and the ferry landing. The ferry is in the middle of the river, and the boathouse is on the right bank on rails that allowed it to be pulled up and down the riverbank. The tie yard is also visible.

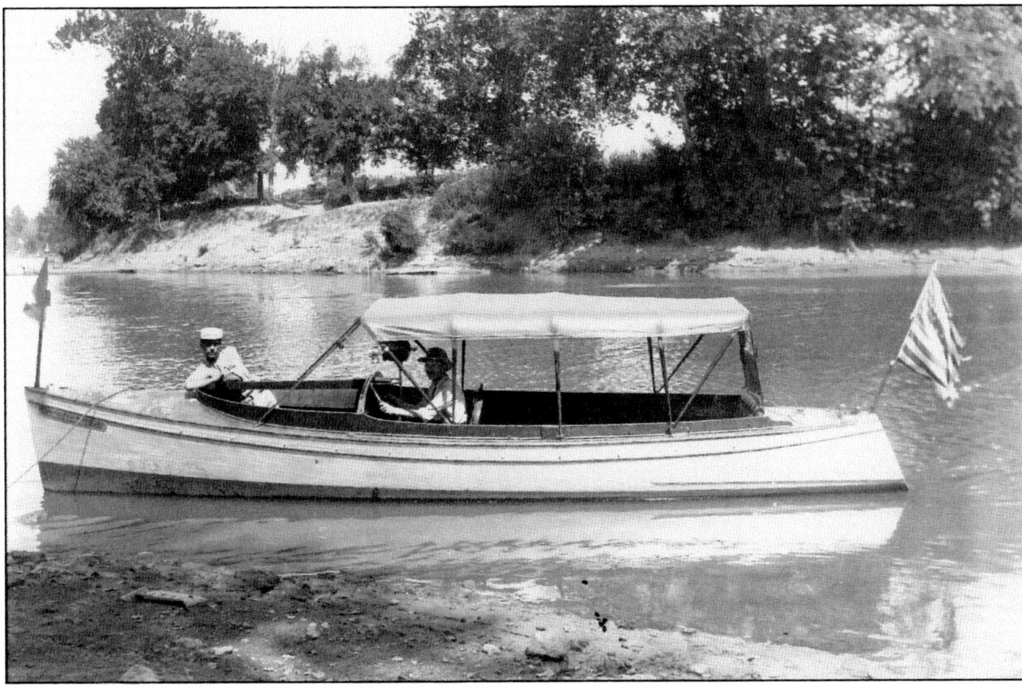

Here, pilot Jess Wilson (right, at wheel) takes this small boat—with passenger Wrey Dennis—on its maiden voyage to Bowling Green on September 1, 1900. It ran a daily round-trip from Morgantown to Bowling Green carrying mail, packages, and passengers.

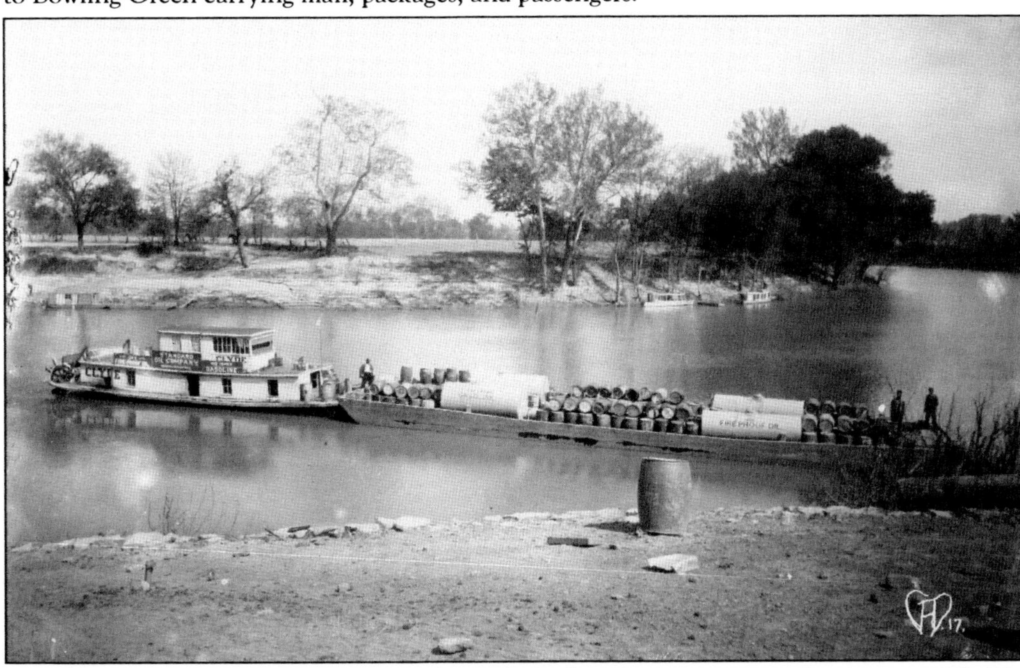

The *Clyde,* sometimes called *Little Clyde,* is docked at the Morgantown landing in 1917. The gas-powered pusher was piloted by Capt. J. Porter Hines for some time. Here, *Clyde* pushes gas and oil barges bound for Bowling Green. Note the two houseboats tied up on the opposite bank of the river.

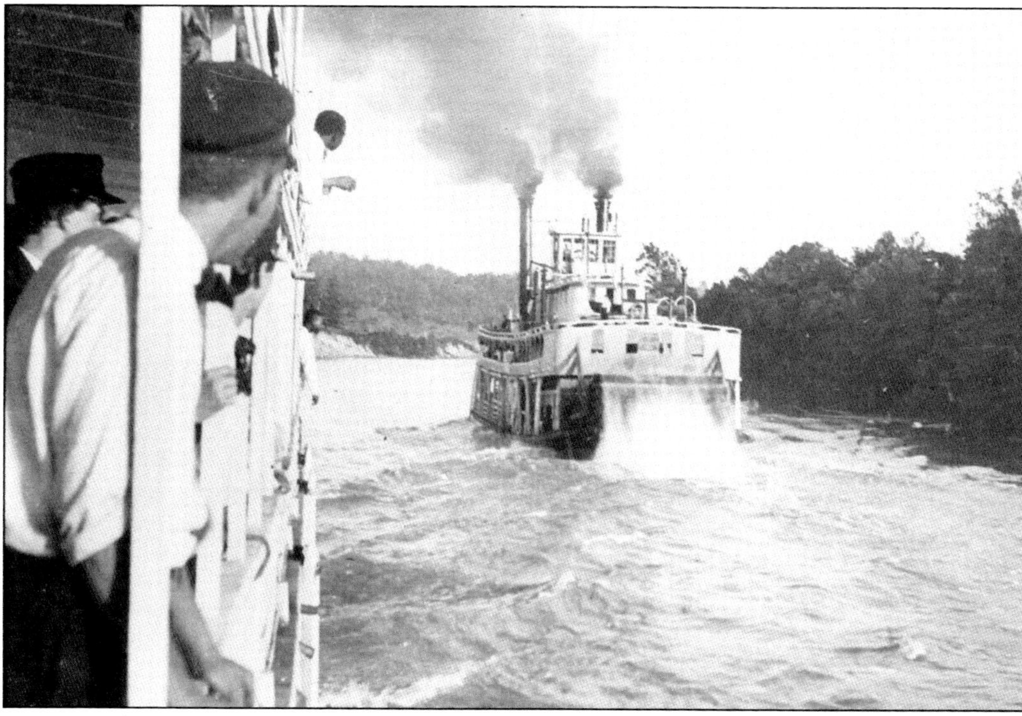

Passengers hang over the bull rail on the bottom deck and the second-level boiler deck rail as these steamers meet on the Green River. It has been surmised that these boats were racing, but that would have been unlikely because of the width of the river. Also, one boat would not have been more than one mile per hour faster than the other.

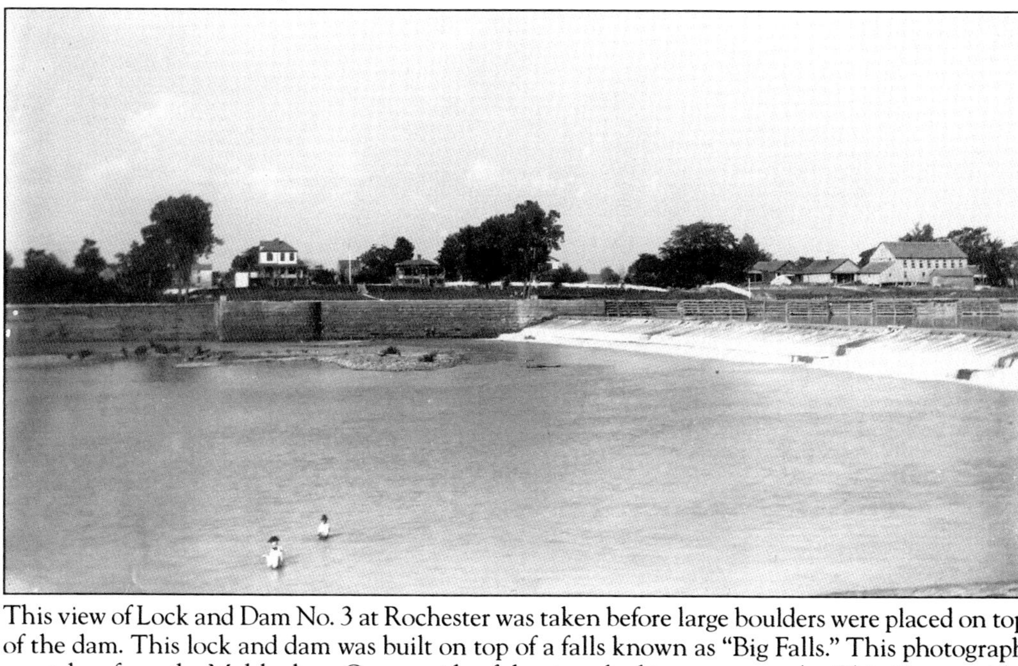

This view of Lock and Dam No. 3 at Rochester was taken before large boulders were placed on top of the dam. This lock and dam was built on top of a falls known as "Big Falls." This photograph was taken from the Muhlenberg County side of the river, looking across to the Ohio County side, with the trees beyond the warehouse at right in Butler County.

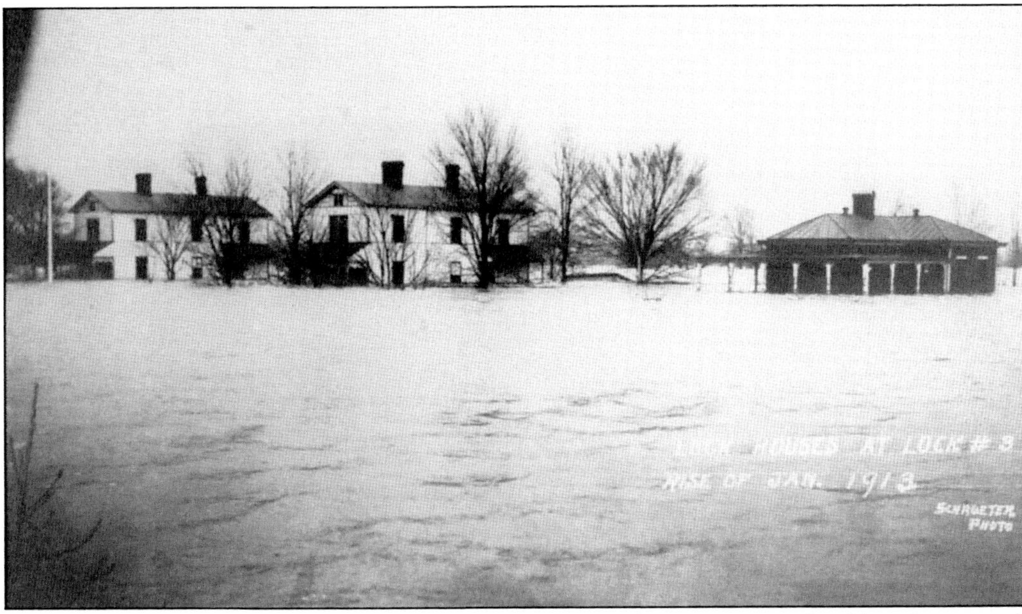

These government houses for Lock and Dam No. 3 at Rochester were on the Ohio County side of the river. This photograph was taken from the Muhlenberg County side during the 1913 flood. The houses were the residences of the lockkeeper and assistant lockkeeper, and the maintenance building is at right. The lock and dam are not visible in the photograph because they were totally underwater.

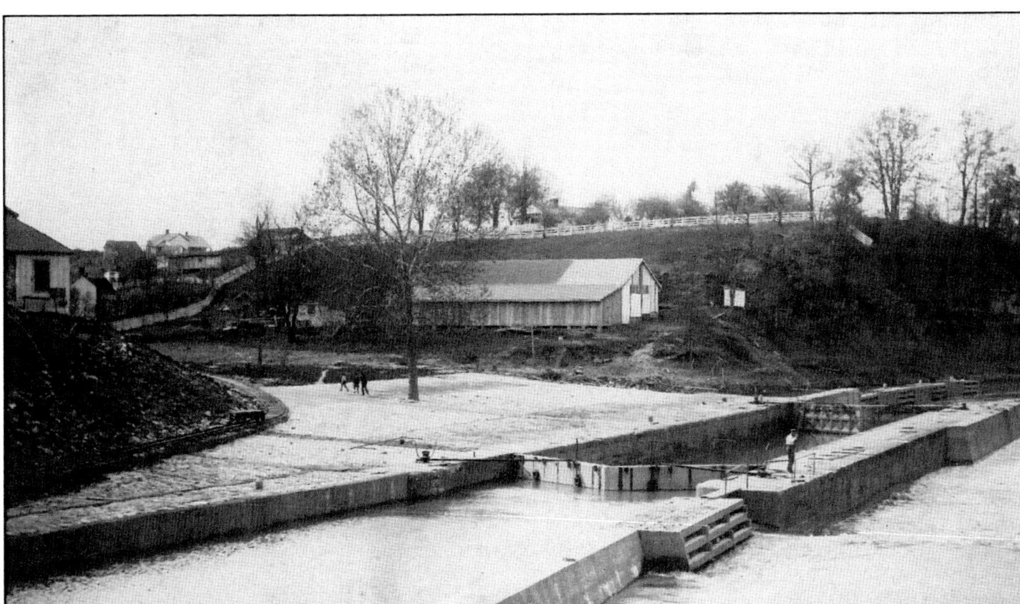

Lock and Dam No. 4 at Woodbury is pictured as it appeared before 1897. The image can be dated as such because of the cobblestone esplanade and the wooden lower guide wall. Additionally, the US Army Corps of Engineers office has not yet been built on top of the hill.

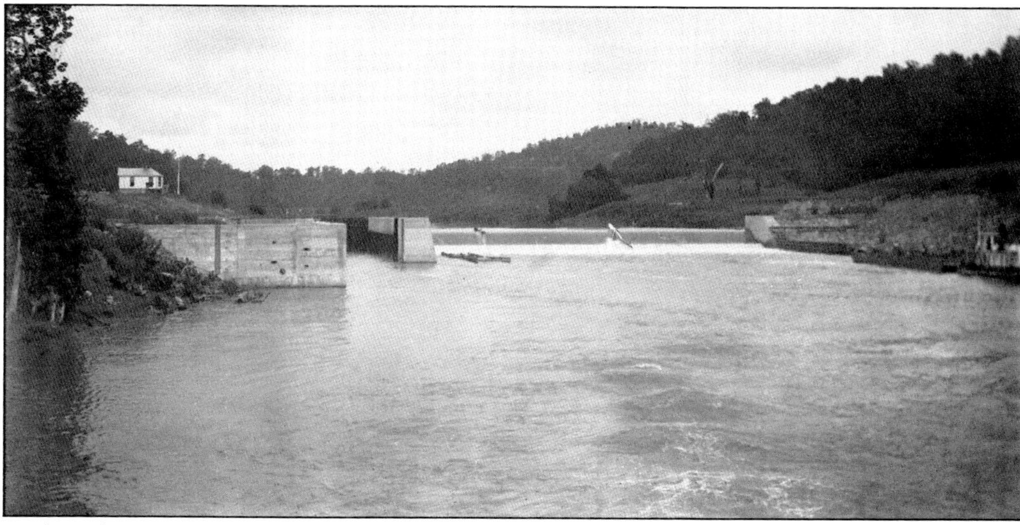

Lock and Dam No. 5, on the Green River near Reedyville, was completed in 1905—the first modern, all-concrete lock and dam on the river. It also featured a larger lock to accommodate Ohio River–sized barges. This lock and dam remained in service until 1951, when it closed due to a lack of traffic after asphalt was no longer shipped from Kyrock by river.

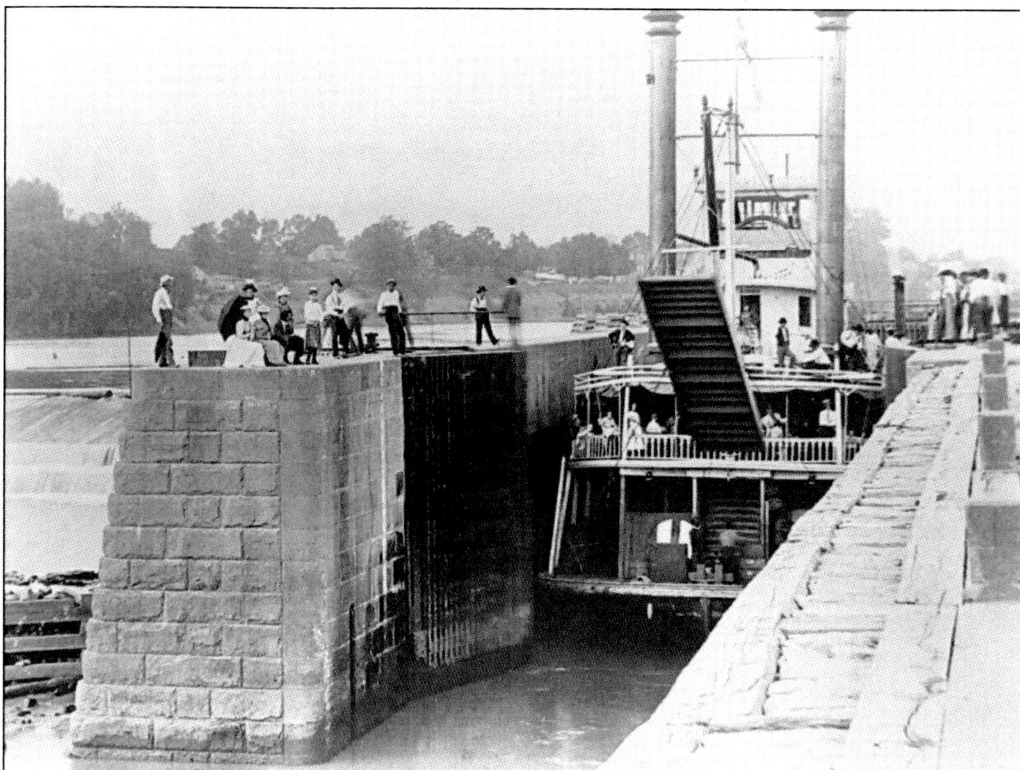

The old locks allowed just enough room for a packet to pass through, as seen here. These older structures, built between 1838 and 1841, were 160 feet long and 36 feet wide. The larger packet boats were up to 35 feet wide and of varying lengths. Note the craftsmanship of the hand-carved masonry in the lock walls; this work was primarily done by slaves.

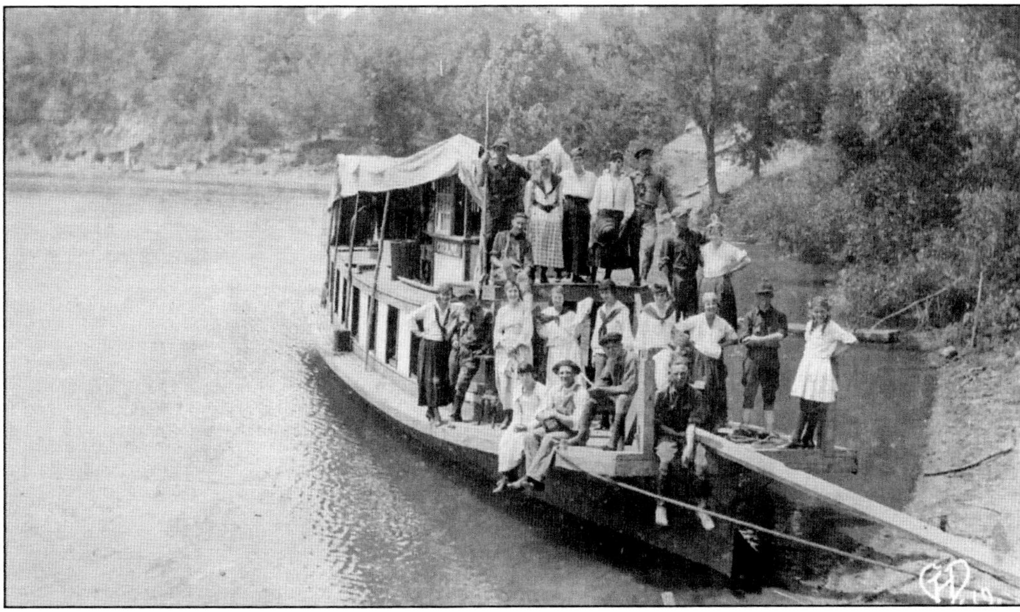

The *Caroline* was built in 1916. Harry Eberman bought the boat to make a daily mail run from Morgantown to Bowling Green. On weekends, youth groups frequently rented the boat for outings like the one shown in this 1919 image. After several years of service, the *Caroline* burned to the waterline. The hull of the boat now rests on the riverbank at Morgantown.

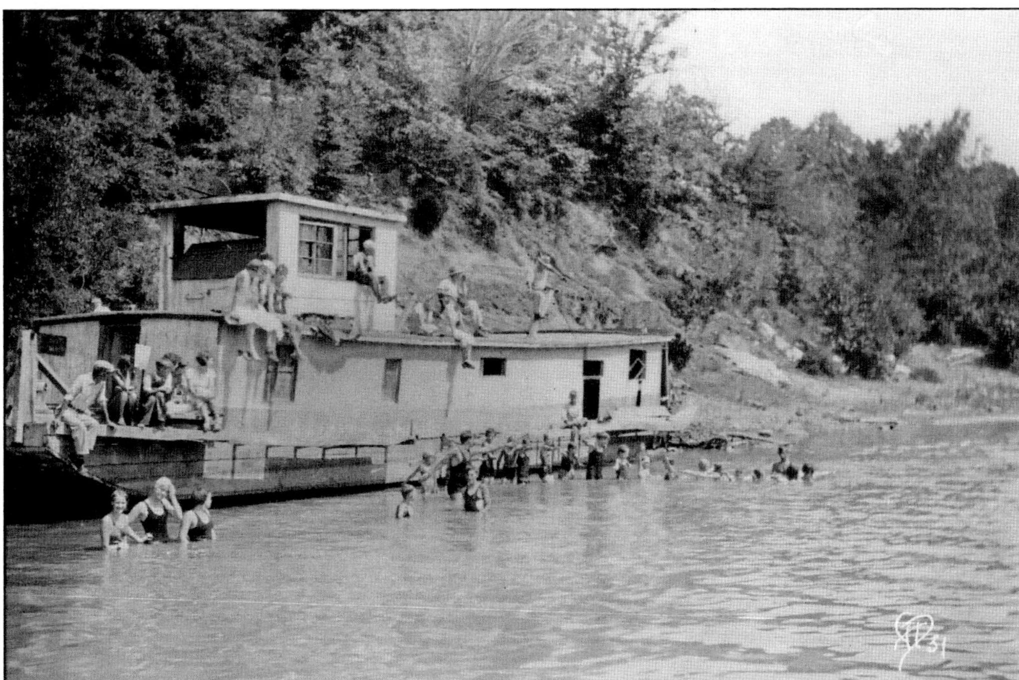

Swimming in the Green River was a favorite summertime activity for the young people of the area, as evidenced in this 1931 photograph from a swimming hole just below the Morgantown landing. The group of children beside the boat is participating in a Red Cross swimming class. Martha Spradlin is the teenager in the middle at left, near the front of the boat.

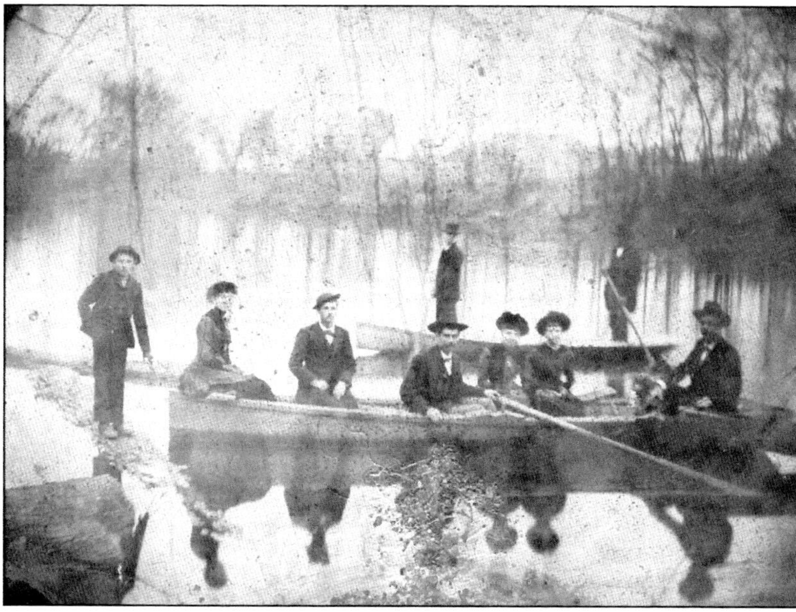

A photograph from 1893 shows a group of young men and women ready for a winter skiff ride on the river. Note that everyone in the picture is formally dressed by today's standards, but wearing acceptable attire for a special outing in that era.

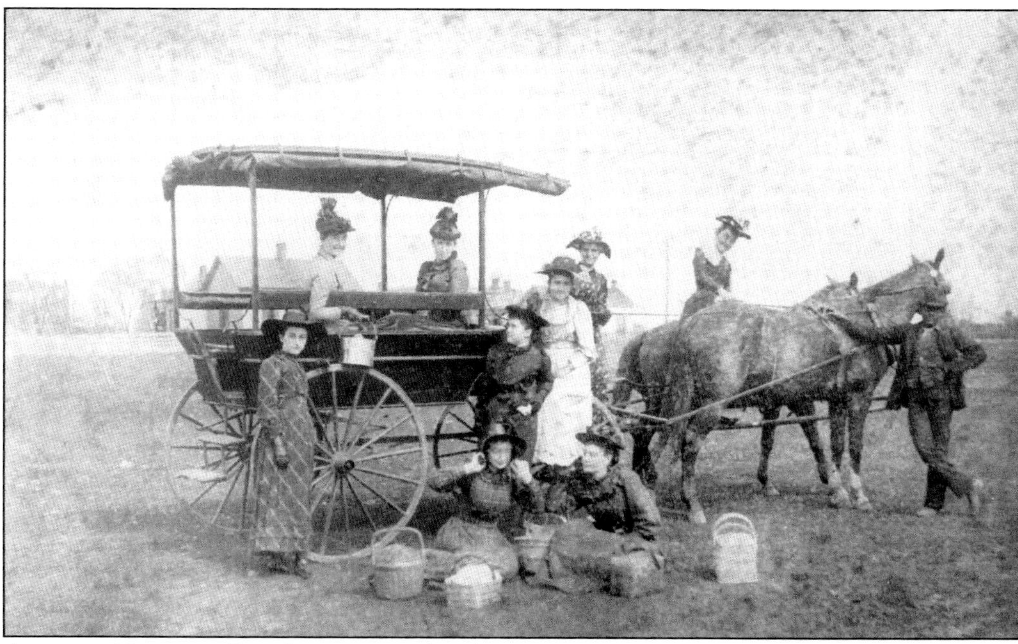

A group of Potter College for Young Ladies (now Western Kentucky University) students enjoys a summer picnic in 1895. The university's connection to the county continues, attested to by the 2011 Dean's and President's Lists students from Butler County, including Amanda Arnold, Denise Ballinger, Bradley Boaz, Brittany Brooks, Kaylyn Cardwell, James Childress, Christine Clark, Charles Drake, Hannah Embry, Janie Embry, Paige Embry, Brittany Evans, Jordan Evans, Kayla Hack, Alisha Hajari, Casie House, Kristen Hughson, Jennifer Johnson, Stephanie Johnson, Amy Keown, Tabitha Keown, Katie Kirby, Ashley McGinnis, Ryann McGuyer, Elizabeth McKinney, Kerissa McKinney, Rebecca Mercier, Jessica Oaks, Cole Overstreet, Casey Phelps, David Patrick Phelps, Lindsey Porter, Adair Schwartz, Danny Shepherd, Frankie Smith, Cade Snodgrass, Kelsey Stinson, Courtney Thompson, Chelsea Tutko, Kelby Tynes, Joshua G. Vincent, and Robert Wilson.

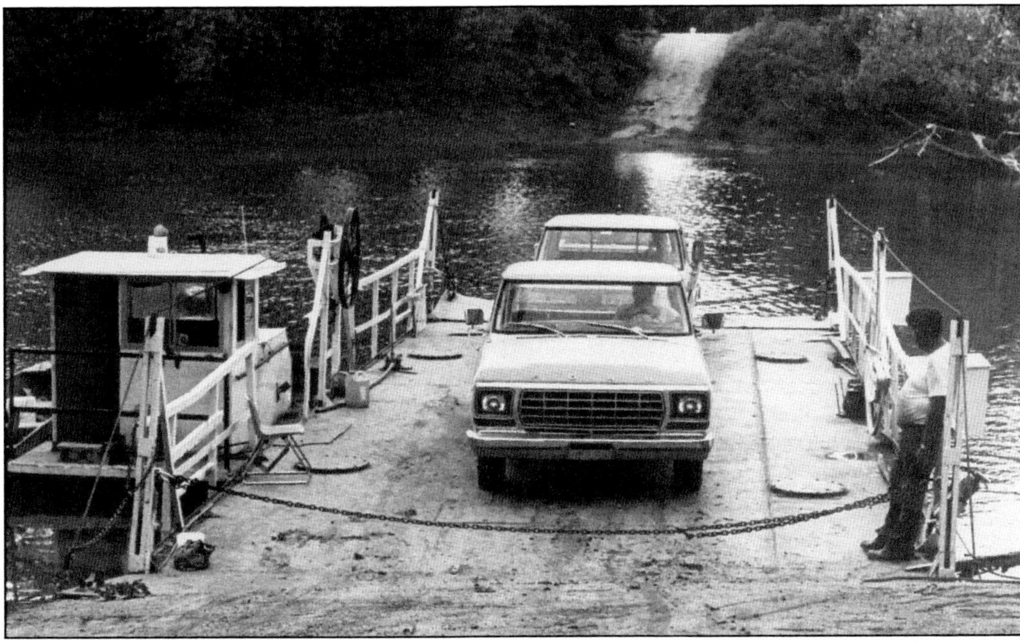

Read's Ferry, the oldest county-owned ferryboat in Kentucky, has been in operation for over 175 years. A ferry is necessary, as Green River snakes through the county, cutting the Little Bend area off from the rest. The county bought the ferry in the 1920s and has since provided free river crossings. Morris Fishburn is the ferryman at right in this 1988 photograph.

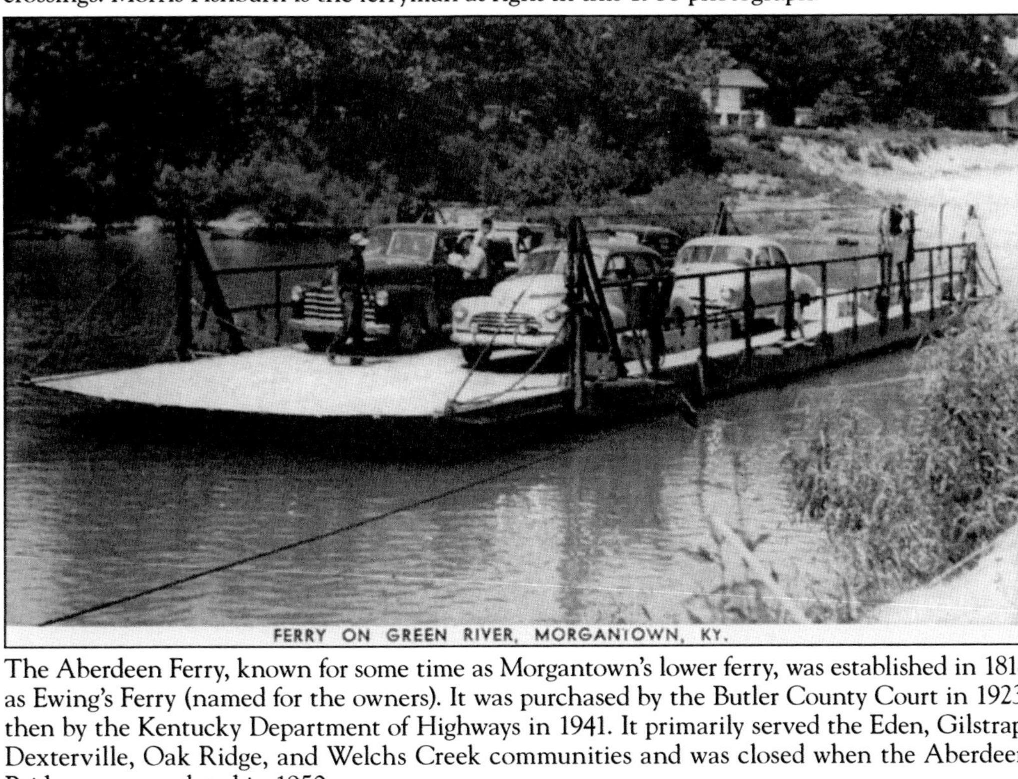

The Aberdeen Ferry, known for some time as Morgantown's lower ferry, was established in 1818 as Ewing's Ferry (named for the owners). It was purchased by the Butler County Court in 1923, then by the Kentucky Department of Highways in 1941. It primarily served the Eden, Gilstrap, Dexterville, Oak Ridge, and Welchs Creek communities and was closed when the Aberdeen Bridge was completed in 1950.

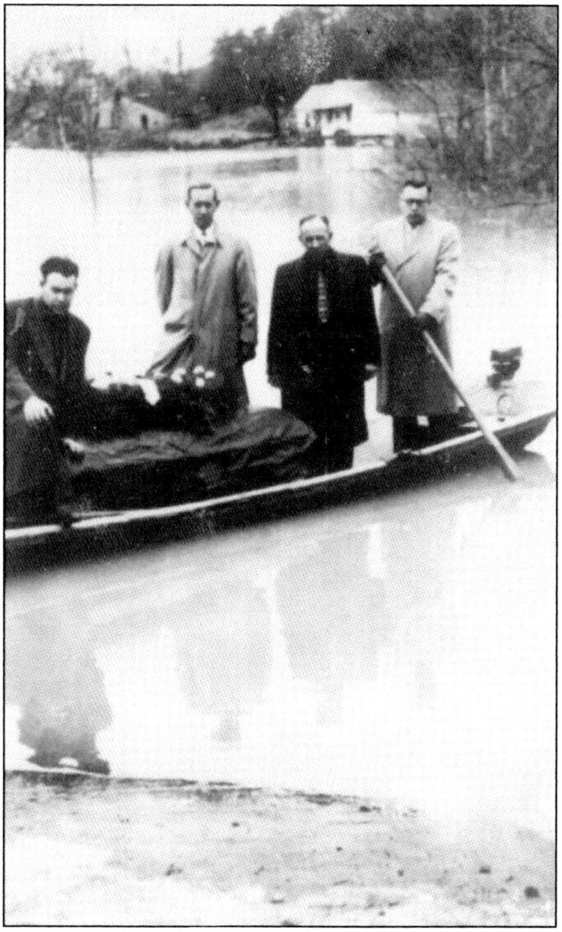

In 1950, the high water did not hinder the interment of river man Capt. Ed Johnson. This group of river men took his coffin across the Green River; they are, from left to right, Albert Johnson, electrical engineer; Leonard Johnson, Mississippi River engineer; Alva Johnson, Aberdeen Ferry operator; and Walter Johnson, riverboat engineer.

This US Army Corps of Engineers house was built in 1913 for the superintendent of the Green and Barren Rivers' Maintenance District at Woodbury. Capt. William Overstreet and his family were the first to occupy the home, which overlooks the Green River. The house, which sits in Butler County Park, has been restored to its original condition and is now home to the Green River Museum.

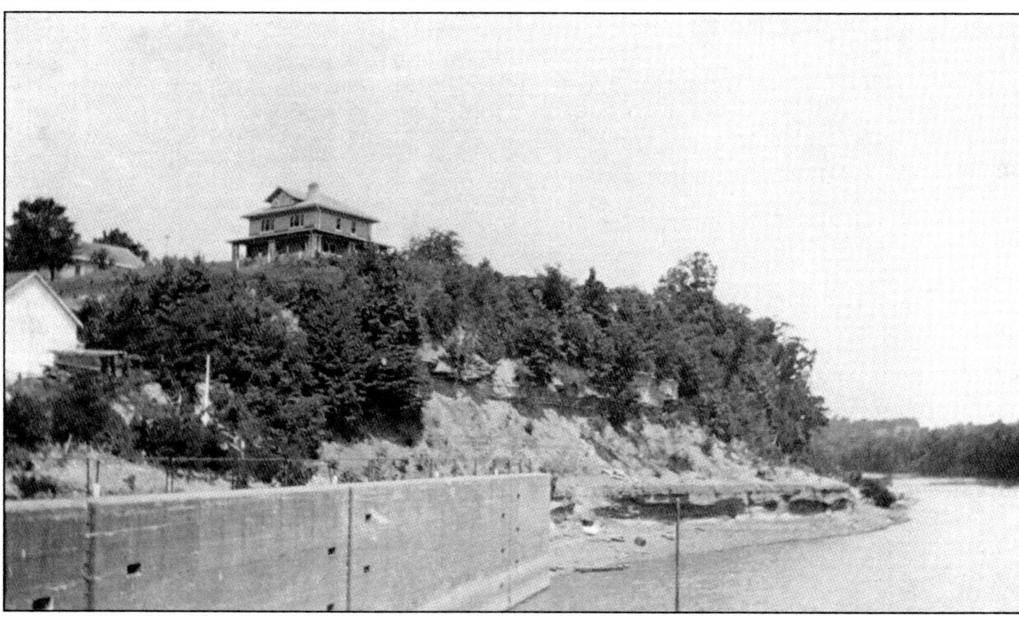

Keith Lawrence (right) helps Billy Jenkins hold up a 91-pound catfish, which Lawrence purchased for his work crew. Today, Butler County is known for its annual Green River Catfish Festival. Anglers come from all over the country to attempt to catch one of the tagged catfish and compete for cash prizes, including a top prize of $50,000.

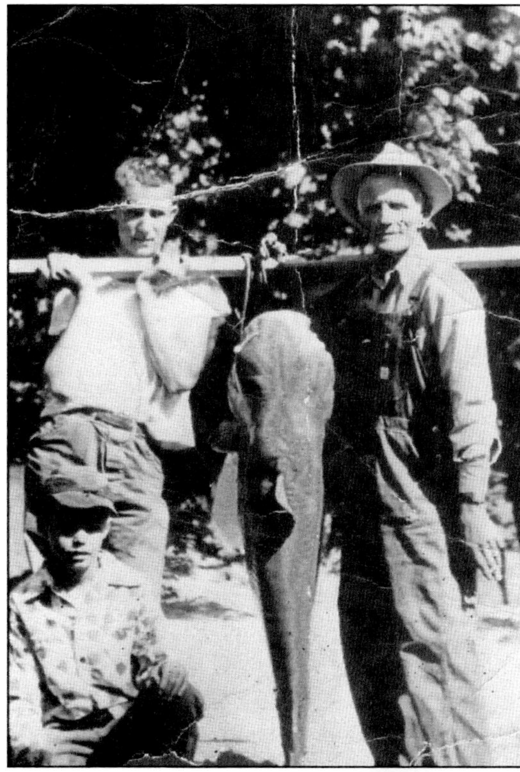

Kentucky's steamboat era reached its peak in the early years of the 1900s, and the excitement created by the arrival of one of these vessels was unmatched. There was always a crowd when a boat like the *Bowling Green* came into the landing, with passengers embarking, flags flying, and whistles and steam pipes blowing.

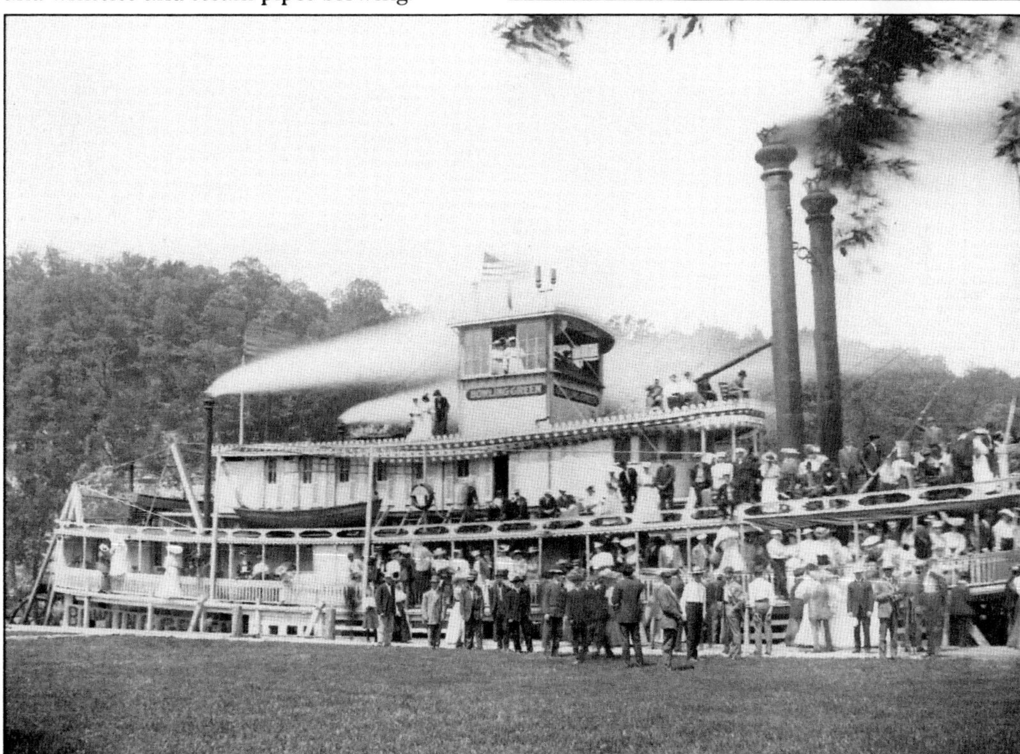

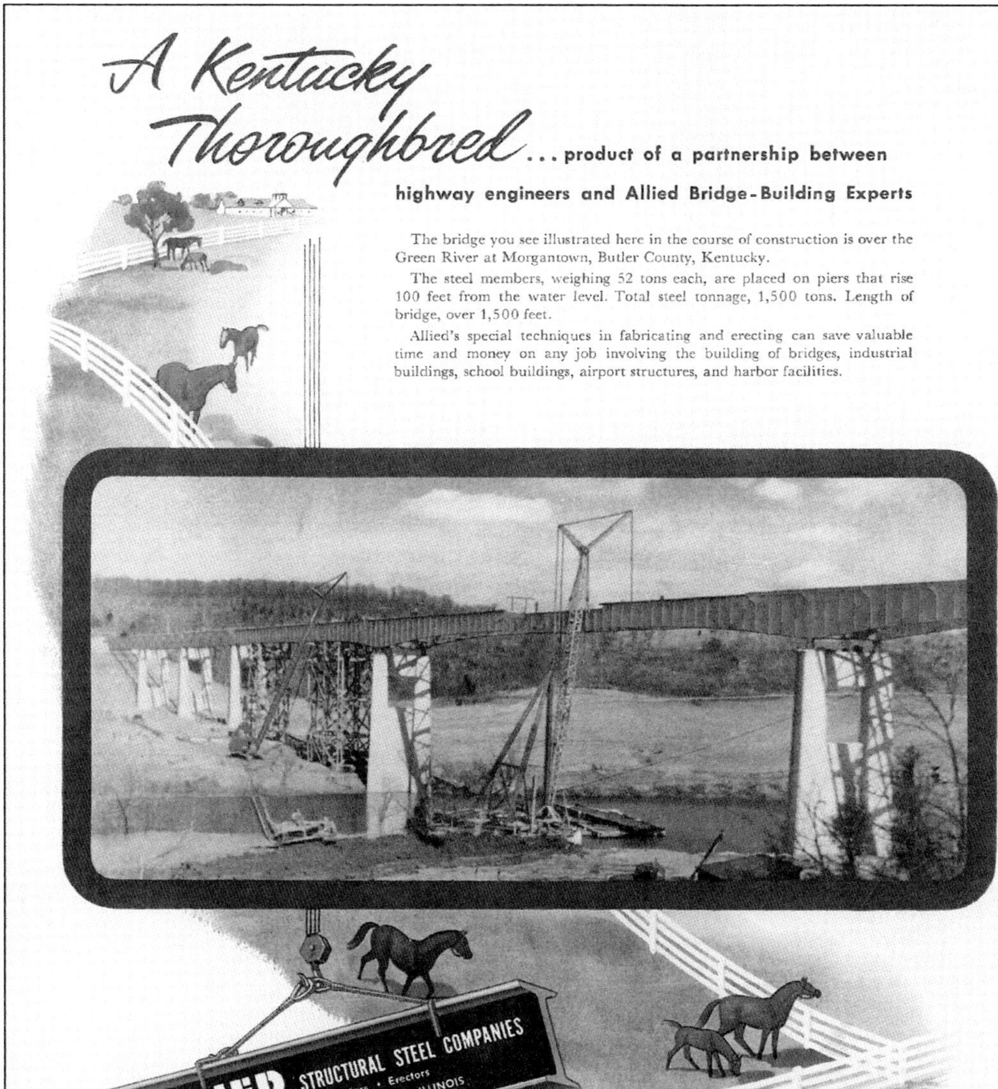

The Aberdeen Bridge opened in 1950 on the new road that would become US Highway 231. At the time it was built, it was the longest single-span steel-beam bridge in Kentucky. Before the bridge was completed, the main roadway from Morgantown to Hartford ran through Logansport, and drivers had to cross the river at Borah's Ferry. People living in the Leonard Oak area used the upper Morgantown ferry. Allied Structural Steel Companies of Chicago was awarded the bridge-building contract and used its construction to showcase their special fabrication techniques. In 2010, the bridge was closed for 55 days while the weathered deck (top layer) was replaced. The Aberdeen Bridge supports over 8,000 vehicles on a daily basis, and the Kentucky Transportation Cabinet has stated that "aside from general maintenance work, the bridge will not require any major renovations for the next 25–30 years."

Three

Civil War Times

Although only a few clashes took place in Butler County, the citizenry, like the nation, was divided on the issue of slavery. About 10 percent of the households in Butler County—almost all of them south of the Green River—were slave owners, including many of the early county leaders. The 1860 presidential election indicated the attitude toward slavery in the county; Constitutional Union Party candidate John Bell, whose party believed in maintaining the Union but took no specific stance on slavery, received the most votes in the county with 500; Stephen Douglas, a Northern Democrat, received 321 votes; and John C. Breckenridge, a Southern Democrat, secured only 119 votes on a platform of secession and continuing slavery. Abraham Lincoln, a Republican and abolitionist candidate (and the eventual winner), collected only five votes—two in Morgantown and three in the Fourth District.

On April 12, 1861, shortly after Lincoln took office, the Civil War began. As of December 31, 1864, Butler County had supplied 508 white and 63 African American soldiers to the Union Army and around one-fifth that number of men to the Confederate Army. There were three or four small skirmishes in Butler County during the war, with the largest occurring at Woodbury when about 250 Union soldiers routed 150 Confederate troops.

Two of the most famous prison escapes of the Civil War were each led by Butler County natives. Thomas Hines planned and led the escape of Confederate general John Hunt Morgan and five officers from the Ohio state penitentiary, while Maj. Andrew Hamilton (along with Capt. Thomas Rose) led 109 Union officers out of Libby Prison in Richmond, Virginia. Both escapes were accomplished by tunneling under the prison walls.

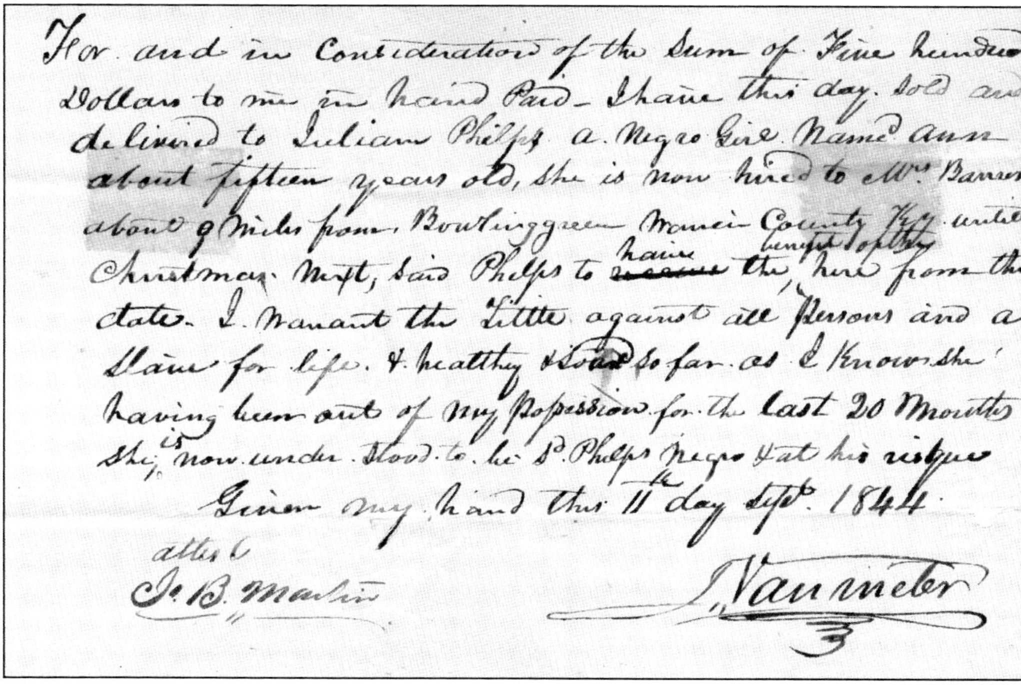

For and in Consideration of the Sum of Five hundred Dollars to me in hand Paid - I have this day sold and delivered to Julian Phelps a Negro Girl Named Ann about fifteen years old, she is now hired to Mrs Barner about 9 Miles from Bowlinggreen Warren County Ky until Christmas next, said Phelps to have the benefit of the hire from this date. I warrant the tittle against all Persons and a slave for life. & healthy & sound so far as I know she having been out of my possession for the last 20 Months she is now under stood to be J. Phelps Negro & at his risque

Given my hand this 11th day Sept. 1844

attest

J. B. Martin

J. Vanmeter

The sale of slaves was not a frequent occurrence in Butler County, but it did happen, as evidenced by this 1844 bill of sale for a 15-year-old "Negro" girl named Ann to Julian Phelps. By 1860, there were 728 slaves in the county.

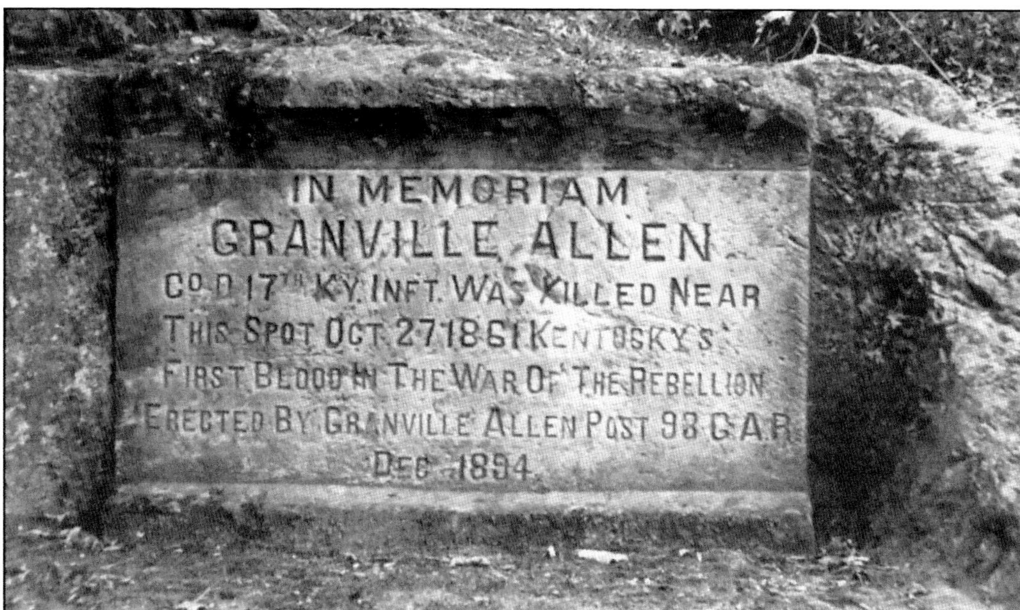

This monument honoring Granville Allen was erected in December 1894 along the old roadway on Big Hill, about a mile out of Morgantown, by the Granville Allen Post 98 of the Grand Army of the Republic (GAR), a Civil War veterans' organization. Although it reads, "Kentucky's first blood in the War of the Rebellion," it would be more accurate to say that Allen was the first man killed in western Kentucky during the war.

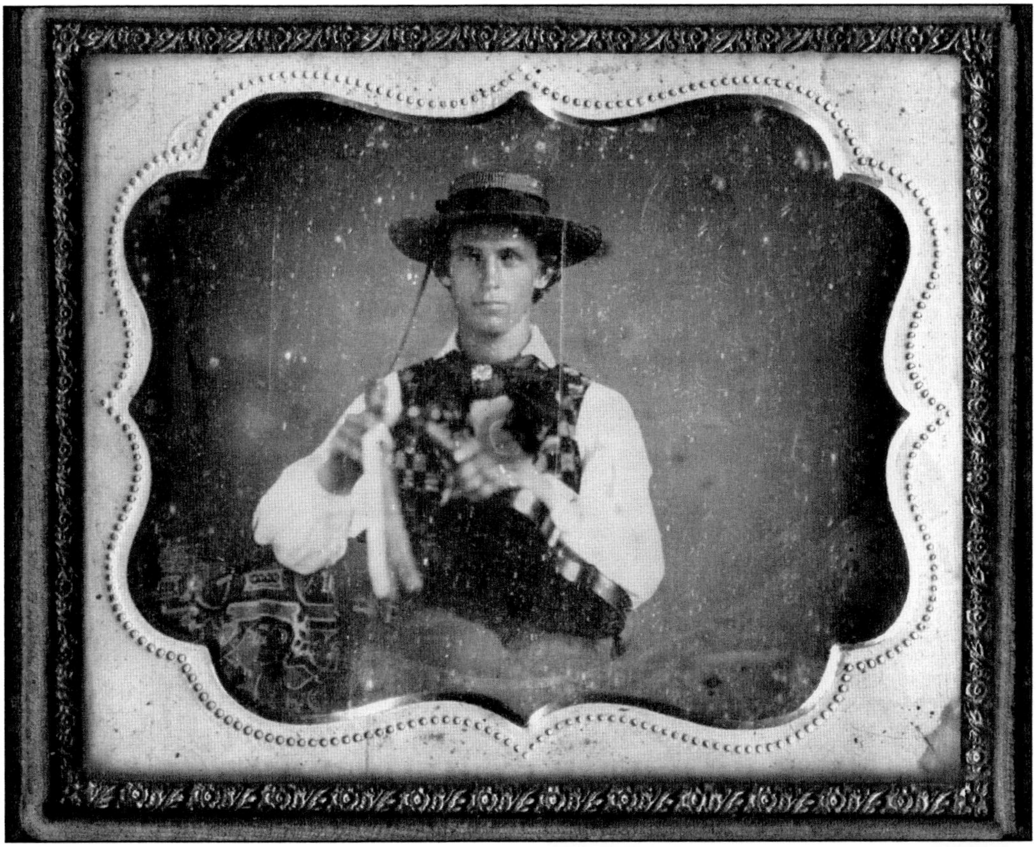

Andrew Hamilton, shown in the above daguerreotype, was originally from Pennsylvania but left for the California gold rush and finally settled in Woodbury. Before the Civil War, he worked for Warren Hines (father of Thomas Hines), boring for oil. Hamilton and Thomas Hines were friends but joined different sides in the war—a hard reality that many friends and family members faced at the time.

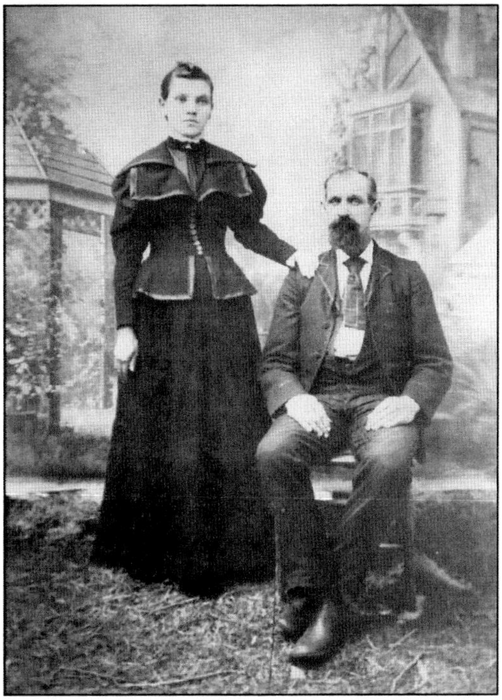

Maj. Andrew Hamilton, pictured in this formal portrait with his wife, Sarah, is celebrated for leading the most famous escape of the Civil War. Hamilton and 109 Union officers escaped from the Libby Prison in Richmond, Virginia, in February 1864. After Libby Prison was moved to Chicago and reconstructed as a national war museum in 1889, Hamilton gave a series of guest lectures and tours there. Hamilton lived in Reedyville after the war and was murdered by Samuel Spencer in Morgantown in 1895.

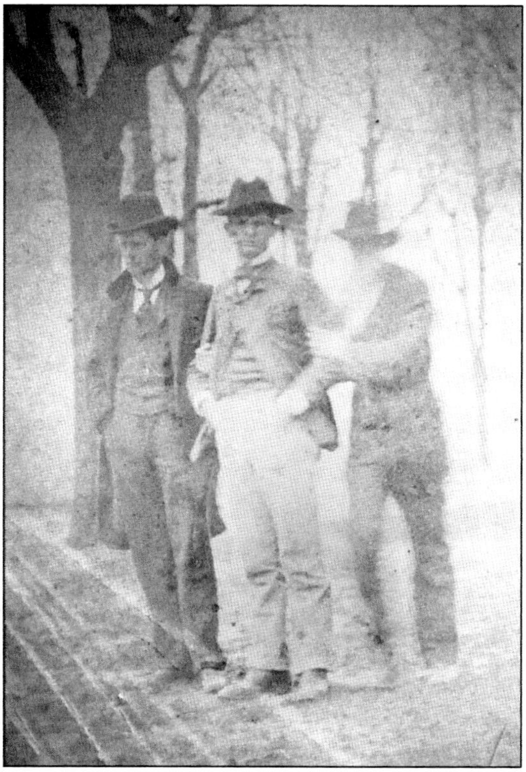

Sam Spencer (center in the picture at left; the other two men are unidentified) was arrested for the murder of Andrew Hamilton. Spencer and Alfred Belcher had confronted Hamilton outside Morgantown, where an argument ensued. Allegedly, Hamilton had brought Spencer's father back from going AWOL during the Civil War, and afterward the elder Spencer was wounded or killed. In his anger, the younger Spencer shot and killed Hamilton. No charges were brought against Belcher, but Spencer served two years in prison.

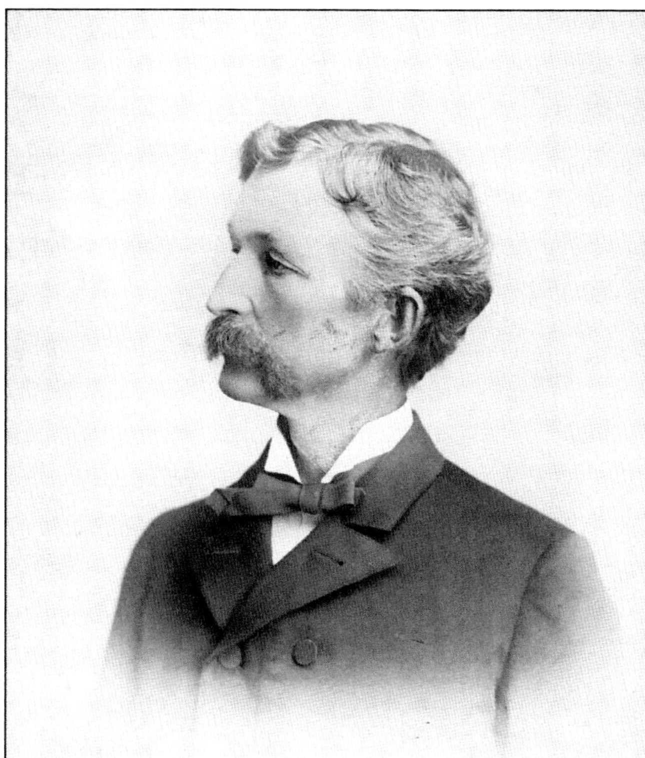

Capt. Thomas H. Hines, known as "the Fox," sat for this portrait after the Civil War. Hines acquired a reputation as "the most dangerous man in the Confederacy," according to various sources, for his covert activities and daring escapades as military commander of the "Northwest Conspiracy," which operated out of Canada. He also led the escape of Confederate general John H. Morgan and five officers from the Ohio state penitentiary.

Andrew B. (pictured) and Joseph Dabbs, the sons of James and Catherine Dabbs of Rochester, joined the Union Army's 11th Kentucky Infantry at Camp Underwood. They fought at Shiloh and at the Battle of Stones River, where Andrew was killed on December 31, 1862. Joseph, who survived the war and settled in Morgantown, was the father of photographer George H. Dabbs.

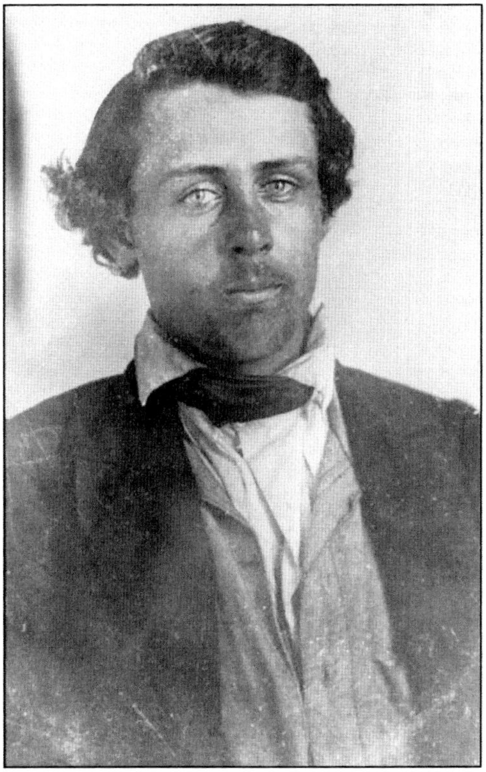

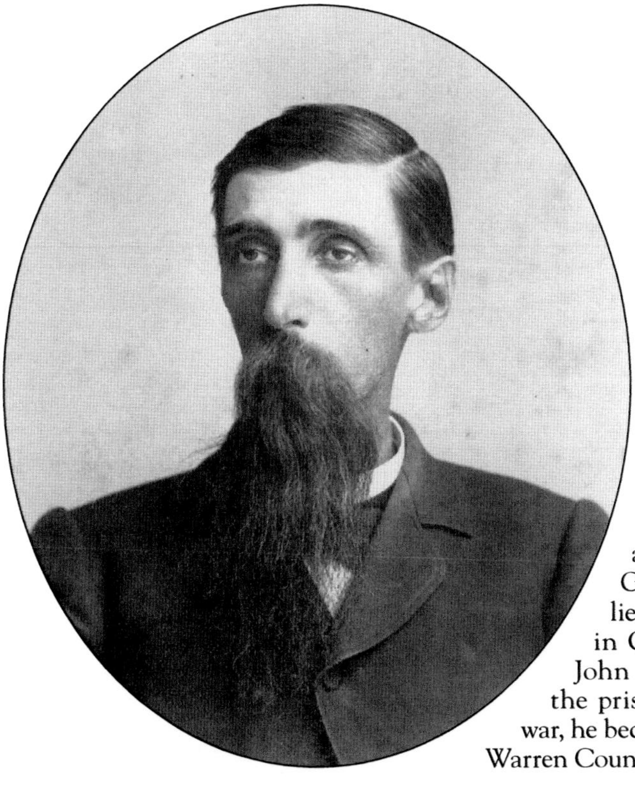

John Monroe Porter was the son of Little Muddy Presbyterian Church pastor Nathaniel Porter, who owned a large number of the slaves in Butler County. John joined the Confederate army when they occupied Bowling Green in the fall of 1861, serving as a lieutenant under Capt. Thomas Hines in Gen. John H. Morgan's command. John was captured in Ohio and sent to the prison on Johnson's Island. After the war, he became the commonwealth attorney for Warren County.

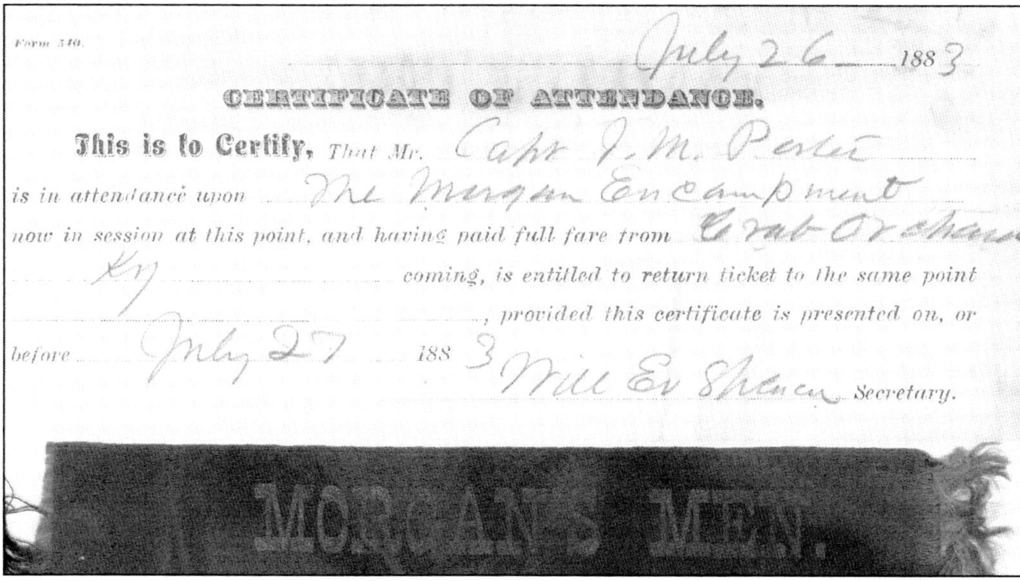
Form 540.

July 26 1883

CERTIFICATE OF ATTENDANCE.

This is to Certify, *That Mr.* Capt J. M. Porter *is in attendance upon* The Morgan Encampment *now in session at this point, and having paid full fare from* Crab Orchard Ky *coming, is entitled to return ticket to the same point*, *provided this certificate is presented on, or before* July 27 1883

Will E. Shane *Secretary.*

MORGAN'S MEN.

John M. Porter attended the July 24, 1883, reunion of "Morgan's Men" at Woodlawn Park in Lexington. About 300 of the survivors, as well as Gen. John Hunt Morgan's daughter Johnnie Hunt Morgan Caldwell, were present for the memorial event. Many dignitaries attended, including officers who fought under and with General Morgan.

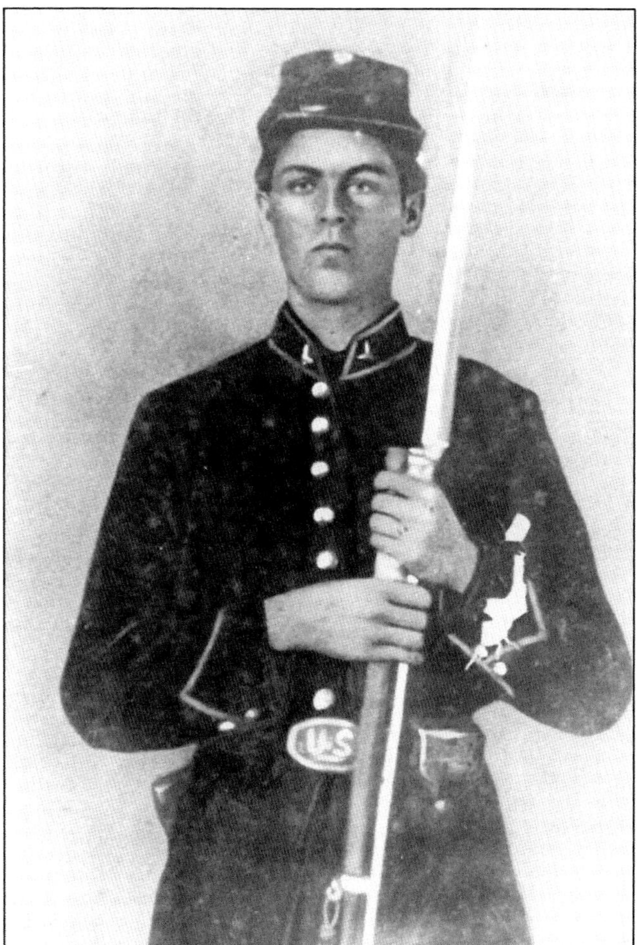

Nicholas W. Johnson was 22 years old when he enlisted in the 2nd Kentucky Cavalry of the Union army in September 1861. He was captured in Georgia in February 1865 and sent to Andersonville prison. Later, he was aboard the *Sultana* when it exploded on the Mississippi, killing some 1,700 Union veterans. Johnson survived, but had scalded arms and legs.

Vincent S. Hay was a leading citizen and landowner in Butler County in the early 1800s. Born in 1808, he taught school in the 1830s and was elected county clerk in 1843, serving four years. He joined the Union army but was captured and died in Andersonville prison in 1863.

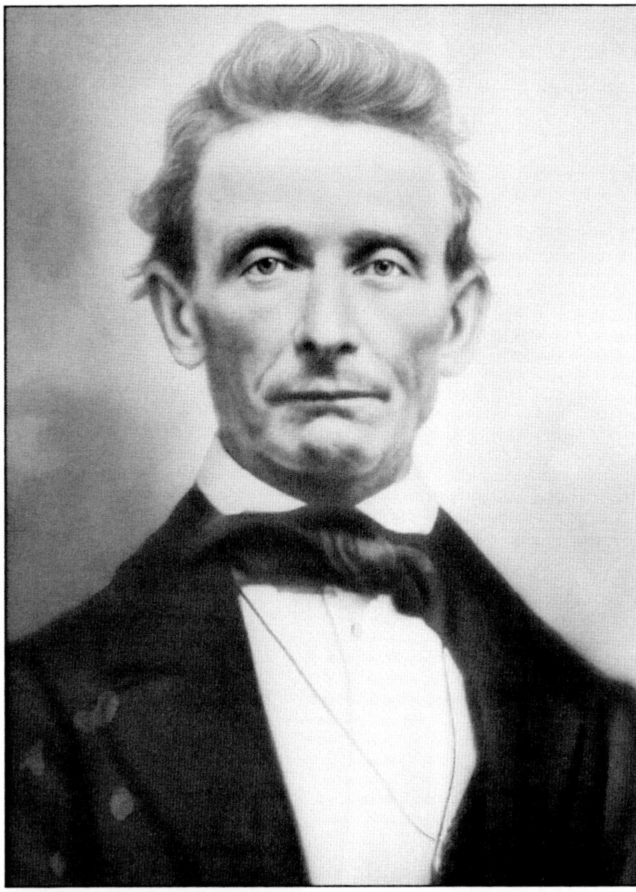

Members of Company G 11th Regiment of Kentucky Volunteers are pictured below at a Grand Army of the Republic reunion in front of Anderson's Dry Goods store in Round Hill. This unit saw action at the Battles of Shiloh, Perryville, and Stones River. The regiment lost 2 officers and 45 enlisted men in battle and 3 officers and 214 enlisted men to disease.

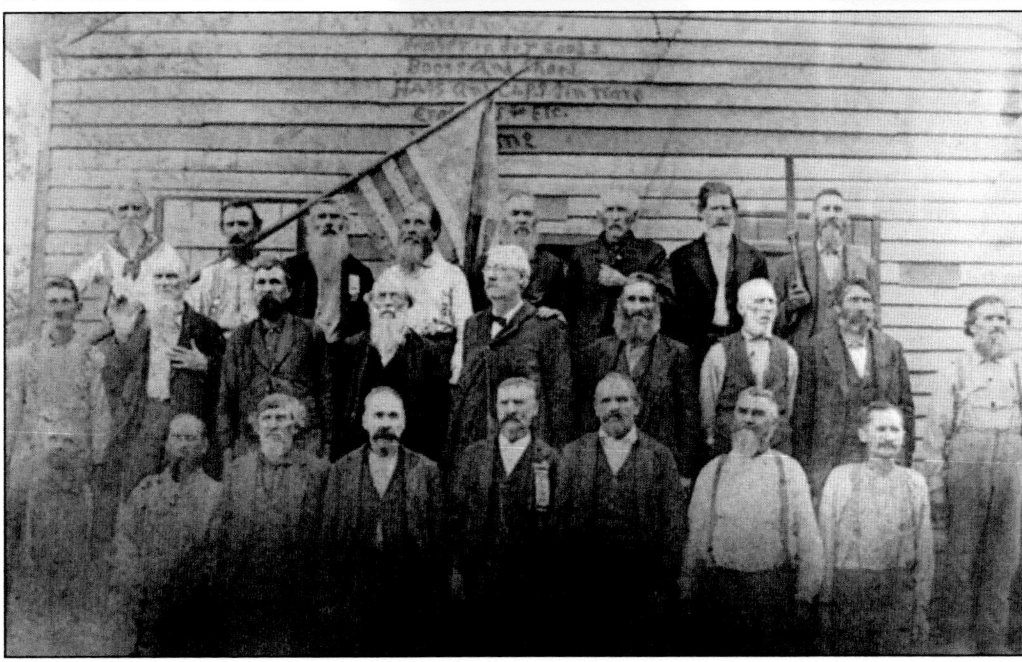

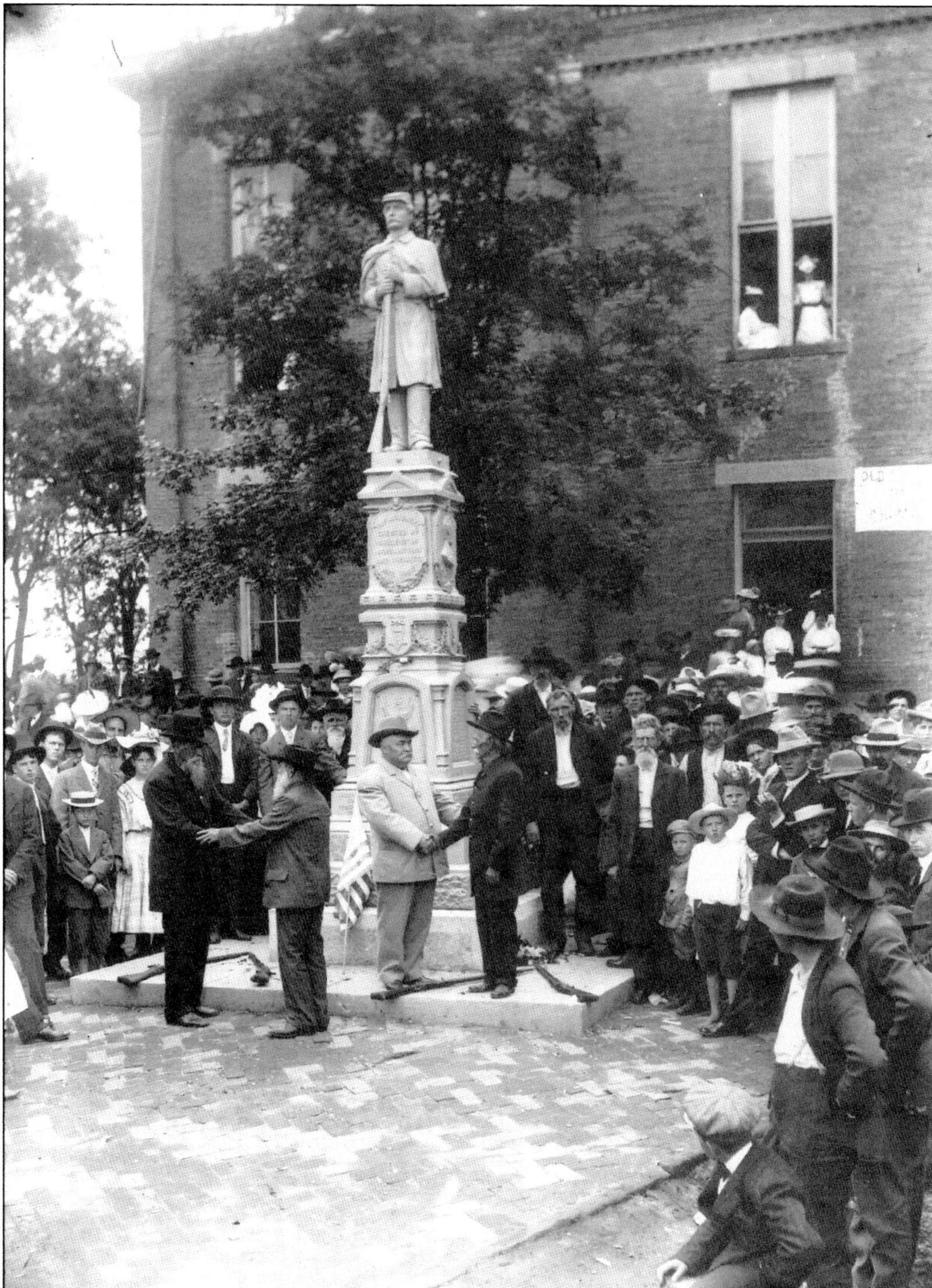

In this May 1907 photograph, Civil War veterans symbolically lay down their arms and extend their hands in friendship. Shaking hands are, from left to right, Henry Vaughn, Robert Hunt, Pleas Ayers, and J.T. Rives. The Confederate-Union Veterans' Monument in Morgantown is believed to be one of only two monuments in the country that honor both Union and Confederate soldiers.

Four

George Dabbs, Artful Chronicler

George Henry Dabbs made many contributions to Butler County through his photography and preservation efforts. Without his photography, a significant part of Butler County history—the riverboat era—might not have been recorded. Dabbs was born on July 6, 1882, the son of Joseph R. and Francis Ann Bunch Dabbs. In childhood, the family moved to Woodbury and then to Morgantown, where Joseph was a saddler by trade. Dabbs was gifted in both art and music and developed a lifelong love for both. His other passions were for Morgantown, the Green River, and his wife, Sallie.

Sarah "Sallie" Elizabeth Glenn was born on September 14, 1880, in Calhoun, Kentucky, to Walker and Ruhama Glenn. After completing her education, she moved to Morgantown and became the first female secretary in the town. She met Dabbs and they fell in love, marrying on September 18, 1904. That same year, the young Dabbs opened a photography studio in the Baldwin building in Morgantown and, over the next 20 years, made his mark with his photography.

Dabbs was commissioned by the *Louisville Courier-Journal* to photograph the maiden voyage of the *Chaperon* to Mammoth Cave and to develop advertisements promoting bonds to support World War I. He was offered a job by the newspaper, but declined after spending a short time in Louisville. In 1926, he closed his photography studio to work for the post office in Morgantown, where he was employed until his retirement in the 1960s. After retirement, he painted and sold several steamboat pictures and prints. In 1985, the Butler County Historical and Genealogical Society developed the George H. Dabbs Celebration of the Arts, featuring a juried art and photography show and the performance of a play, *Mr. Dabbs and the Magic Belle*, which was written by local theater founder and actor Ken Jenkins (who later had a recurring role on the television show *Scrubs*) in Dabbs's honor.

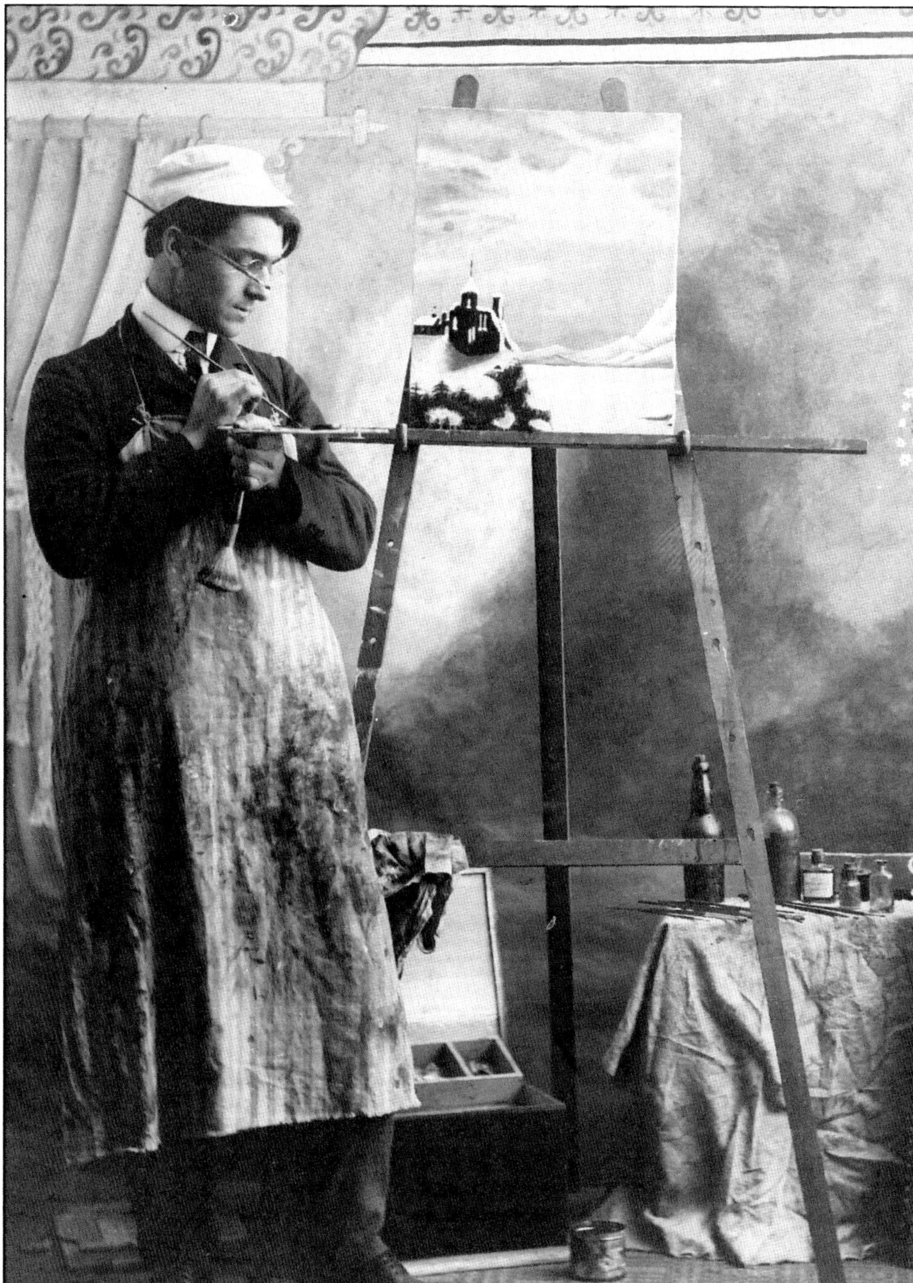

George H. Dabbs—artist, musician, photographer, and poet—was born on July 6, 1882. Dabbs operated his photography studio, Enterprise Studio, in Morgantown from 1903 to 1924 and had a special gift for choosing subjects that were important to record for posterity. He also recognized the camera's ability to capture a moment in time; through his camera's lens, viewers can get a glimpse of the bygone riverboat era in Morgantown and the Green River country, as well as a record of many events and people. After years of dedication to the betterment of Morgantown and Butler County, Dabbs died on June 29, 1967. Many people were proud to say "George Dabbs made this" or "George Dabbs was my friend."

This family portrait shows the Walker Glenn family of Calhoun, Kentucky, in McLean County, which was also on the Green River. The oldest daughter, Sarah Elizabeth Glenn (upper right), married George H. Dabbs, and they had two children, George Jr. and Katherine Glenn Hill.

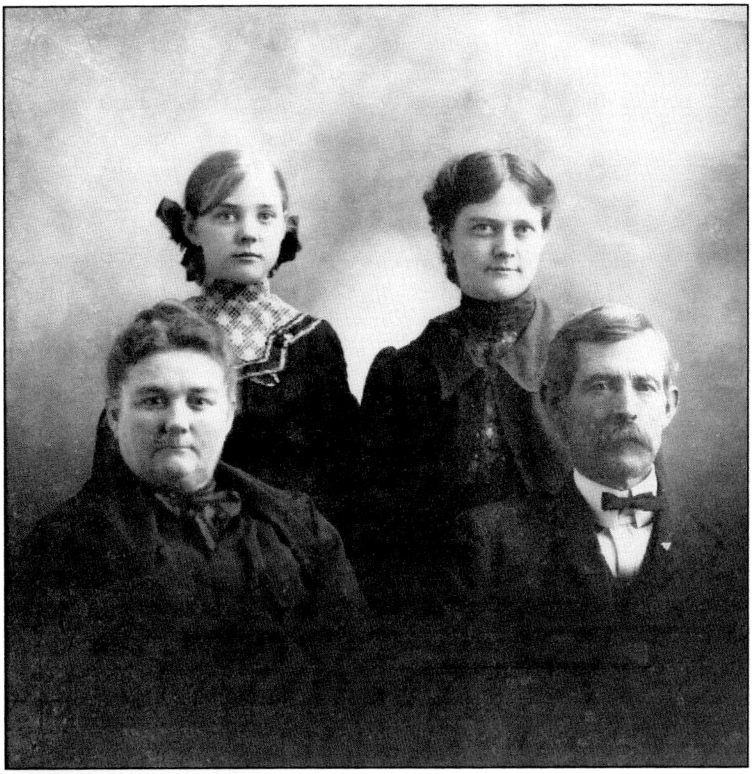

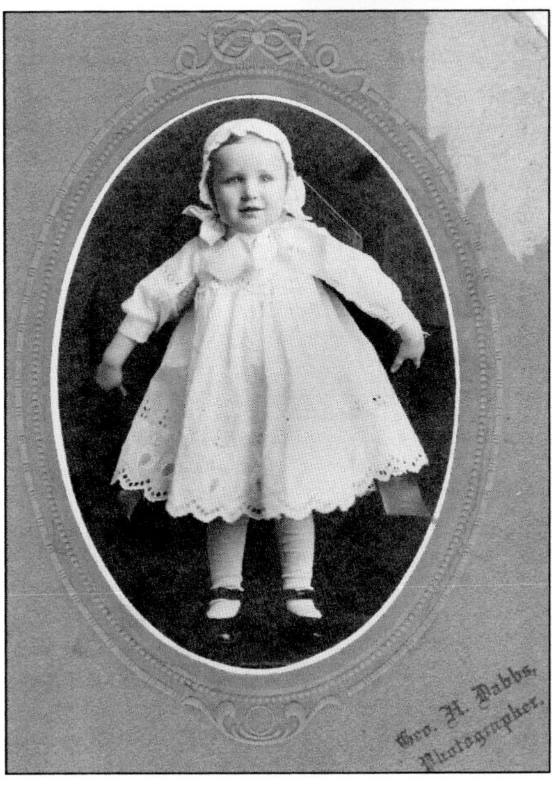

One of the many portraits made by Dabbs in the early 1900s shows an Austin child whose first name is unknown. The Victorian dress and shoes offer a clue that this was a girl in a very early photograph. The cabinet card image is stamped "Geo. H. Dabbs, Photographer."

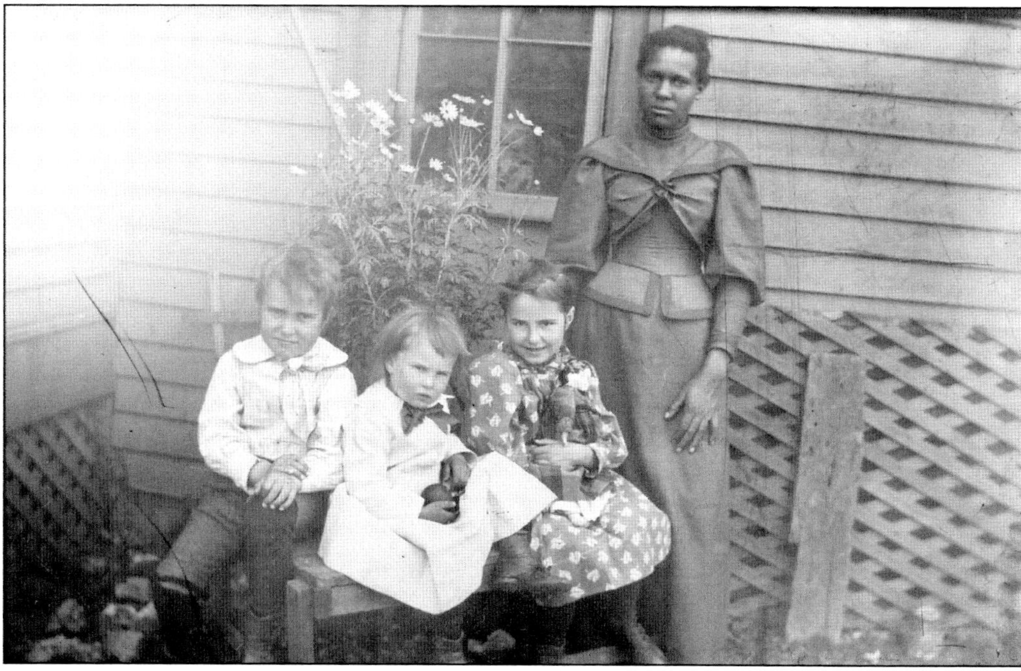

In this Dabbs photograph, an unidentified African American nanny cares for her employer's children, a common scene in well-to-do households around 1900. Dabbs had a special fondness for Butler's African American citizens and hated any form of racial prejudice. This attitude is reflected in the many photographs he made of citizens of all backgrounds.

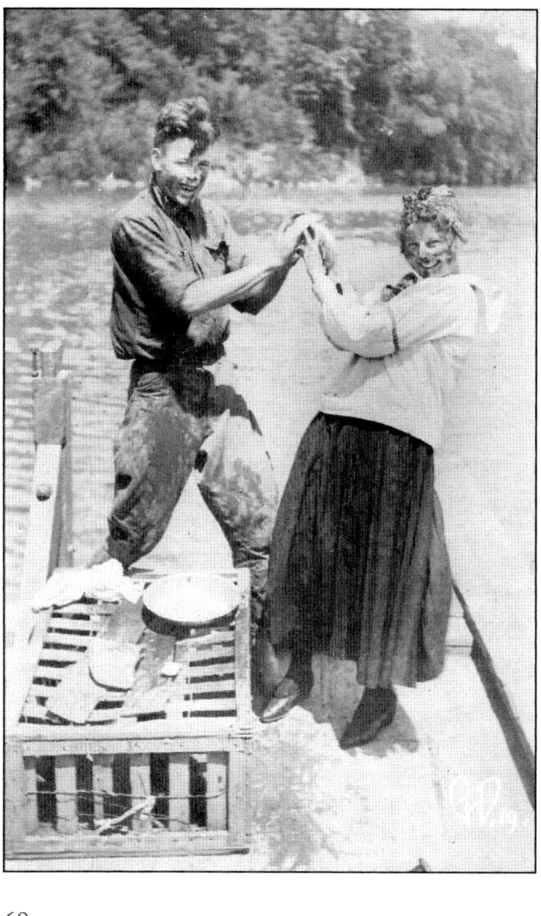

Throughout their lives, George and Sallie Dabbs maintained a special love for each other, their friends, Morgantown, and the Green River. One of their favorite pastimes was being on the river with friends for weekend cruises. As seen in this 1919 photograph of an unidentified couple, Dabbs recorded the good times enjoyed by all.

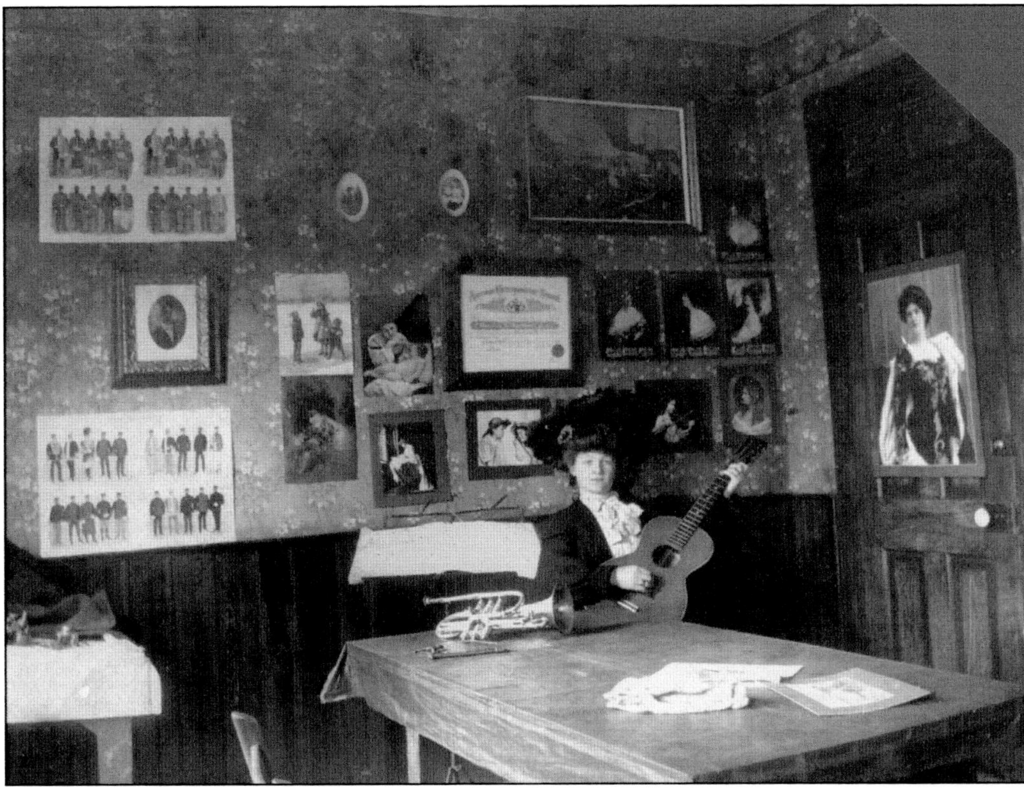

The reception area of George H. Dabbs' studio, pictured above around 1904, was a feast for the eyes. Many of his interests are represented, including the music stand, trumpet, and framed photographs and paintings. Dabbs also was proud of his diploma from the American Correspondence Normal school of Dansville, New York. (Courtesy of Special Collections: Ekstrom Library, University of Louisville.)

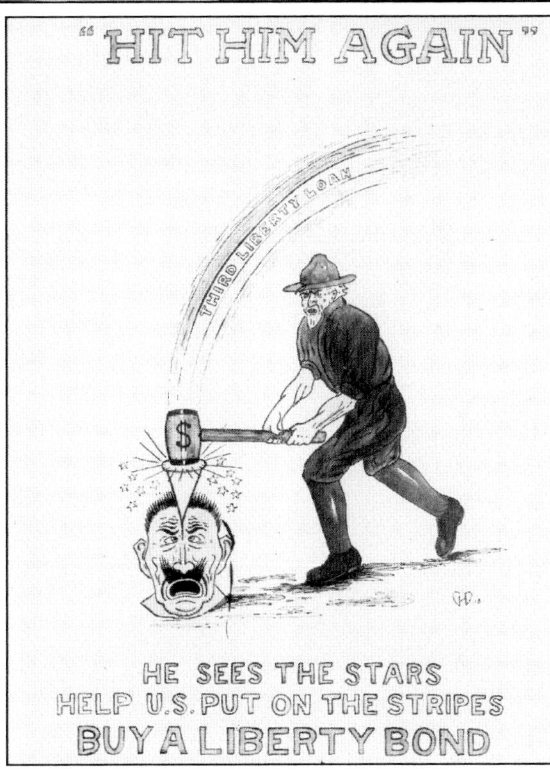

At right is a 1918 pen-and-ink advertisement that ran in the *Louisville Courier-Journal.* George Dabbs was commissioned to create this advertisement and others to sell bonds during World War I. He also did other freelance work for the *Courier-Journal.*

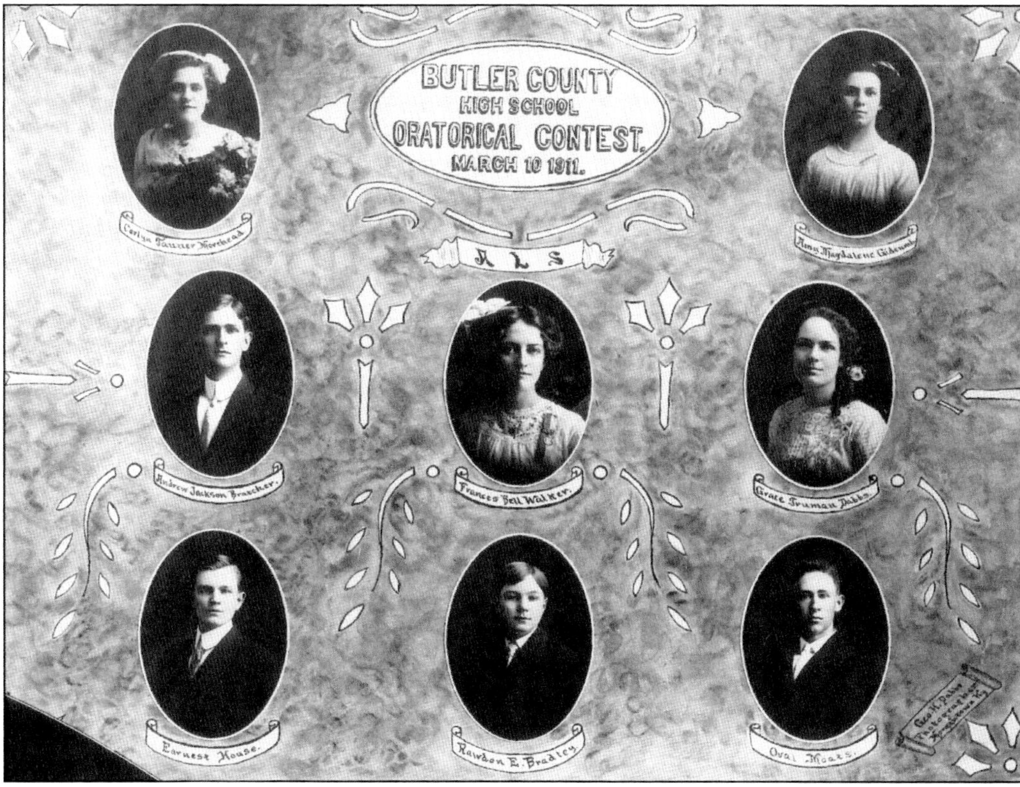

The Butler County High School oratorical contest on March 10, 1911, might have been forgotten if not for the foresight of George H. Dabbs. Members of this group who entered notable professions include Andrew Jackson Bratcher, circuit judge from 1945 to 1969; Grace (Truman) Dabbs Dean, choral director/vocal teacher at Lexington's Lafayette High School; and Oval Moats, county court clerk from 1914 to 1920.

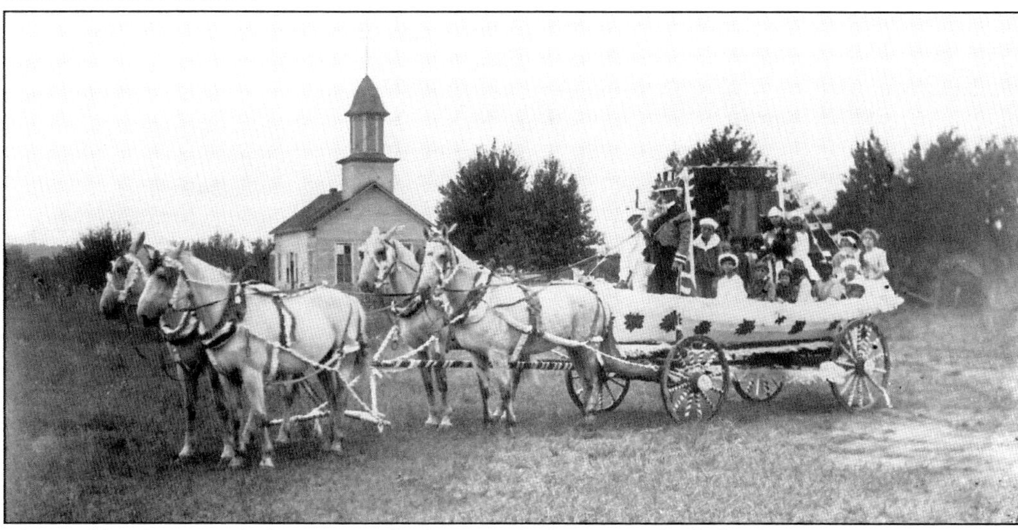

This Dabbs photograph shows a nicely decorated school float built for the Butler County School Fair and parade on October 15, 1915. Note that the four white horses are decorated with ribbons on their bridles and harnesses, as are the spokes of the wagon wheels. The driver is Grady Norris.

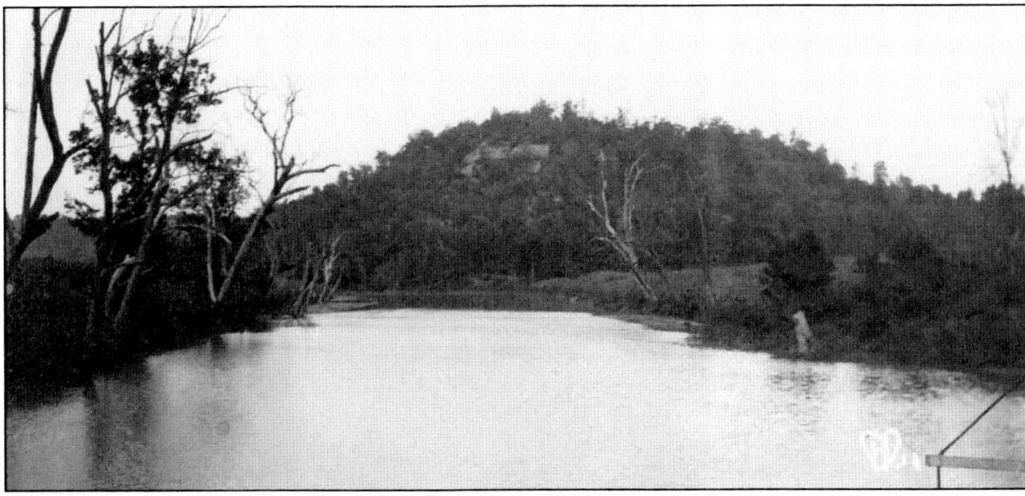

Dabbs never tired of taking photographs of his beloved Green River and other outdoor scenes. His interests in steamboats and river folklore were lifelong pursuits. This photograph, taken from the boiler deck of a steamer, is believed to be of "Buzzards Bluff," located high above the right bank of the river about halfway between Morgantown and Woodbury.

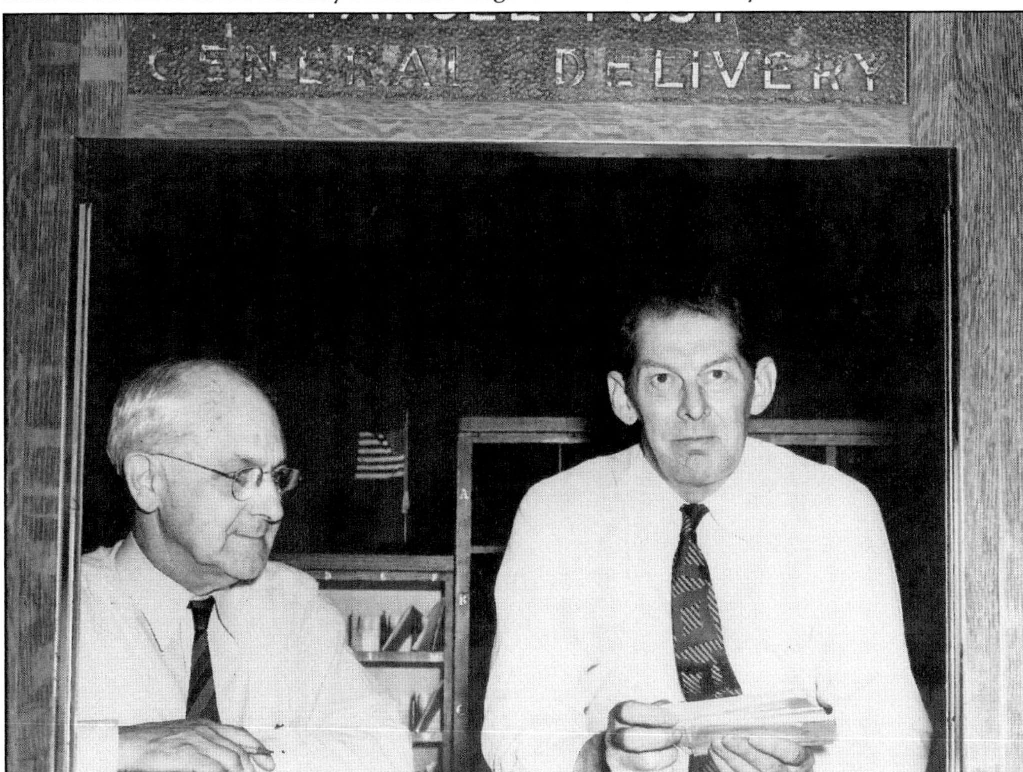

Dabbs (left) is pictured with fellow employee Clyde Helm in the Morgantown post office, where they served as clerks. After closing his studio in 1926, Dabbs worked for the postal service until he retired in the 1960s. After his retirement, he painted several of his riverboat photographs and sold them directly to clients; four of them were made into commercial prints.

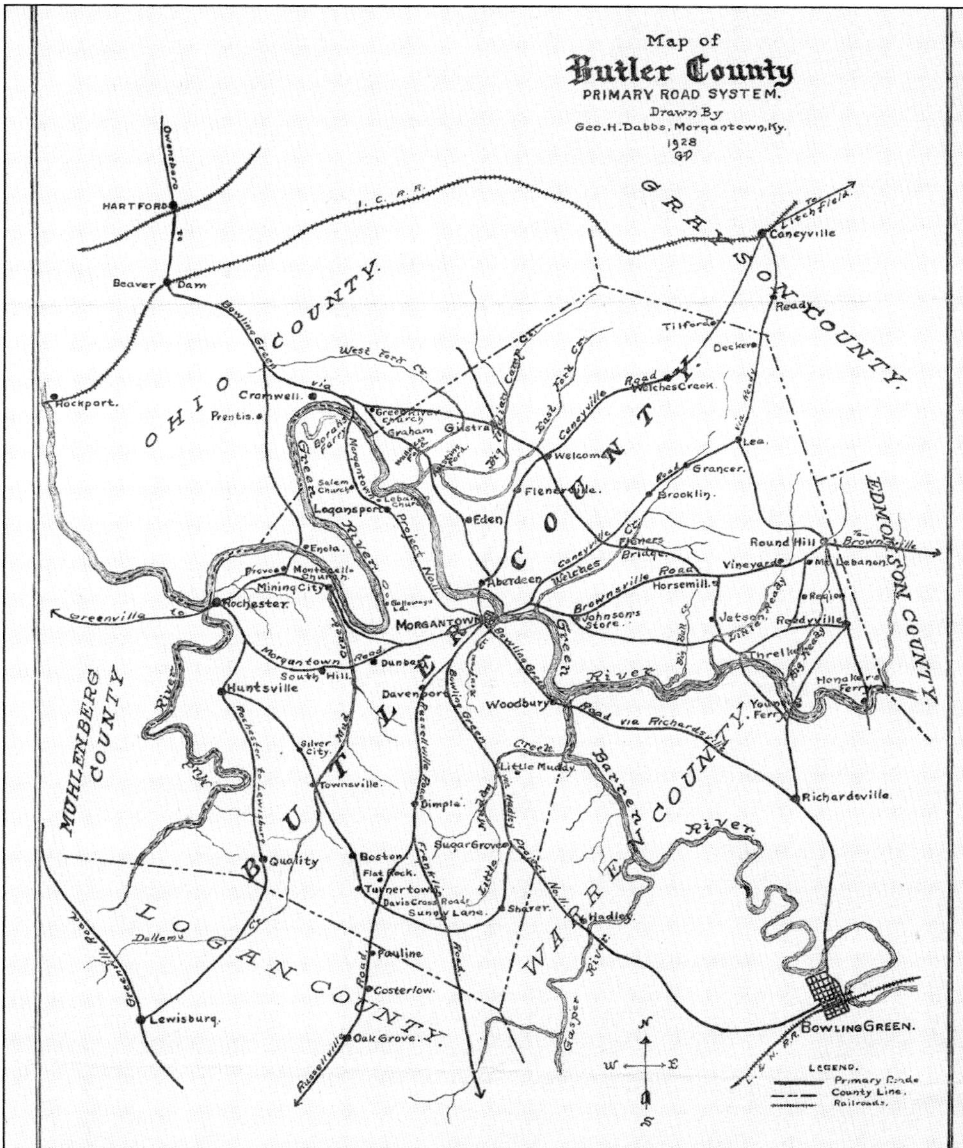

The above map shows the Primary Road System of Butler County as now designated.

The proposal is for Butler County to put up One Dollar for every Three Dollars the State puts up.

If Butler County votes to issue $150,000 in Bonds for the purpose of building hard surfaced roads, the State's part will be $450,000. This making a total of $600,000 worth of roads built and to be maintained for all the time by the State.

As an artist, Dabbs did other commercial work, including this 1928 drawing of a proposed Butler County road system. Few of the present-day roads match this drawing. Of particular note are the Russellville and Franklin Roads and the Beaver Dam roadways via Welcome, Horse Mill, Threlkel, and the Richardsville-to-Bowling Green road. Also, note the lack of a connecting route from Aberdeen to the Brownsville Road.

Five

School Days

The first documentation of a common school in Butler County was in a deed dated September 1, 1854. The school was located between Big Muddy and Brushy Fork Creeks in southern Butler County. The 1850 census listed five teachers in the county: Samuel Forgy, Thomas Rust, George and James Hill, and Curran Norman. Superintendent Elwood Neel adopted the first uniform textbook law for the county in July 1886. The books approved were: *McGuffey's Revised Reader and Speller*, *Ray's New Arithmetic and Algebra*, *Harvey's Revised Grammar*, *New Eclectic Geography: Kentucky Edition*, *New Eclectic Copybooks*, and *Eclectic Physiology*.

Butler County had several institutions of higher learning before 1900, including Rochester High School and Normal Institute, Butler County Seminary, Green River Normal, Little Muddy Academy, and Rochester Seminary. In 1902, records listed eighty-four white districts (with a total enrollment of 5,459 students) and six African American districts (with 296 students).

In 1908, the state legislature enacted a law requiring the establishment of a public high school in each county by 1910, which Butler County met in 1911. Rochester already had an independent public high school. In 1928, the communities of Boston and Reedyville built high schools, which were both closed in 1940. Rochester consolidated with Butler County High School in 1953, leaving Morgantown's school as the only high school in the county. Black students who wanted a high school education were transported to other counties, at school expense, until county schools were desegregated in 1961. Beginning in 1954, all of the county's elementary schools were consolidated into four larger elementary schools. In 1991, a new high school was built, and the old building was remodeled into a middle school. The fourth and fifth district schools were consolidated into a single North Butler Elementary School in 2005.

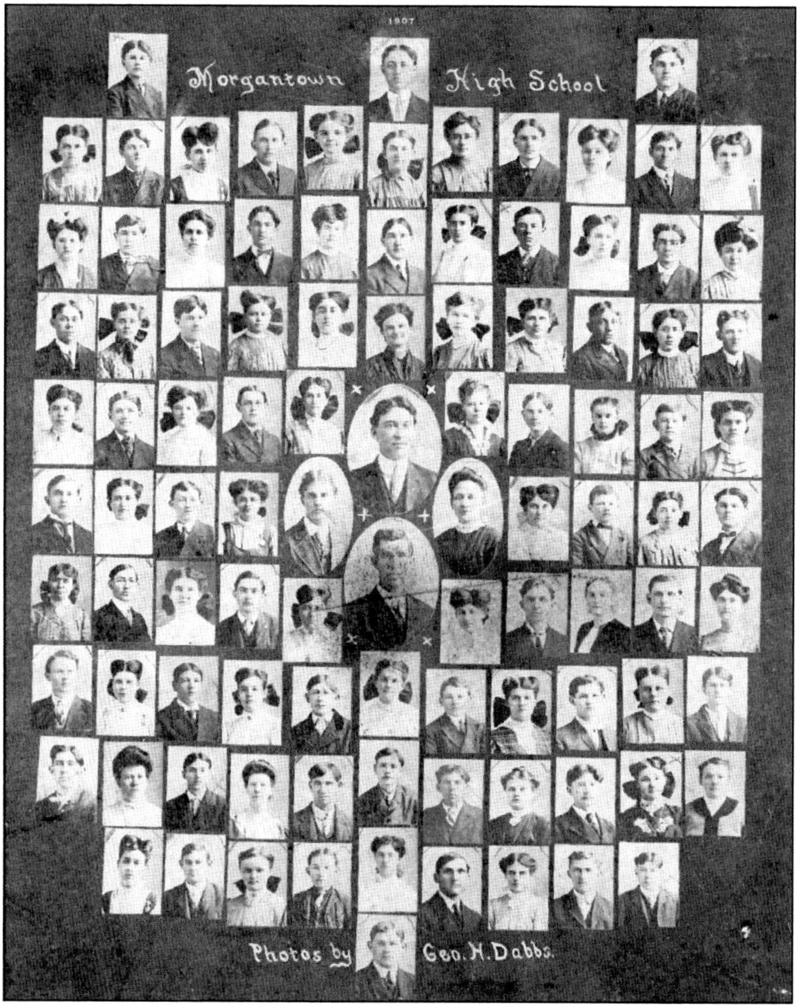

In 1907, the Morgantown High School did not have a yearbook, but George H. Dabbs provided the school with the next best thing—a collage with each student's portrait grouped into a single photograph. There are 94 students and four teachers in this image.

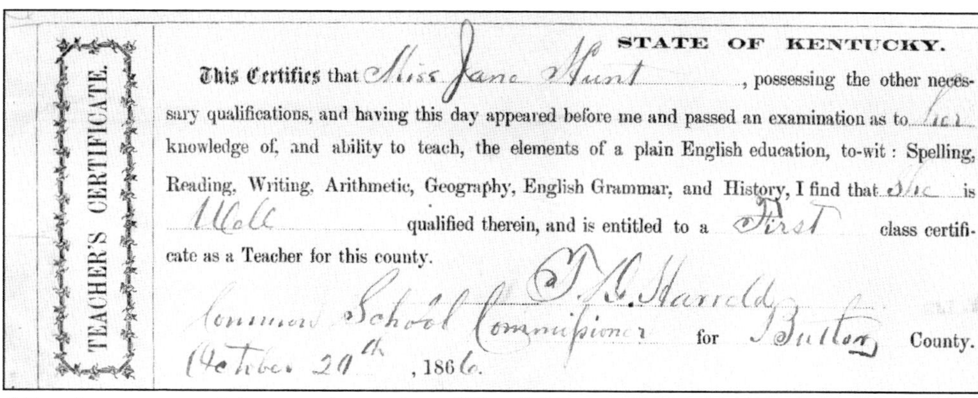

TEACHER'S CERTIFICATE.

STATE OF KENTUCKY.

This Certifies that Miss Jane Hunt, possessing the other necessary qualifications, and having this day appeared before me and passed an examination as to her knowledge of, and ability to teach, the elements of a plain English education, to-wit: Spelling, Reading, Writing, Arithmetic, Geography, English Grammar, and History, I find that she is Well qualified therein, and is entitled to a First class certificate as a Teacher for this county.

T. G. Harreld
Common School Commissioner for Butler County.
October 20th, 1866.

After the issuance of this certificate, Jane (Wood) Hunt taught at Old Hickory School in Butler County. The school lasted four months, and she was paid $25 per month. By spending a week with each family, her board was furnished by the community. The rules for female teachers were strict; the rule book stated, "women teachers who marry or engage in unseemly conduct will be dismissed."

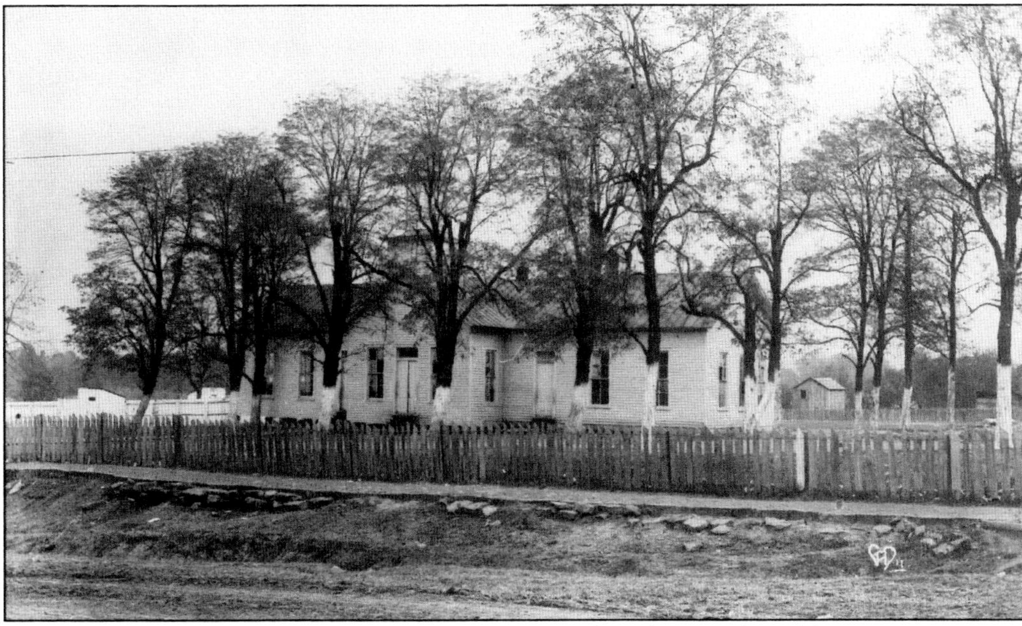

The Morgantown Seminary was built around 1854 on three lots purchased from Vincent S. Hay. This three-room building had a cupola that housed the school's bell; as attendance increased, the "bell room" on the front was eventually used as a classroom. This building was moved in 1910 to allow the larger, modern brick high school to be built on the site.

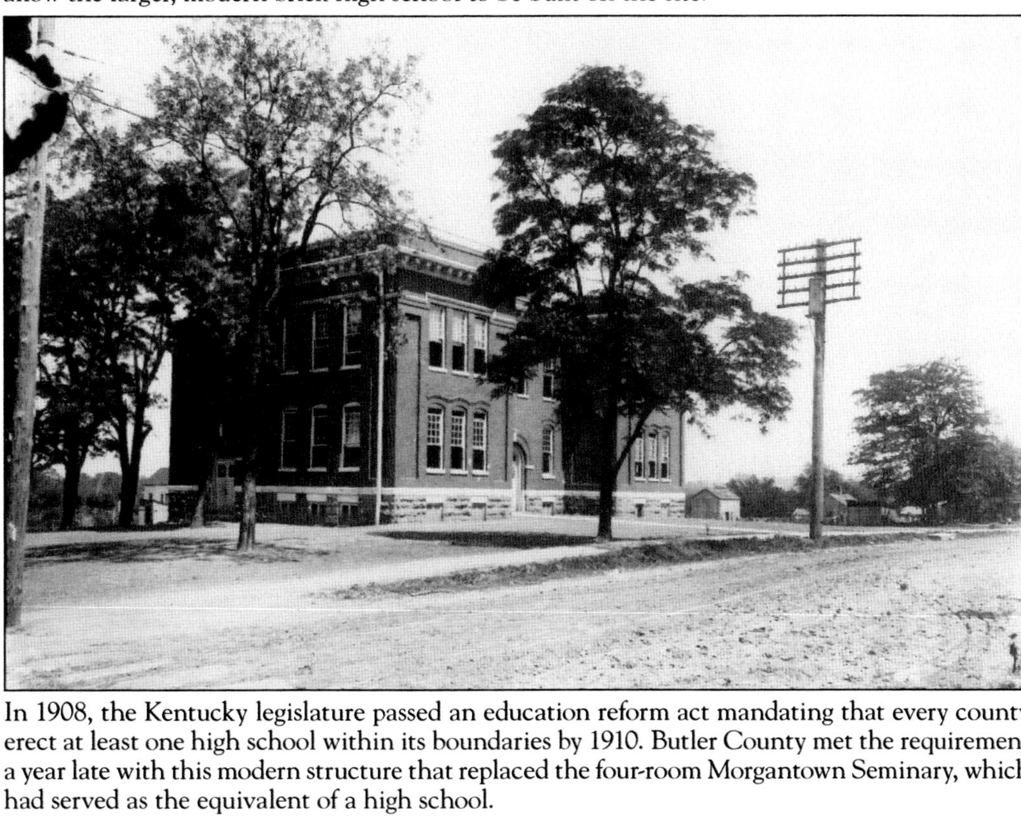

In 1908, the Kentucky legislature passed an education reform act mandating that every county erect at least one high school within its boundaries by 1910. Butler County met the requirement a year late with this modern structure that replaced the four-room Morgantown Seminary, which had served as the equivalent of a high school.

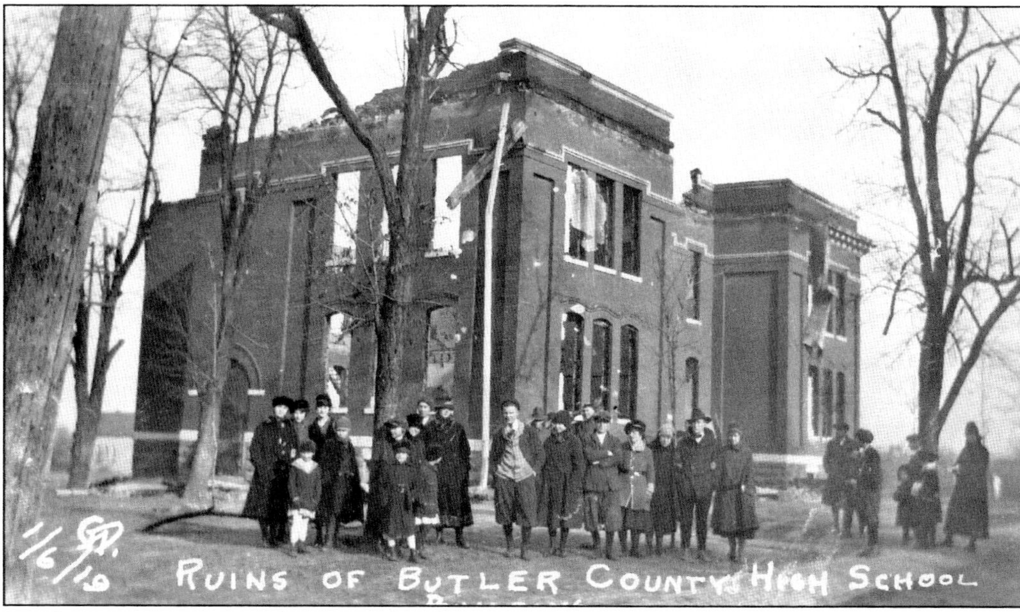

Residents came out to see the ruins of Butler County High School after a fire completely destroyed the building on January 6, 1919. At the time of the fire, the building had only been in use for nine years. This location is now home to the Butler County Board of Education building.

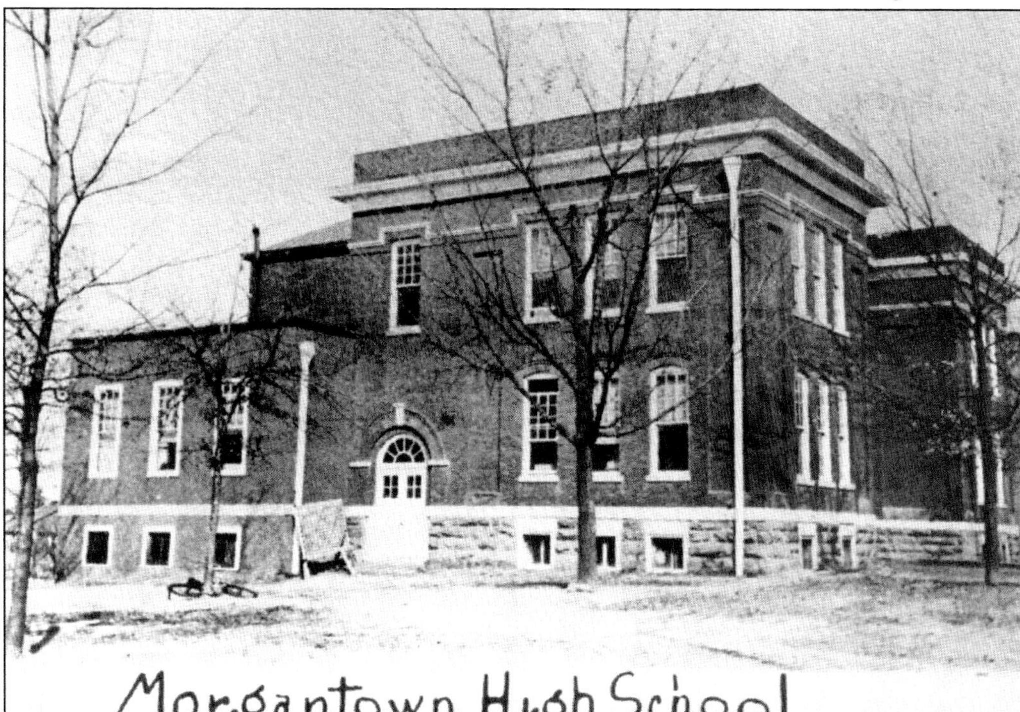

Butler County's high school was reconstructed in 1920. The structure, renamed Morgantown High School, was built on the same foundation using the same design but with a one-room, single-story addition on the rear left side. More classrooms and a gymnasium/auditorium were added in 1935. This building served as a high school until 1952 and as an elementary school until 1971.

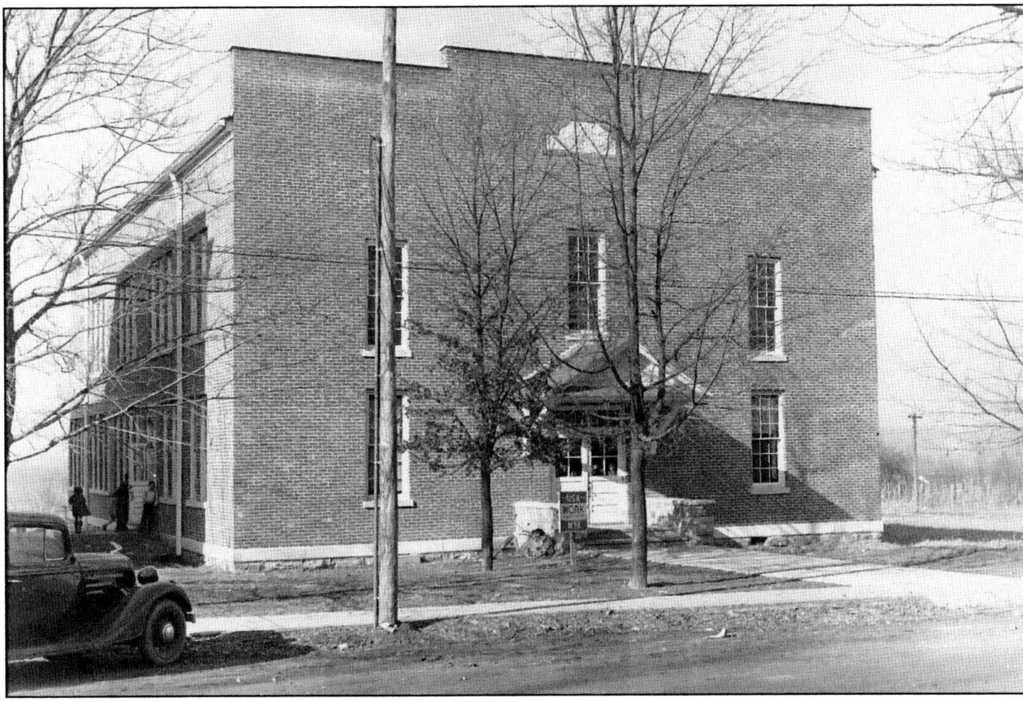

This photograph shows the old Morgantown High School, with an auditorium/gymnasium on the second floor and classrooms on the lower level. Built in 1935, it was a WPA project that cost $19,084. It was sponsored by Morgantown and Butler County, who paid $3,582 while the federal government picked up the rest of the cost. This building burned down in the early 1970s.

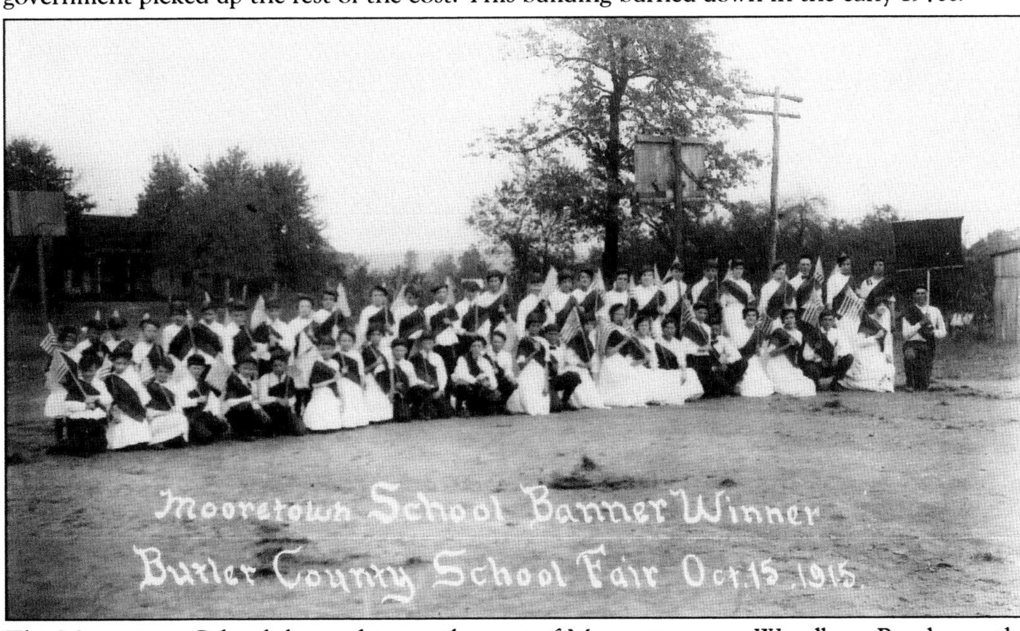

The Mooretown School, located two miles east of Morgantown on Woodbury Road, was the banner winner of the 1915 Butler County School Fair. Although they are not pictured above, John Monroe Moore, who became an important bishop in the Methodist church, was a former student, and Kentucky governor William S. Taylor was once a teacher at Mooretown.

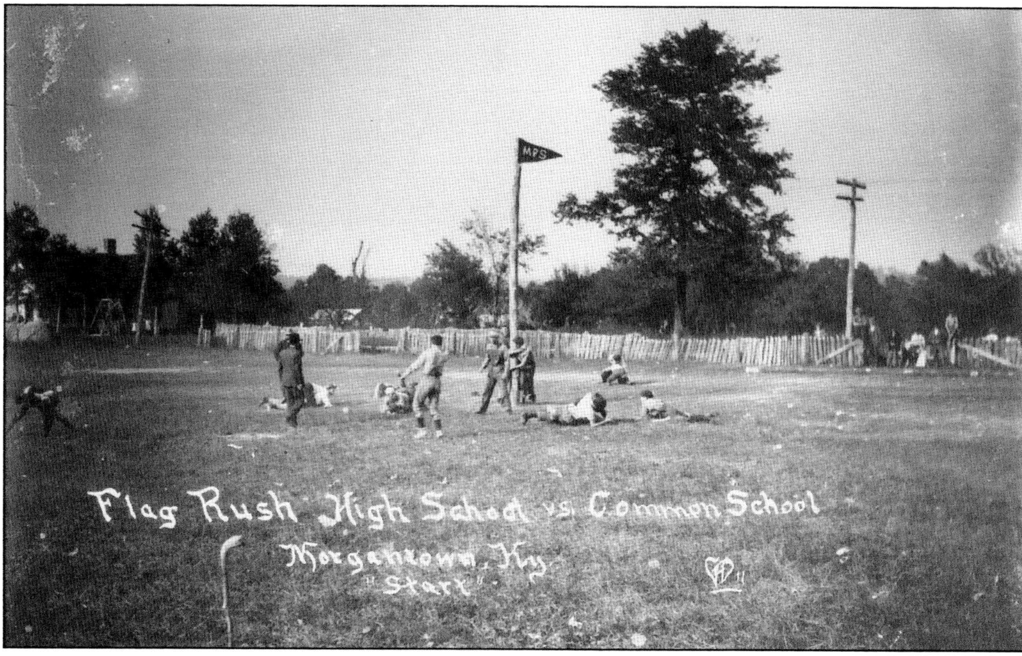

This photograph shows a flag rush game between Morgantown High School and the Common School at Morgantown. Flag rush was a game in which each school defended their pole and flag. Common schools were tuition-free schools; other learning institutions in the early 1900s were subscription schools supported by students' tuition fees.

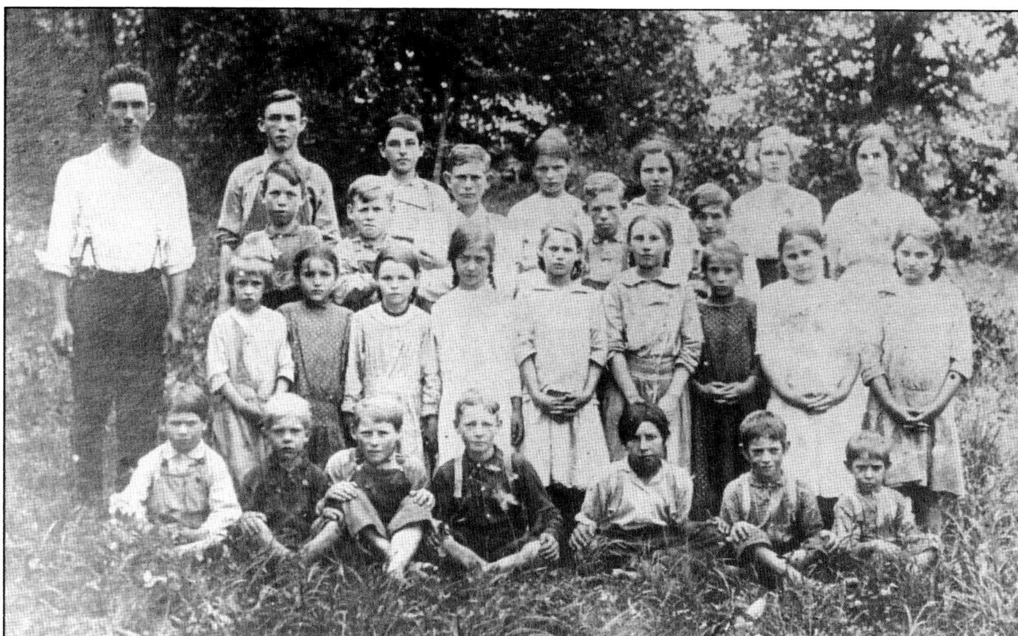

Students at the Howard School, located on the north side of Green River, pose for a group photograph in the early 1900s. Around that time, there were as many as 90 school districts in Butler County, including seven African American districts; all but Morgantown and Rochester were served by one-room schools.

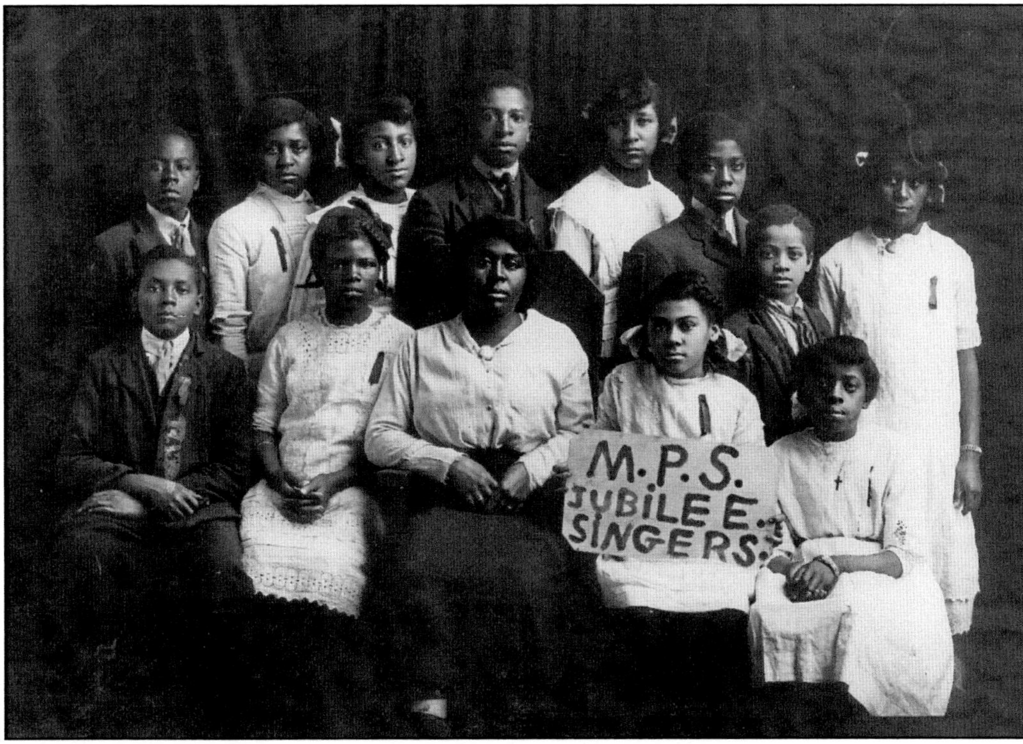

This photograph appears to be of the Morgantown Public School Jubilee Singers. Jubilee groups were very popular African American performers who sang traditional and gospel music. The only identified member is Morgantown's Pearl Ratcliffe (seated, second from left).

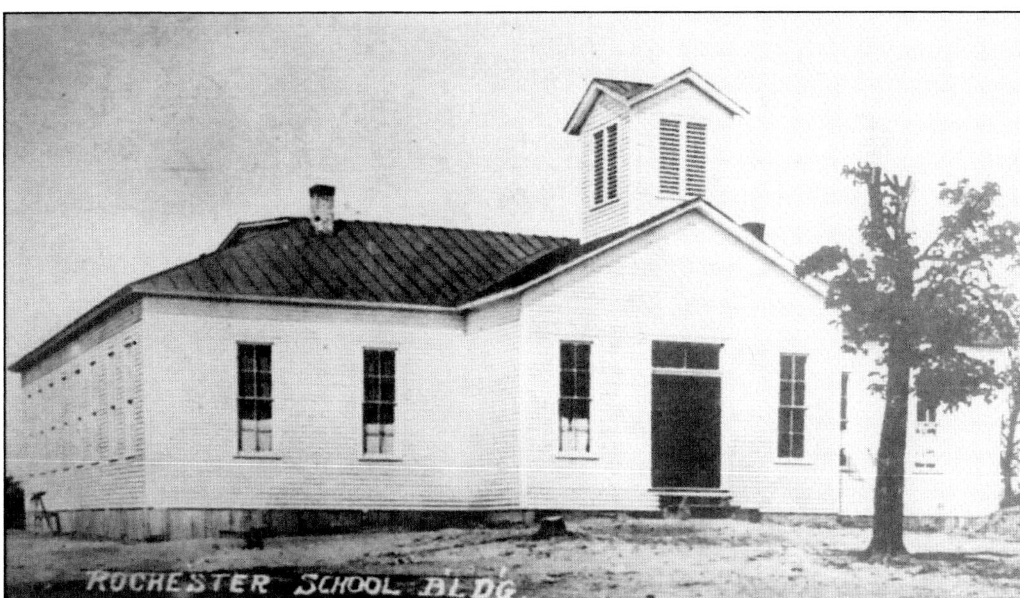

This new building, which was completed in 1916, replaced the Rochester School building that burned down in 1914. In 1934, the trustees voted to consolidate it with the Butler County schools.

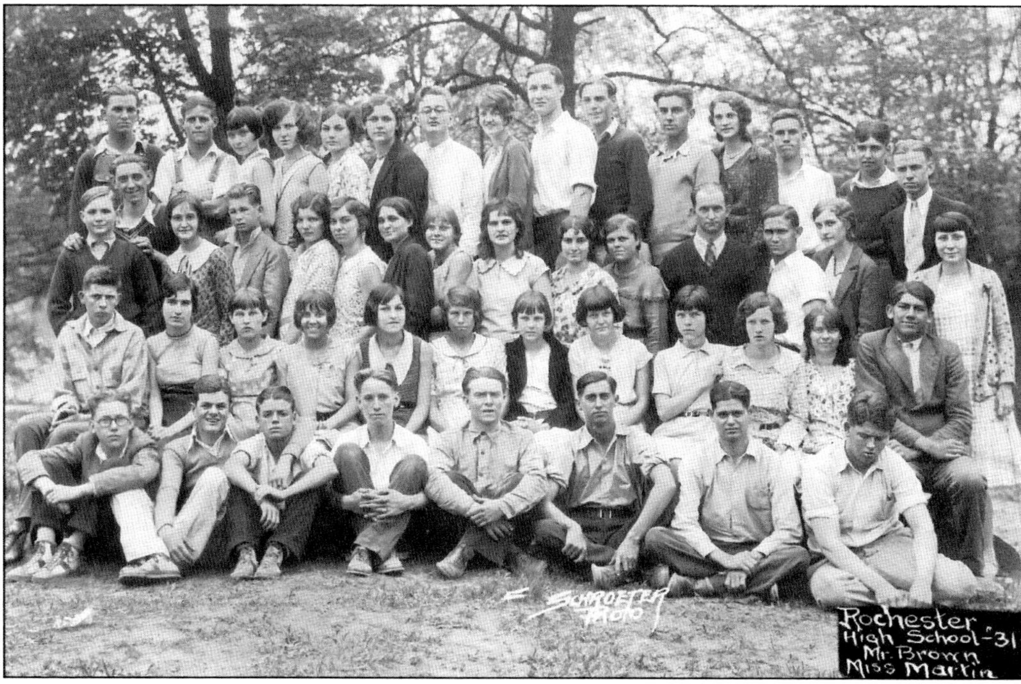

Schroeter Floating Studio captured this image of Rochester High School students in 1931. The teachers standing on the far right are R.P. Brown and Ruth Martin. Rochester operated an independent school system until 1934.

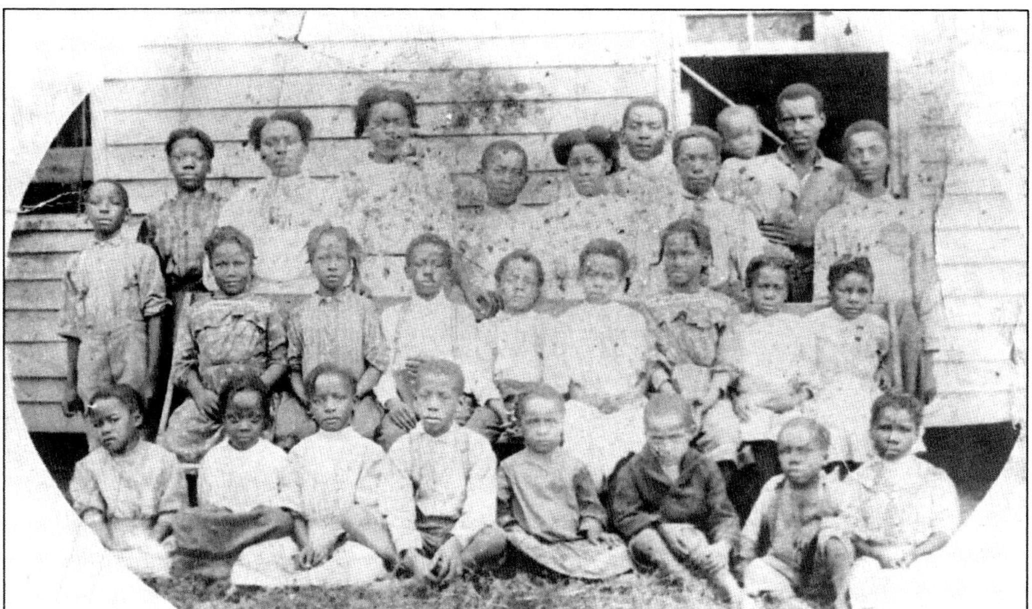

Students at the Rochester School in 1911 included (first row, fourth from right) Slaughter Ray; (second row, sitting, from left to right) Allene Ray, Bertha Wilson, unidentified, Wesley Mason, and four unidentified students; (third row) B. Smith, Pearl Ray, teacher Mae Bailey, Ollie Porter, Franklin Porter, Jessie Cushenberry, Arthur Porter, Estile Smith, Willie Robinson (holding son Edgar), and unidentified.

The Woodbury School is shown in this c. 1903 image by Schroeter & Rorst, taken when the school was new and the pride of its community. Woodbury is located about 4.8 miles from Morgantown. The only identified student in the photograph is Bonnie Wand Drake, born in 1895, who is ninth from the left in the first row. (Courtesy of Barbara Drake Bresler.)

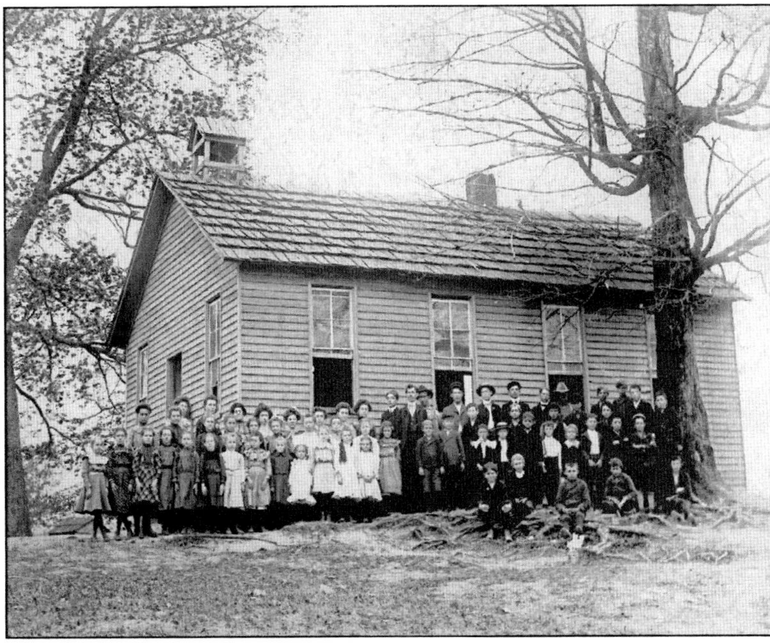

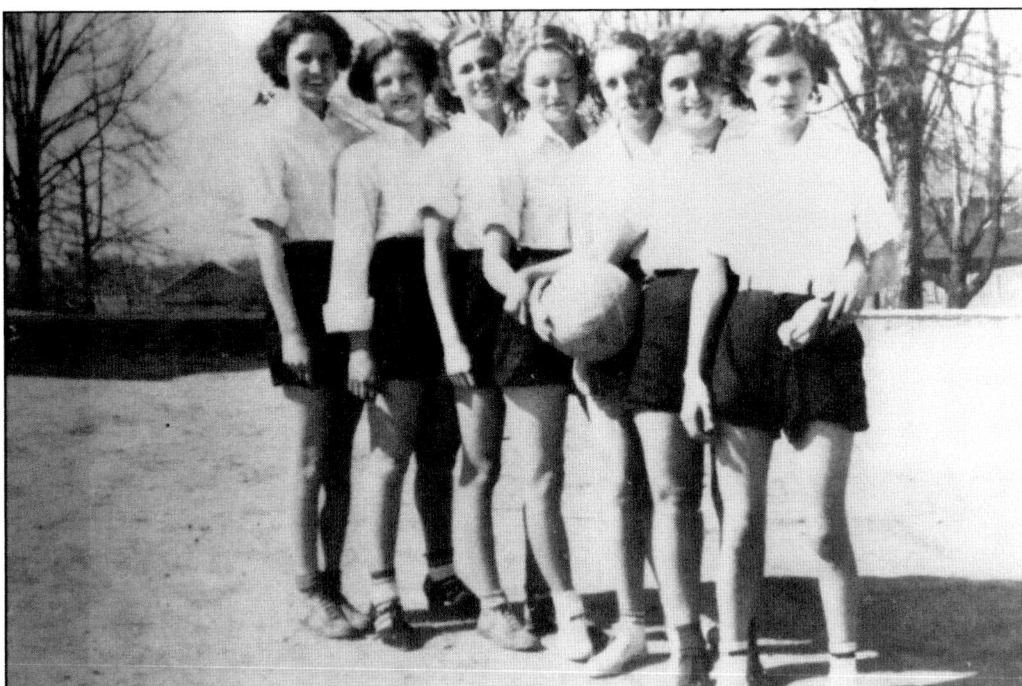

Rochester High School was socially progressive, as shown in this photograph of the 1938–1939 girls' basketball team. The team members are, from left to right, Hazel Barbee, Wilma Green, Glenda Barbee, June Smith, Marjory Brown, Edna Woods, and Ruth Freeman Baker. For a time, girls' teams were not allowed to compete at the state level; in fact, the 1932 Kentucky High School Athletic Association (KHSAA) tournament was the last time women competed until Title IX was enacted in 1972.

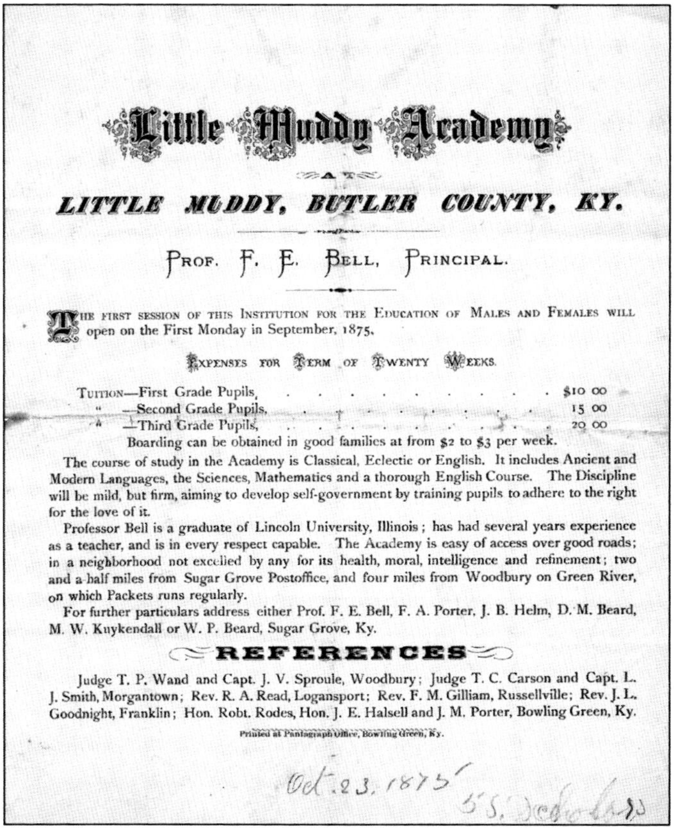

Little Muddy Academy

AT

LITTLE MUDDY, BUTLER COUNTY, KY.

PROF. F. E. BELL, PRINCIPAL.

THE FIRST SESSION OF THIS INSTITUTION FOR THE EDUCATION OF MALES AND FEMALES WILL open on the First Monday in September, 1875.

EXPENSES FOR TERM OF TWENTY WEEKS.

TUITION—First Grade Pupils,	$10 00
" —Second Grade Pupils,	15 00
" —Third Grade Pupils,	20 00

Boarding can be obtained in good families at from $2 to $3 per week.

The course of study in the Academy is Classical, Eclectic or English. It includes Ancient and Modern Languages, the Sciences, Mathematics and a thorough English Course. The Discipline will be mild, but firm, aiming to develop self-government by training pupils to adhere to the right for the love of it.

Professor Bell is a graduate of Lincoln University, Illinois; has had several years experience as a teacher, and is in every respect capable. The Academy is easy of access over good roads; in a neighborhood not excelled by any for its health, moral, intelligence and refinement; two and a half miles from Sugar Grove Postoffice, and four miles from Woodbury on Green River, on which Packets runs regularly.

For further particulars address either Prof. F. E. Bell, F. A. Porter, J. B. Helm, D. M. Beard, M. W. Knykendall or W. P. Beard, Sugar Grove, Ky.

REFERENCES

Judge T. P. Wand and Capt. J. V. Sproule, Woodbury; Judge T. C. Carson and Capt. L. J. Smith, Morgantown; Rev. R. A. Read, Logansport; Rev. F. M. Gilliam, Russellville; Rev. J. L. Goodnight, Franklin; Hon. Robt. Rodes, Hon. J. E. Halsell and J. M. Porter, Bowling Green, Ky.

Printed at Pantagraph Office, Bowling Green, Ky.

Oct. 23. 1875

55 Scholars

Little Muddy Academy boasted of 55 scholars in this advertisement from October 23, 1875. The subscription school was coeducational, and its references came from many of the leading citizens of the county. The building, constructed in 1830, still stands today as the Little Muddy Community Center.

The Butler County School Fair of October 15, 1915, was an exciting event. This photograph was taken on the playgrounds behind Morgantown High School. The building in the background was the center bell room portion of the old seminary. It was moved there when the modern brick high school was built in 1910 and was used as a primary school until it was torn down in 1942.

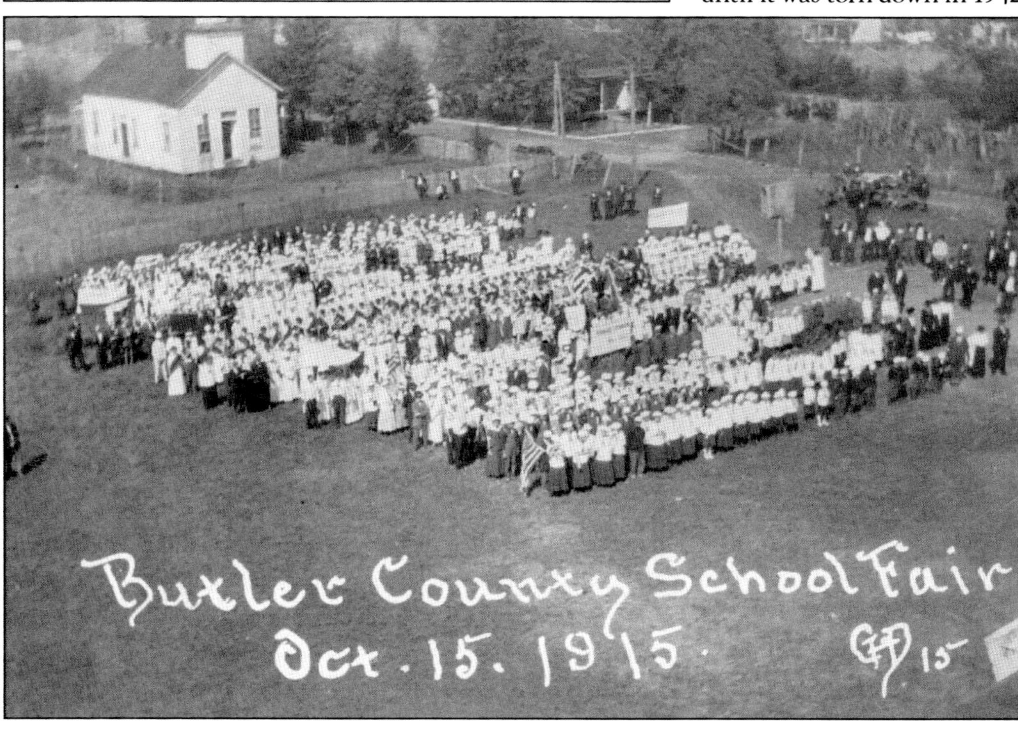

Six

Morgantown

After some debate about where the county seat of Butler County should be located, it was finally decided that it should be on Funkhouser Hill. The town was laid out and christened Morgan Town in 1810, in honor of Revolutionary War hero Gen. Daniel Morgan. Col. John Porter was influential in naming the town, having fought under Morgan in the Battle of Cowpens, a turning point in the war. Morgantown was officially incorporated in 1813, and the town grew slowly in the beginning, with a population of 101 in 1860. The opening of the river to the steamboat trade did not initially help Morgantown much, as there were only 202 inhabitants in 1880. However, by 1900, its population, at 588, had almost tripled. It has grown slowly since—its 2010 population was 2,544. George H. Dabbs described his dreams for Morgantown in the following poem:

I've lived my life, the better part,
Served its people, practiced art,
With fondest hope someday to see
The dear old town what it ought to be.
When I view its cemetery, its illustrious dead,
I think with pride of the lives they led,
Its men of letters, of law, of grace,
The ones who labored to build the place,
Methinks I hear from the grassy mounds,
The weird and troubled and doleful sounds,
Pleading, as it were, from days that are gone,
"Pick up the torch folks! Carry on!"
"Keep fast the faith, and make it the rule
To care for the home, the church and the school;
Hold sacred the law, its majesty and grace
And keep the old town a desirable place."
So let us like men, like citizens bold,
Regard with all honor the place we hold;
Let's "Carry On" without fear or frown,
And have a bigger and better "old Morgantown."

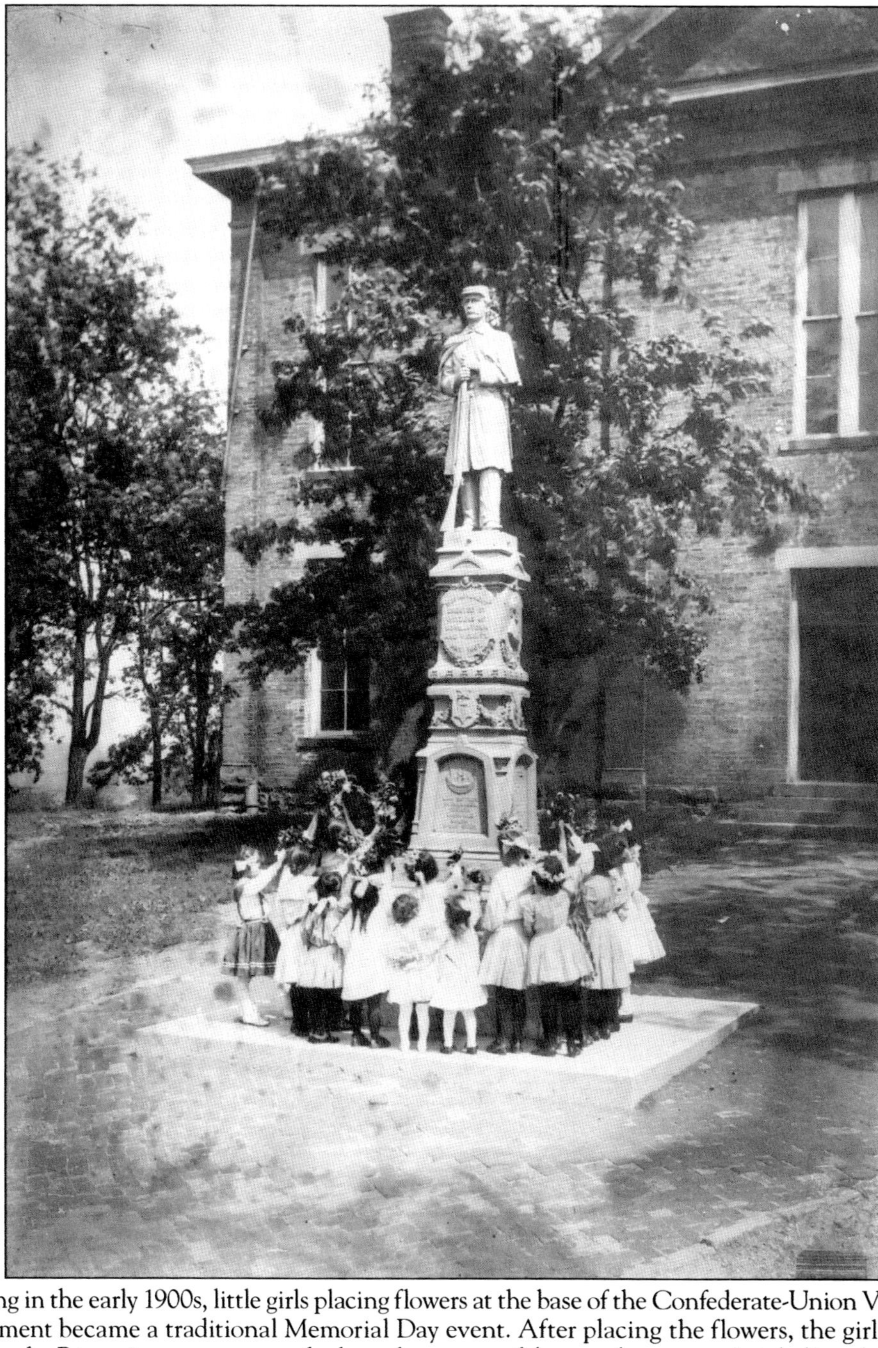

Starting in the early 1900s, little girls placing flowers at the base of the Confederate-Union Veterans' Monument became a traditional Memorial Day event. After placing the flowers, the girls would walk to the Riverview cemetery and adorn the graves of deceased veterans. It is believed that the tradition started as a part of the dedication of the monument in May 1907. This photograph was George H. Dabbs's favorite. Through photographs like this, Dabbs sought to illustrate the biblical injunction, "but this one thing I do, forget those things which are behind, and reach forth to those things which are ahead." He wanted all people to come together and work toward a better Morgantown and community. This monument still stands on the grounds of the Butler County Courthouse; it was listed in the National Register of Historic Places in 1997.

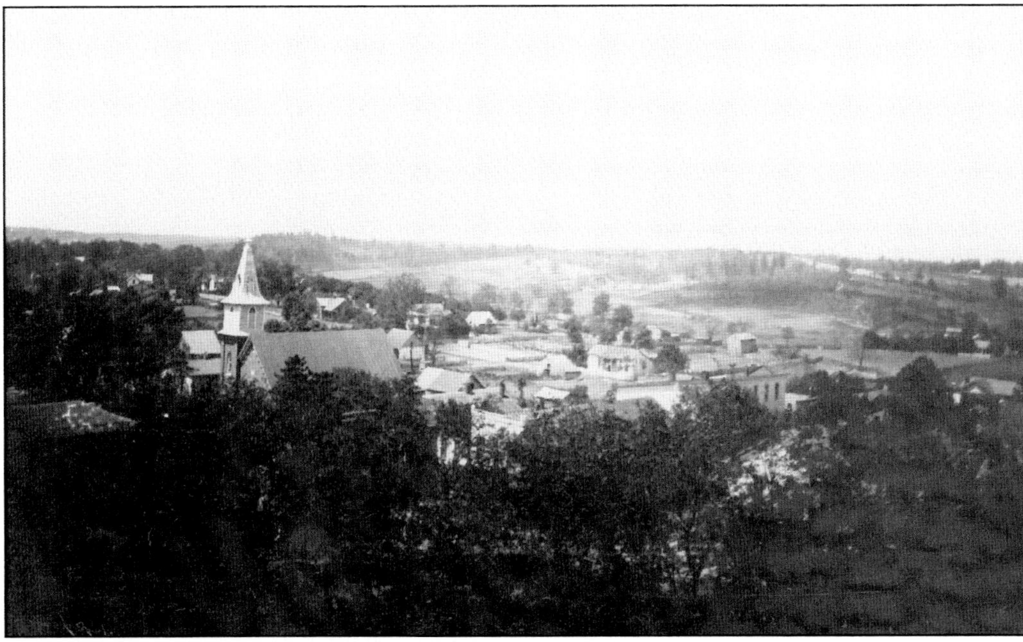

This pre-1915 view from the top of the Butler County Courthouse overlooks Morgantown in a northwesterly direction. A city park is now located in the field in the upper center of the image. The home just right of center is on South Tyler Street and still stands.

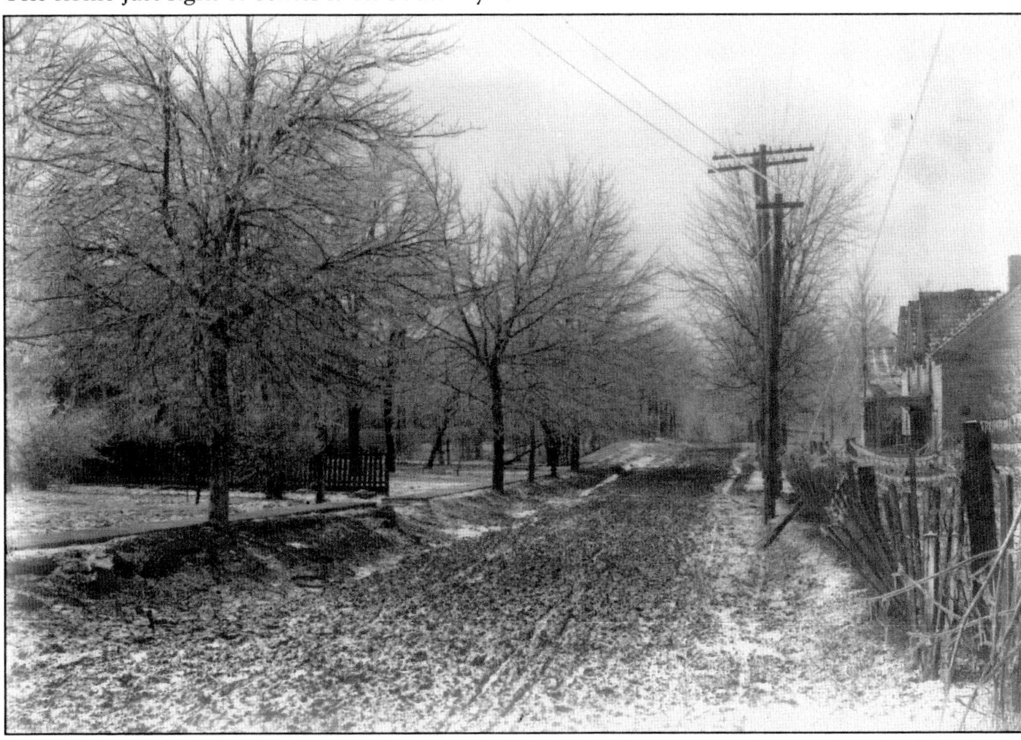

This winter scene looking south on Tyler Street was taken after 1905 (when the telephone poles were installed). The three-dormer house at right still stands on the northeast corner of Morrison and Tyler Streets and is now the home of Danny and Nellie Webb.

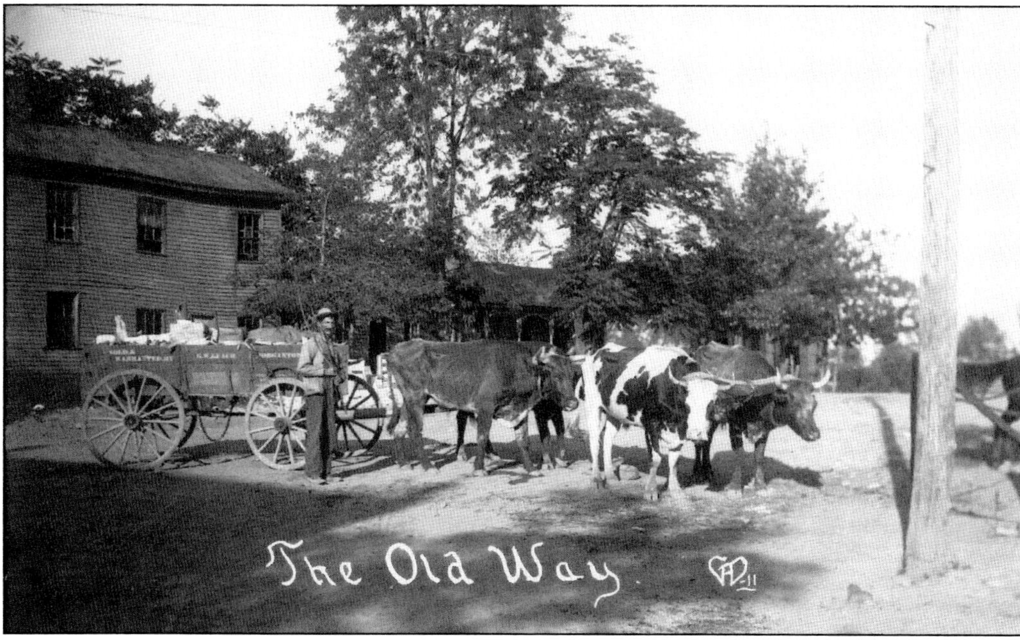

In 1911, more than 100 years ago, George Dabbs described the oxen-drawn wagon in this image as "the old way." Apparently, the horse had replaced the ox as the preferred method for transporting farm products by that time, and by the 1920s, the animals had been replaced by automobiles. The driver is Bud Blancett. G.W. Leach Hardware is in the background, in the present-day location of Wan's Clinic.

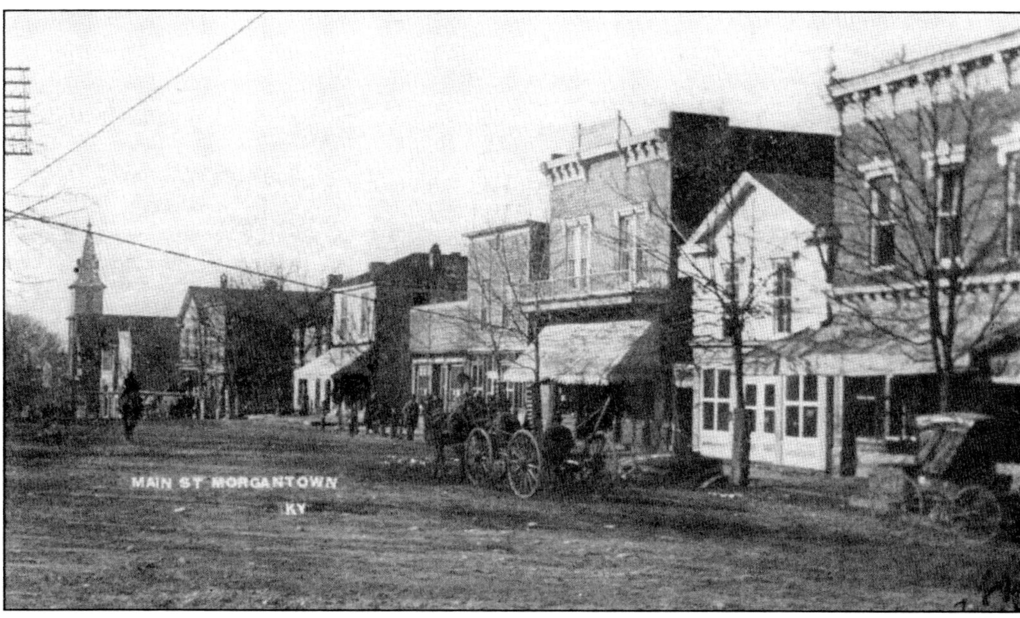

This 1905 image shows the shops and churches along Morgantown's main street—Butler Street—including, from left to right, the First Baptist Church, John Carson Bank, W.A. Kelly's shop, Dockery's Drug, unidentified, Cook's Grocery, the Richmond Hotel (behind Cook's Grocery), Beesley's Drug, Cliff Moore's shop, Kip Ruley's store, Liege Phelps grocery, and J.A. Tanner Dry Goods.

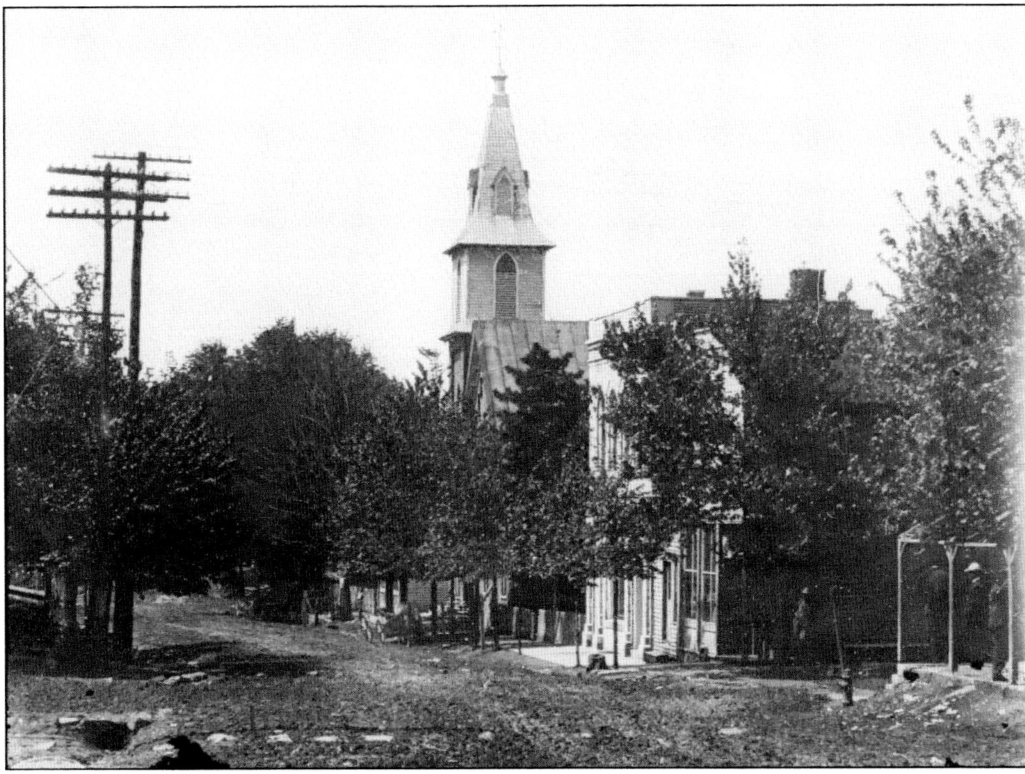

This 1900 photograph shows the intersection of South Butler and Logan Streets, with the First Baptist Church on the right of the street. This building was completed in December 1897 and burned down on January 18, 1915. The John Carson Bank is beside the church, and W.A. Kelly's shop is on the corner.

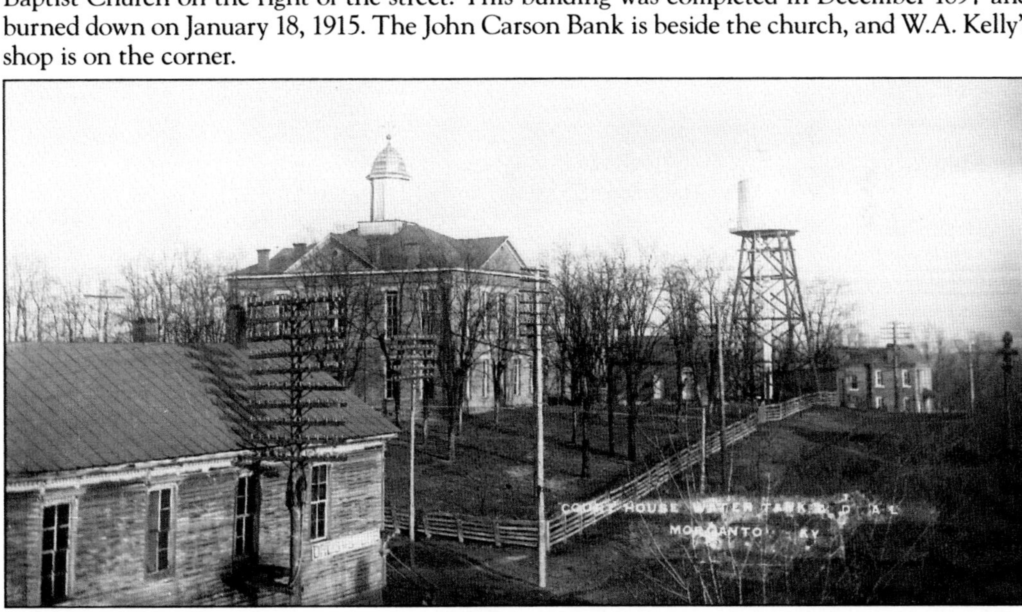

This photograph can be dated to between 1905 and 1912 because of the telephone poles and the water tower. The tower was part of the Morgantown Water Works, which collapsed in May 1912 and was not replaced. Dockery's Drug is in the lower left corner, and the building to the right of the water tower was the Butler County jail.

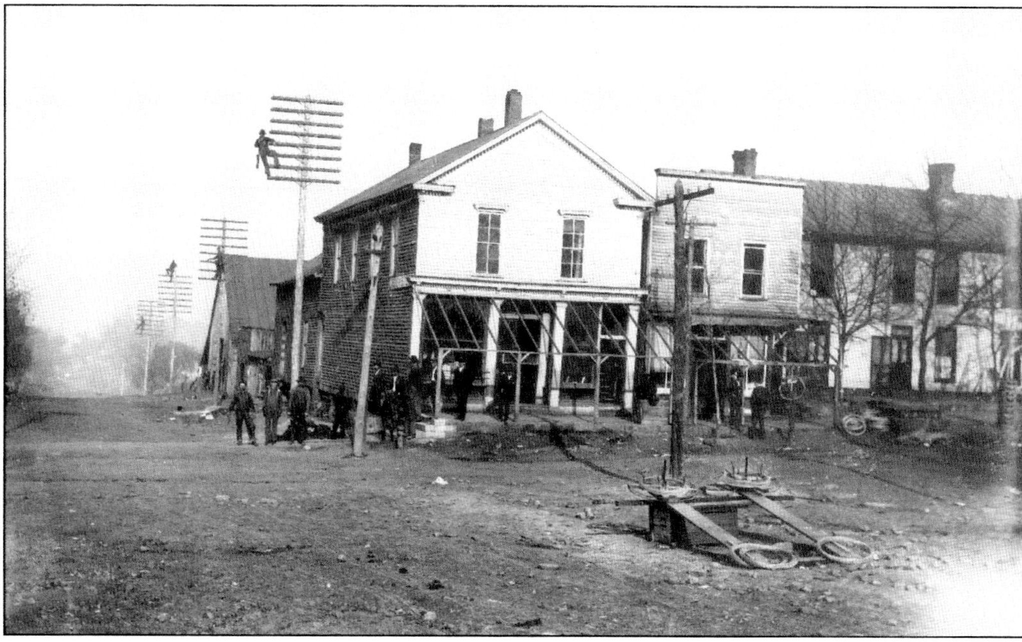

The construction of Morgantown's first telephone system is shown in this early 1900s photograph. Dockery's Drug is on the corner of Butler and Logan Streets, and Hammer's Restaurant and the Richmond Hotel are to the right of the drugstore. Behind Dockery's Drug is Mauzy's livery stable. The back room of Dockery's Drug, complete with a Victrola and a piano, was a popular teenage hangout at the time.

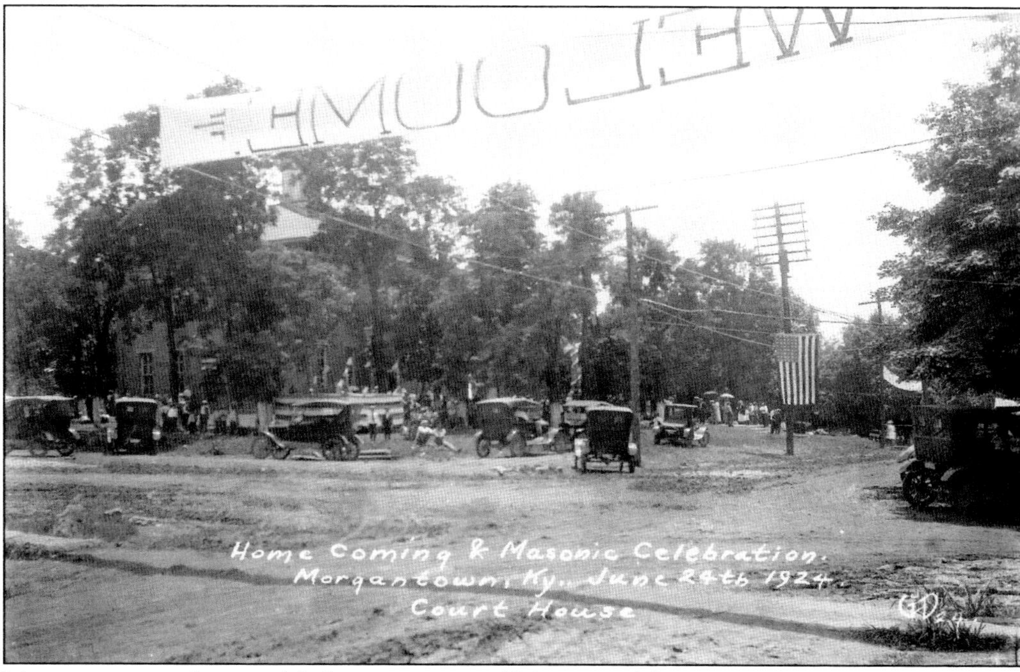

Morgantown was decorated for homecoming and Masonic celebrations on June 24, 1924. It appears that Model T Fords were abundant in those days, and parking was done at random. It would be two more years before Morgantown had an improved, macadamized road through town.

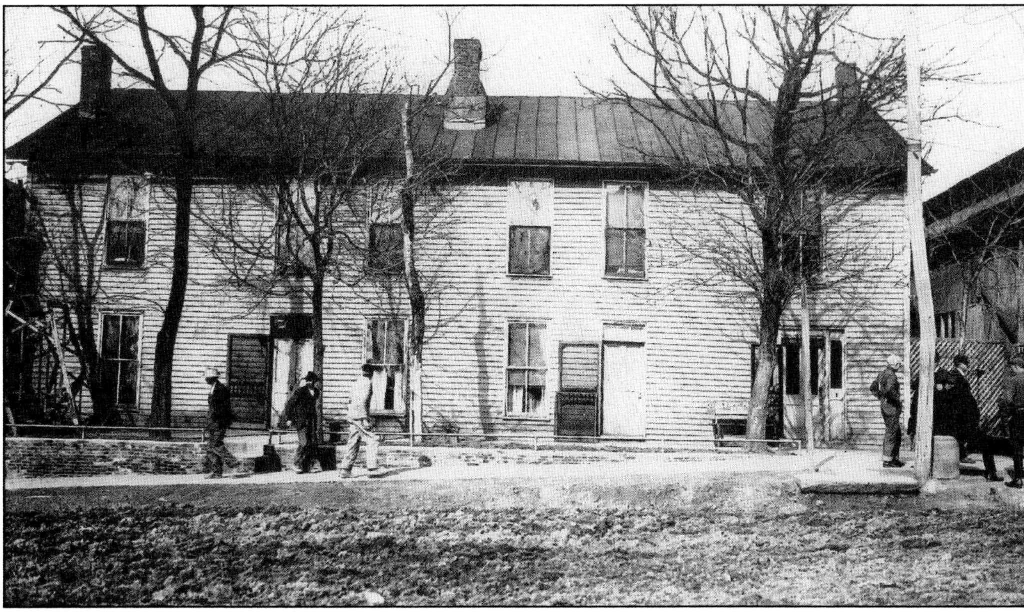

The Richmond Hotel is shown here without the front porch addition. The Richmond was one of Morgantown's finest early-1900s lodging establishments. Because it was directly across the street from the county courthouse, it attracted many out-of-town lawyers, judges, and other travelers. The hotel was destroyed by fire in 1946.

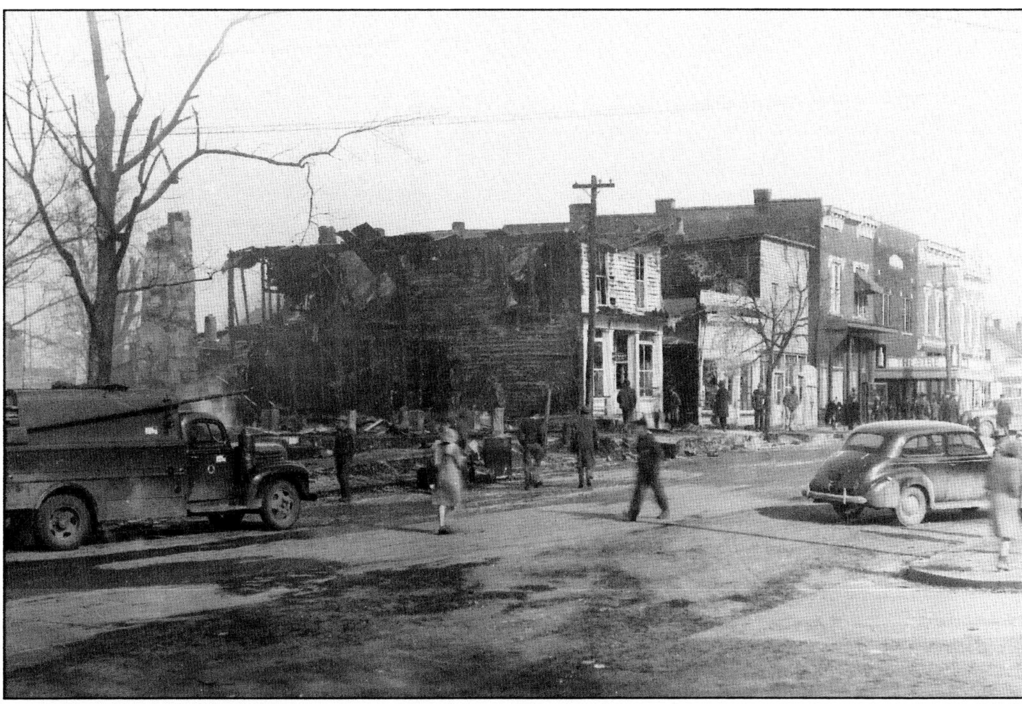

In 1946, townspeople gathered to see the ruins of the Richmond Hotel in Morgantown. "Ma Bell" was already on the scene, as evidenced by the Bell telephone repair truck at left. The building next to the Richmond is Cook's (Romans') grocery, which was heavily damaged by the fire.

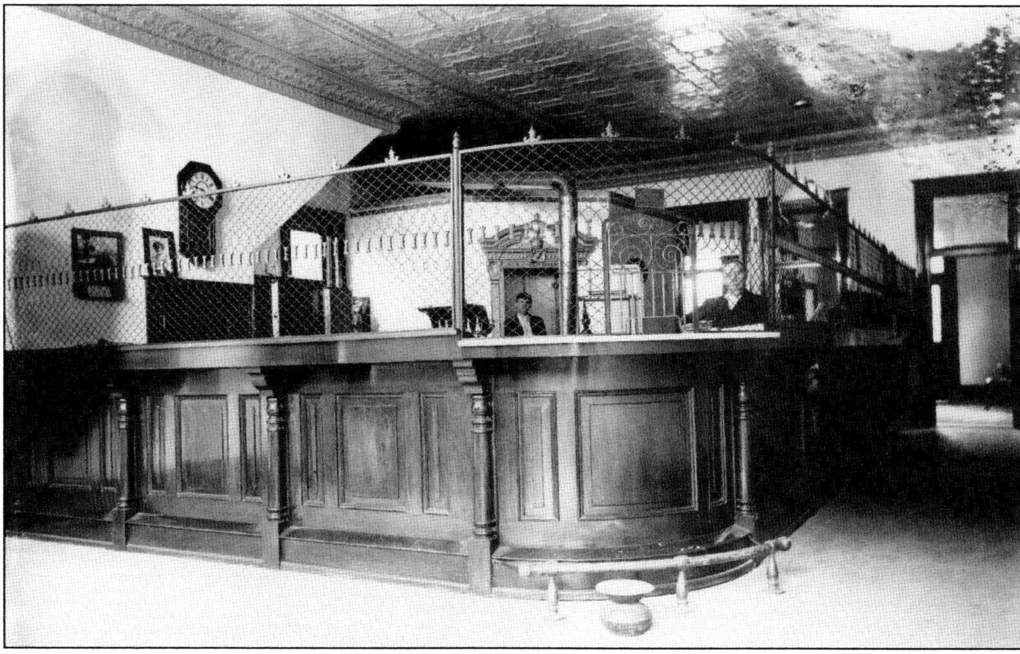

The interior of the John Carson Bank had an ornate appearance for its time. Carson served as circuit court clerk from 1882 to 1886 before opening the bank, which failed during the Great Depression. Carson (left) is pictured here with James R. Phelps in a quiet moment.

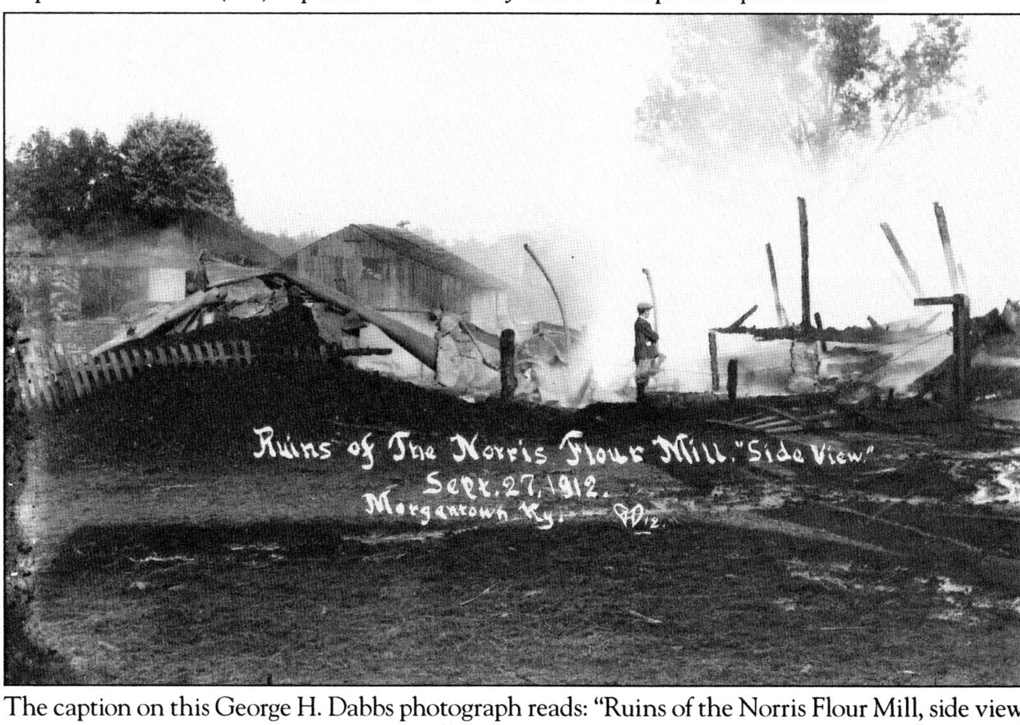

The caption on this George H. Dabbs photograph reads: "Ruins of the Norris Flour Mill, side view, Sept. 27, 1912, Morgantown, Ky." The mill, located on the corner of Morrison and Tyler Streets, was later rebuilt by R. Bunyon House and was operated by various owners into the late 1970s, when it burned down again. The last operators of the mill were Arthur and Paul Ingram.

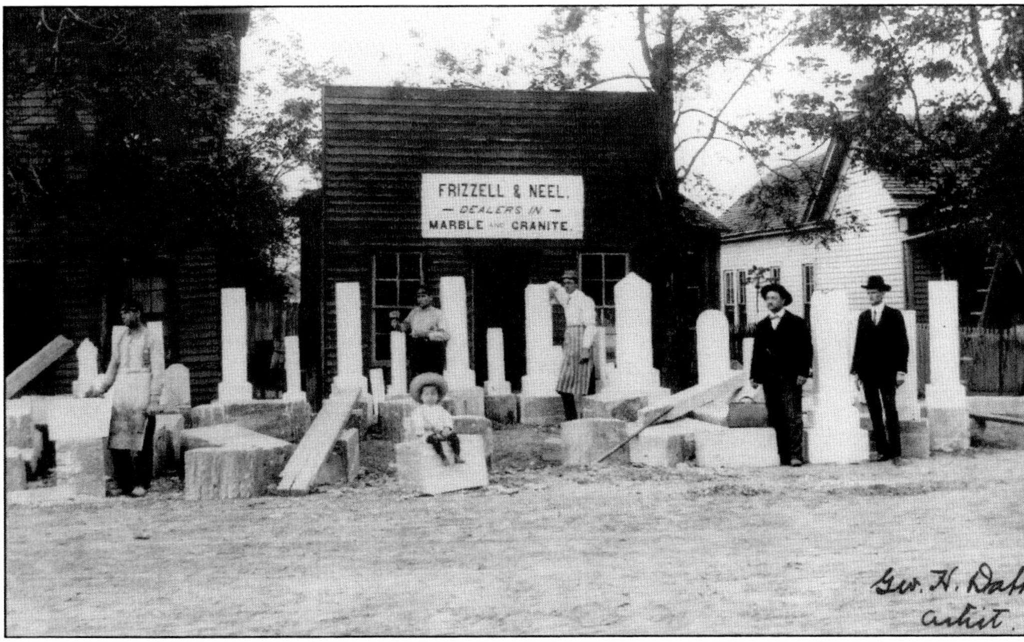

Frizzell and Neel Monument Company was located on Ohio Street. This photograph was taken around 1904, as verified by Dabbs's signature (shortly after that time, Dabbs began using the "GHD" mark). The two men in suits at right are owners John Frizzell (left) and Elwood Neel (right).

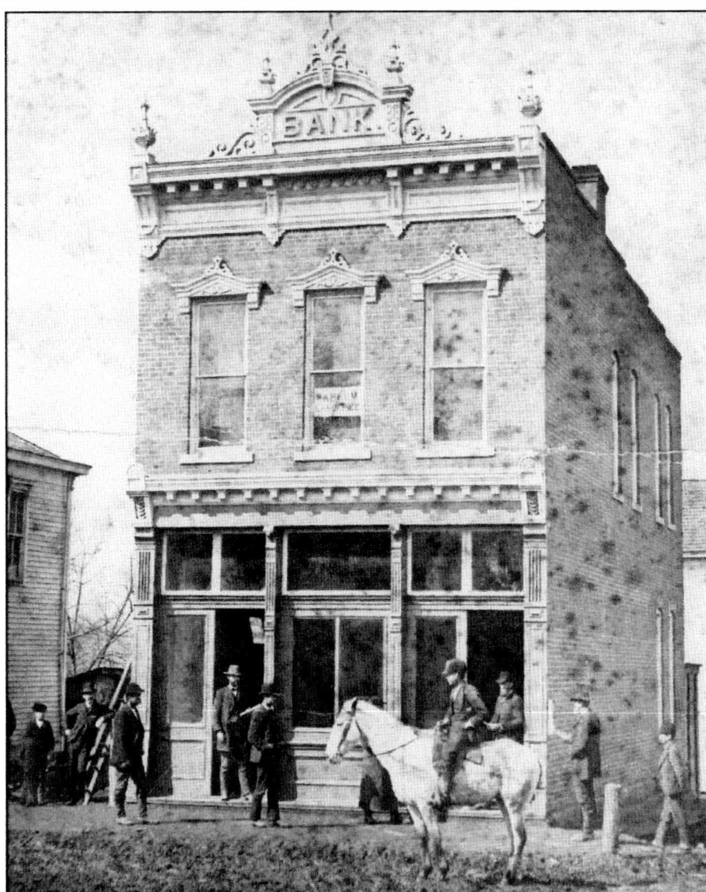

The Morgantown Deposit Bank, the first brick building in Morgantown, was constructed in 1885 on the corner of Butler and Ohio Streets. It was the second bank in Morgantown, the first being a private bank established in 1819. The W.A. Helm law office was located on the second floor. Helm was the bank's attorney and served as president in 1916.

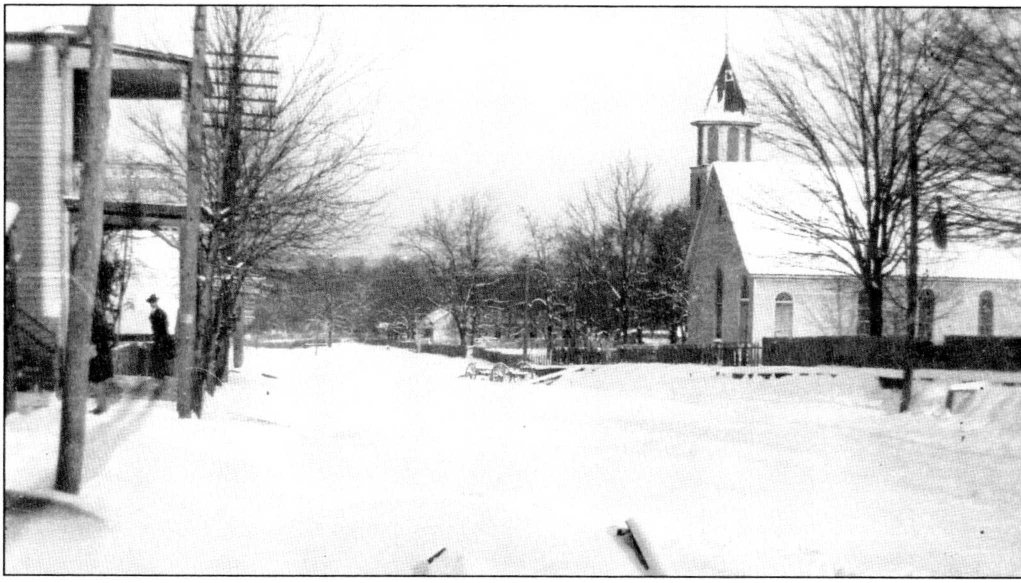

The Union Church is visible at right on Ohio Street on this snowy day in the early 1900s. Prior to the construction of the second county courthouse in 1872, all denominations held church services in the old courthouse. The court forbade worship in the new courthouse, so residents joined together to build Union Church. The first *Green River Republican* newspaper office is at left.

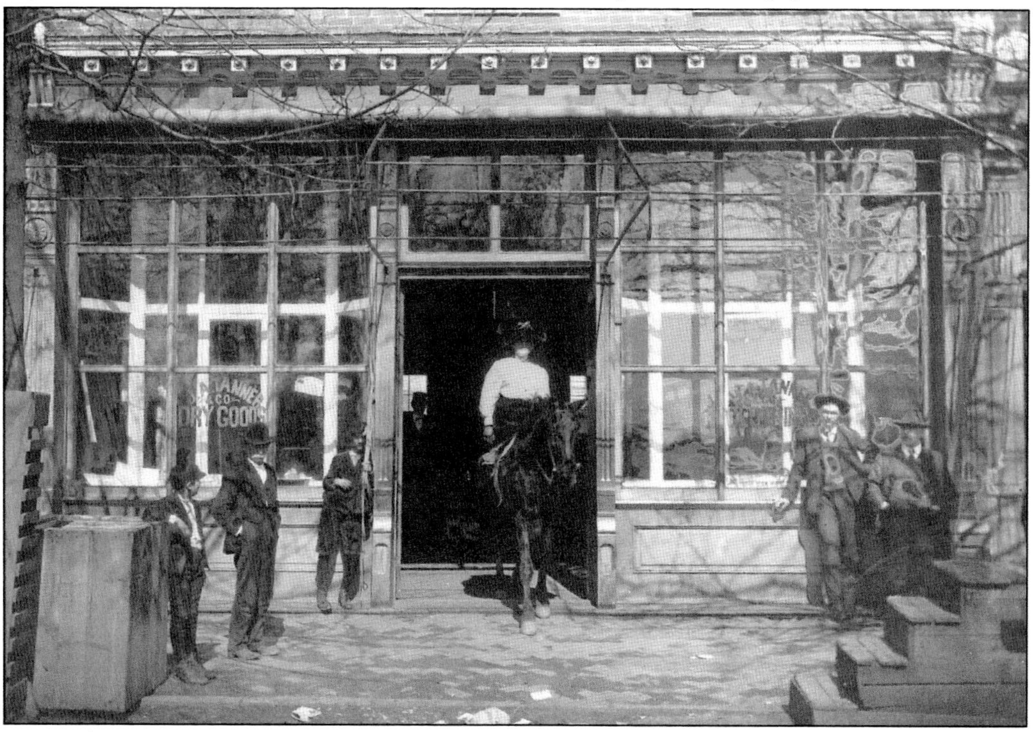

May Helm rides out of the J.A. Tanner Dry Goods Store on her horse. Tanner's store was built in the early 1890s. As was popular at the time, the storefront was had cast-iron framework surrounding the windows and supporting the brick veneer on the front of the second floor. This building currently houses Five Seasons Flowers and Gifts.

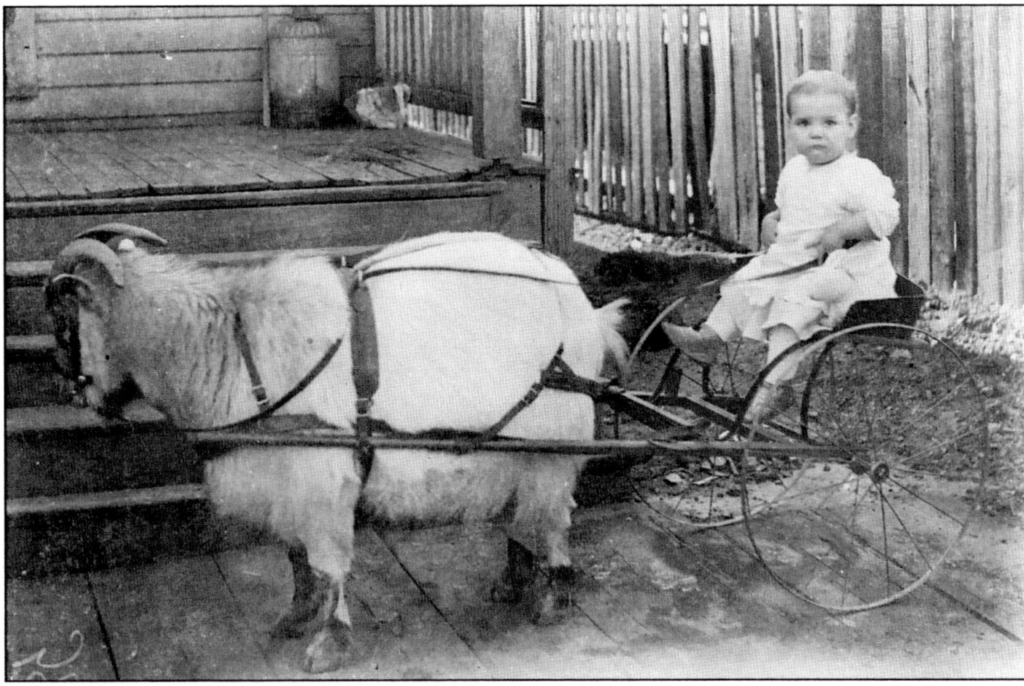

In this April 4, 1918, image, one-year-old Myrtle Clare Bailey is posed on a fun mode of transportation. At the time, families commonly trained goats to pull carts bearing children.

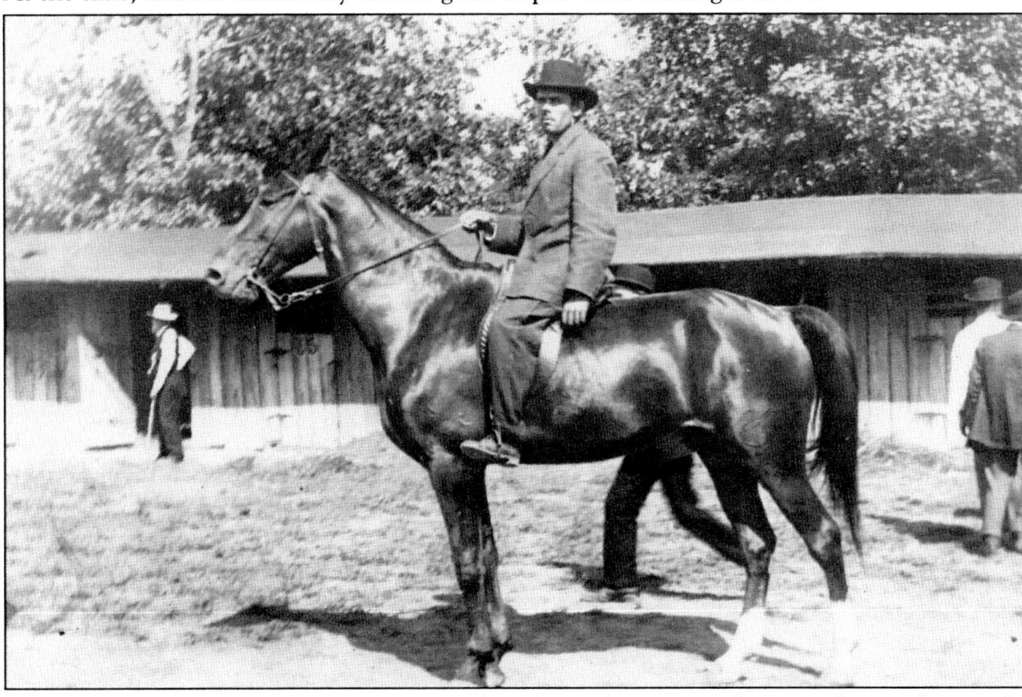

John C. Smith sits atop a fine looking steed at the Butler County fairgrounds. Smith gained a reputation as a tough "take no foolishness" marshal, a needed stance in the 1930s and 1940s, when Morgantown was considered a rough place. Once, Smith had a shoot-out with a man named Blanchard on Main Street just because he told him to get out of Morgantown.

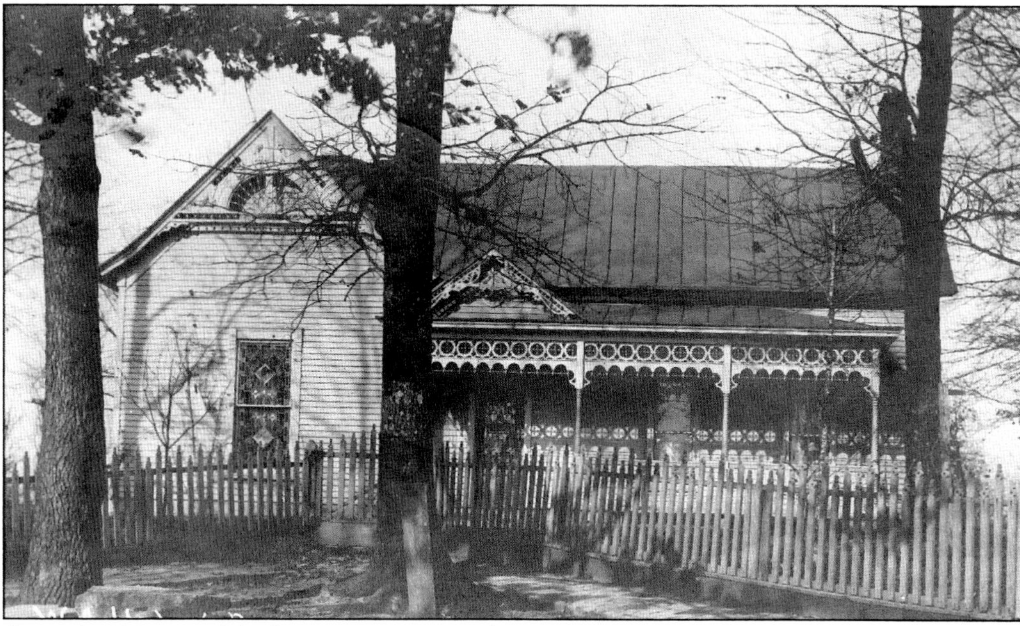

Around 1900, one of the largest, most ornate homes in Morgantown was the W.A. Helm house. Helm was an attorney, a leader in the Democratic Party and a delegate to its 1892 national convention, and president of Morgantown Deposit Bank. This home, located on South Tyler Street, is now the Helm House Bed and Breakfast.

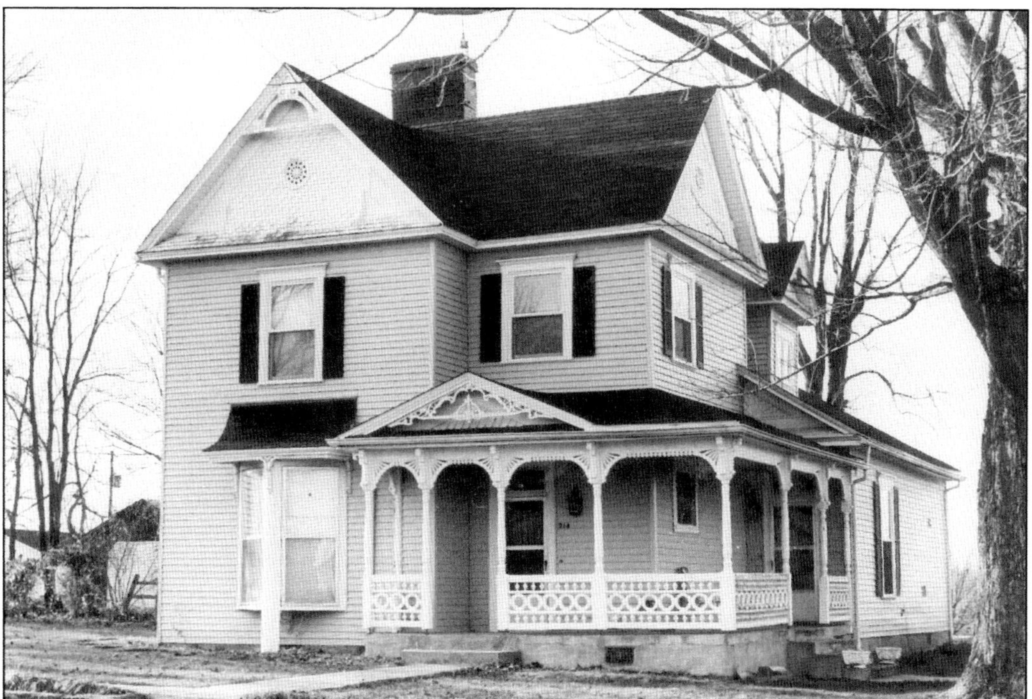

The J.D. Render home on Tyler Street was one of the finer homes in Morgantown when it was built in 1905. It was constructed from a Sears, Roebuck home kit shipped in by river and was also the first house in Morgantown sold on time payments. It was destroyed by fire in the 1980s.

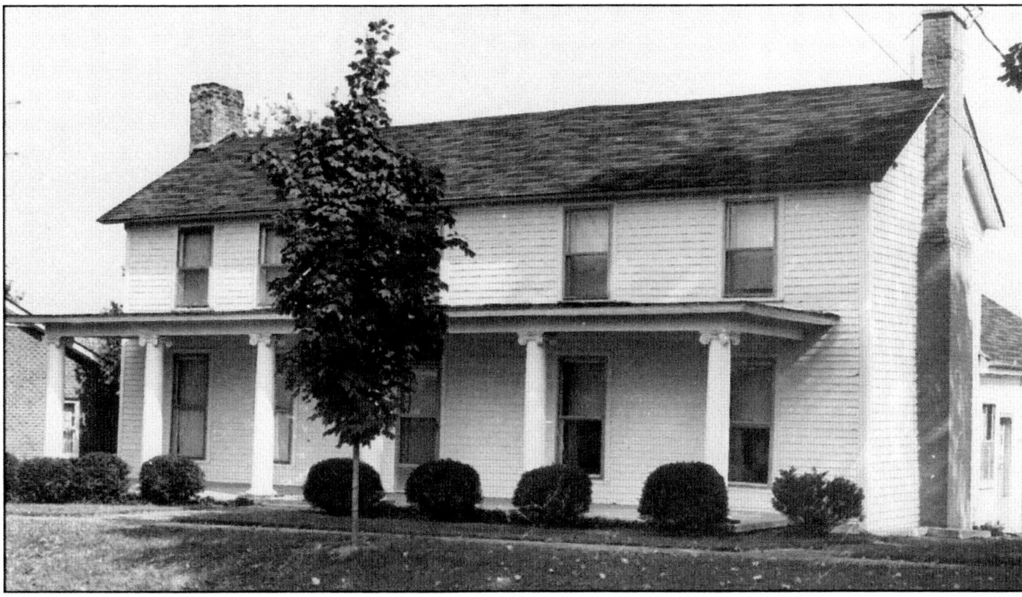

William F. Leach moved from Ohio County in 1856 to establish himself in the blacksmithing business. He built the original part of this home—the back ell, which is thought to be the oldest house in Morgantown. It is located on Roberts Street behind the Methodist church, near where Leach's blacksmith shop once stood. Legend says that Gen. John H. Morgan flew the Confederate flag from an upstairs window in 1862.

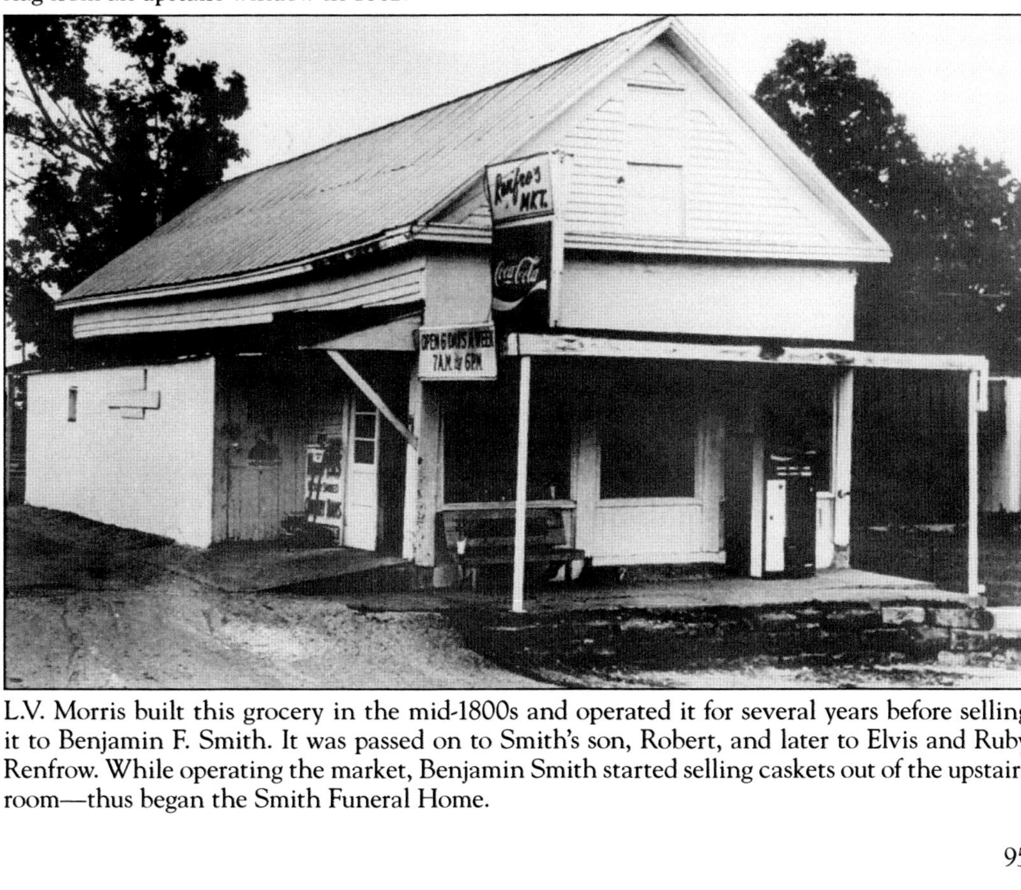

L.V. Morris built this grocery in the mid-1800s and operated it for several years before selling it to Benjamin F. Smith. It was passed on to Smith's son, Robert, and later to Elvis and Ruby Renfrow. While operating the market, Benjamin Smith started selling caskets out of the upstairs room—thus began the Smith Funeral Home.

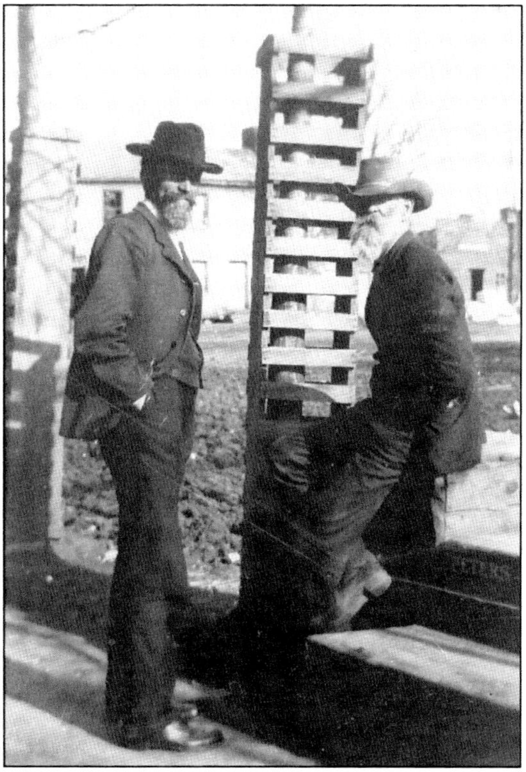

Two unidentified men enjoy conversation and pose for a photograph on the sidewalk of Butler Street in 1890. The photograph was taken in front of J.A. Tanner Dry Goods, looking toward Ohio Street. The Frizzell and Neel Monument Company is in the background at right. Notice the stile, which was used for assistance when mounting and dismounting horses.

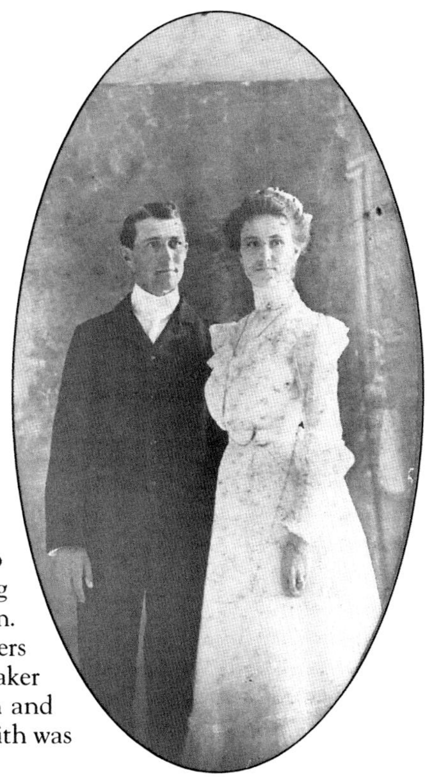

This portrait of two unidentified people is stamped "photo by L.A. French, Morgantown, Ky.," which is intriguing because there is no record of an L.A. French in Morgantown. According to the 1870 census, there were five photographers in the county: James Shaver in Sugar Grove, Calvin Whitaker and Samuel Terry in Morgantown, and Charles Ryan and Murray M. Smith in Woodbury. By 1880, Murray M. Smith was the only one remaining.

Granville and Zelphia Rone stand in front of their home in Morgantown. Granville was considered a wealthy man in the black community. He owned a farm at the edge of town, near the end of Porter Street; he and Zelphia were both born into slavery. "Gran" lived to the age of 99 and "Zelph" to the remarkable age of 114.

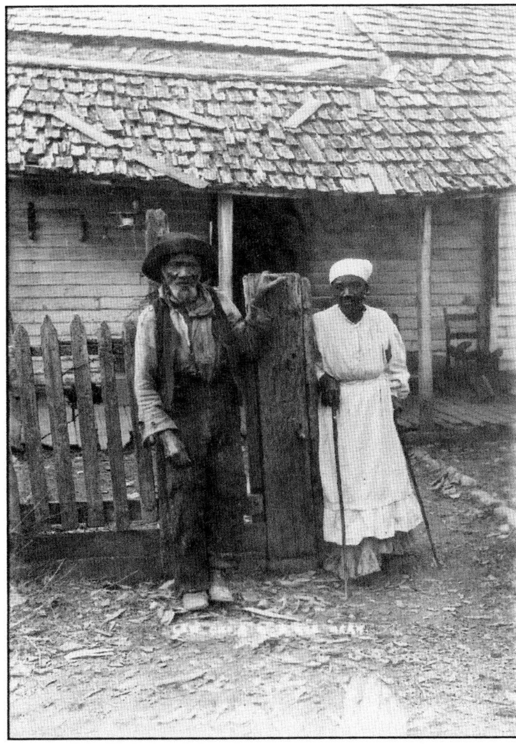

This fashionable group of men, pictured in the *Green River Republican*, seems well prepared for a trip to California with two spare tires and a lantern strapped to the side of their Model T Ford. Fred Morphew is driving and Wes Sharer is in the passenger seat. Justus Carson is behind the driver; the other passenger is Wes Sharer's brother.

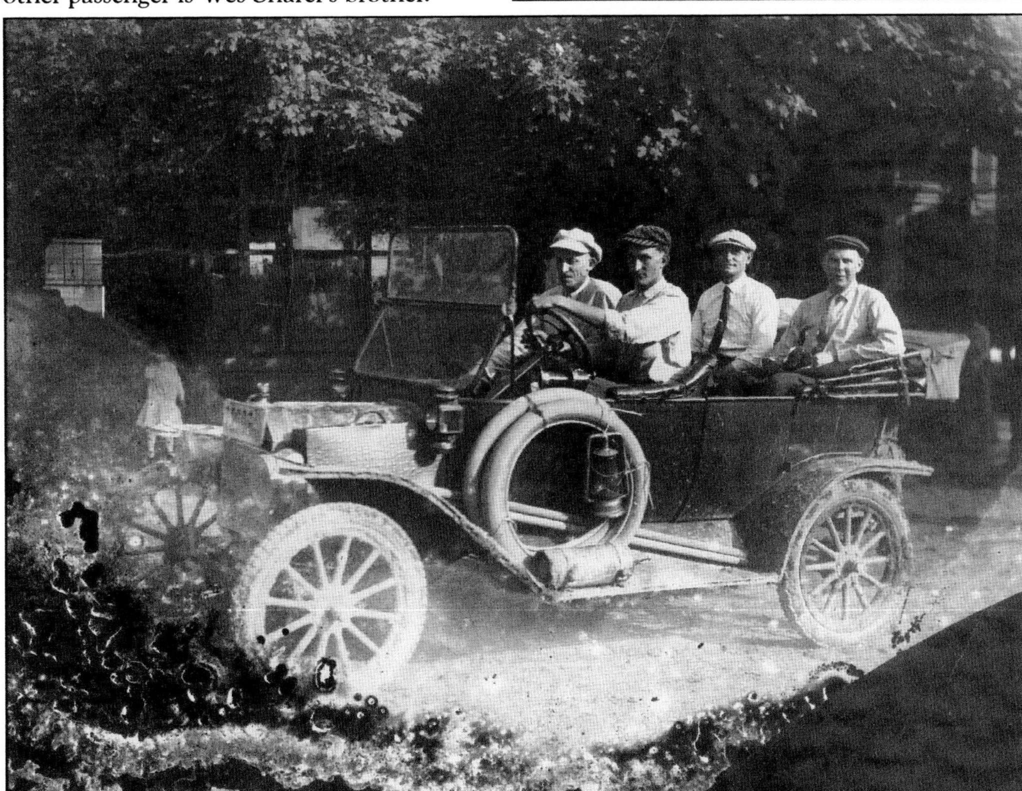

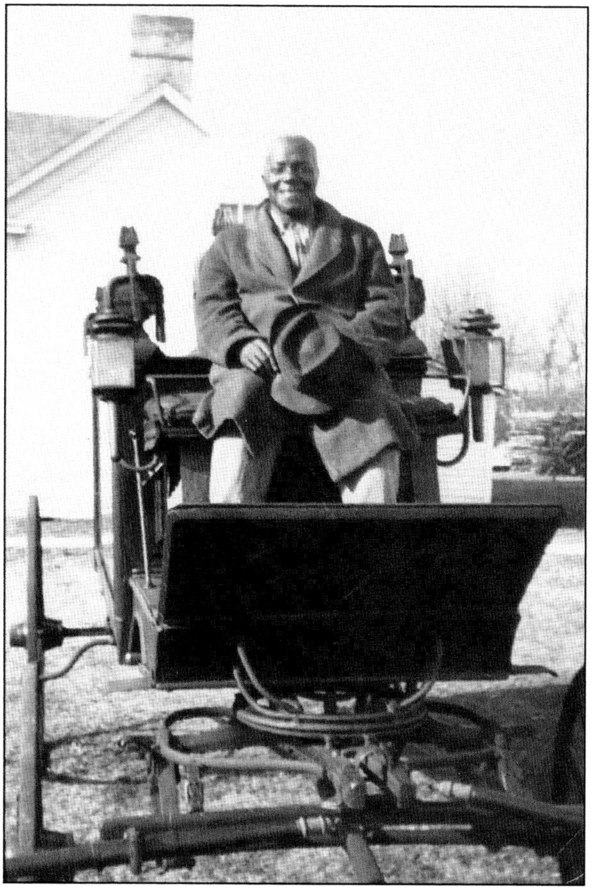

James G. White was a liveryman who drove the hearse owned by Smith Funeral Home before the days of the automobile. After the business stopped using the hearse in the 1920s, White went to work as a chauffeur. Dwight C. Smith, the last Smith to own the hearse, remembered that "Jim always had a big smile."

This group of Morgantown youths is participating in an American Red Cross swimming and lifesaving class. Harold Kelly, the teenage boy kneeling at left, is administering lifesaving techniques. The photograph was taken at the Morgantown landing, which was a favorite swimming hole in town.

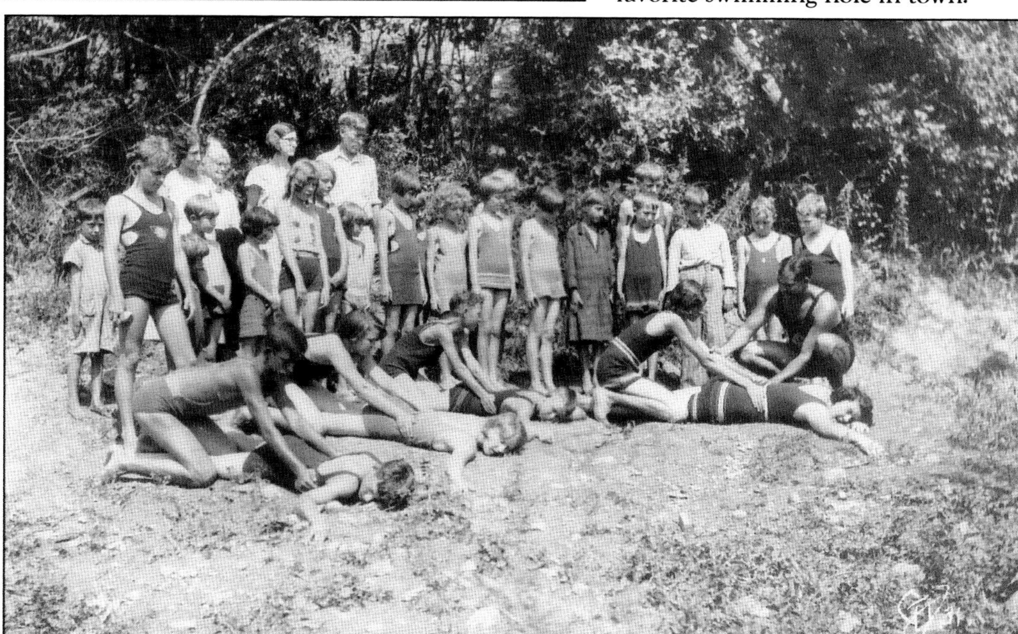

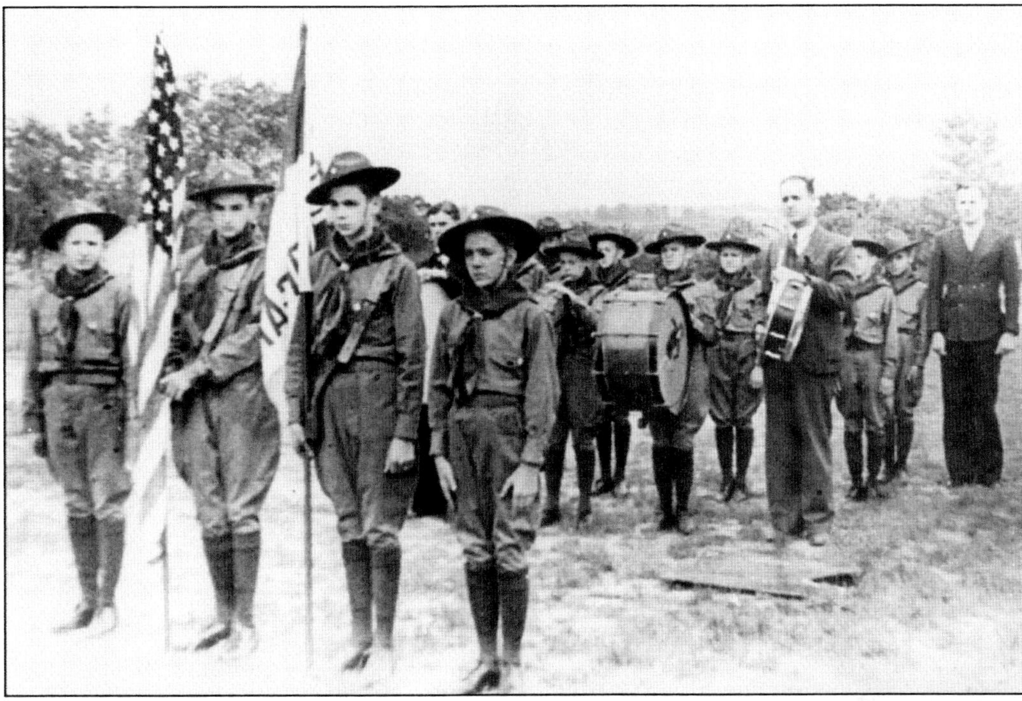

A mid-1930s Boy Scout troop poses in full uniform in Morgantown. One of the troop leaders, Dwight C. Smith, stands at right with a drum in his hand. The only identified Scout in the photograph is A.C. Hocker, who is holding the American flag. Smith owned the Smith Funeral Home and was active in community events throughout his life.

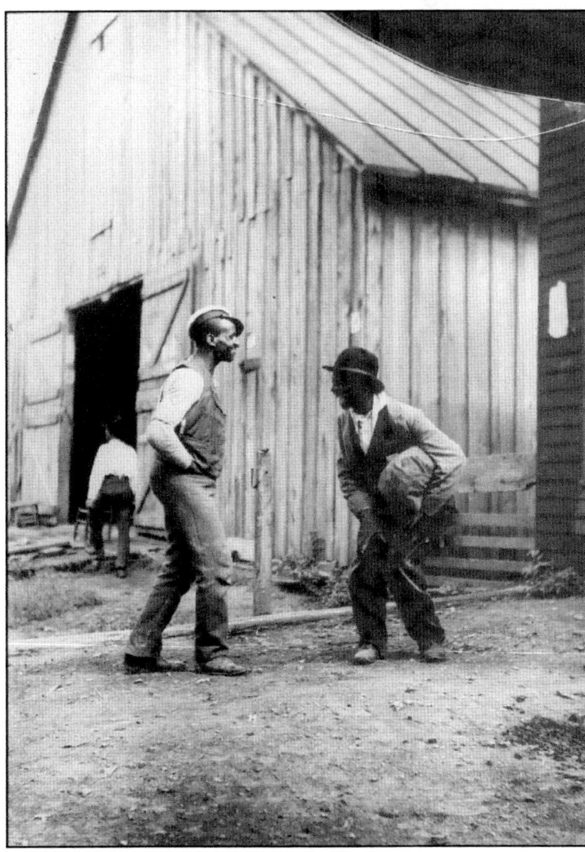

Eldon Bailey (left) and Mote Helm enjoy a moment by Mauzy's Livery stable on "Dogwalk" (now G.L. Smith Street). Both Bailey and Helm turned the press for the *Green River Republican*. The corner of the building at far right is the back of Dockery's Drug.

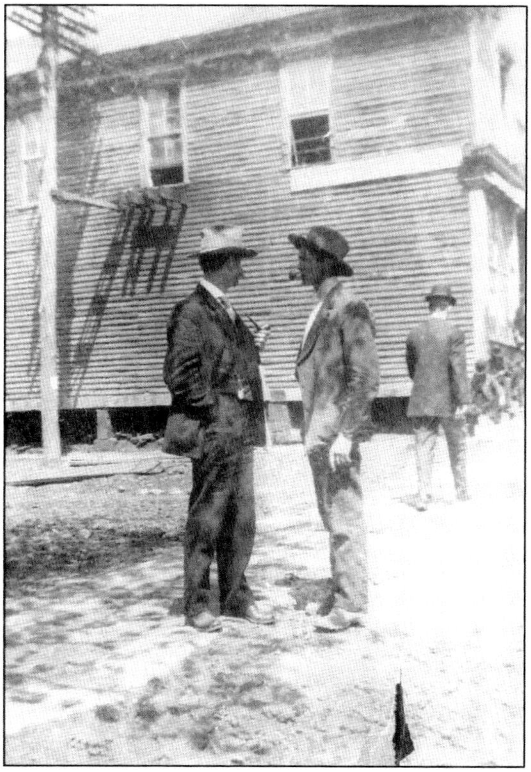

James W. Cook (left), who served as the Butler County tax commissioner from 1922 to 1926, stands at the corner of Butler and Logan Streets talking with Joe Bunch. Dockery's Drug is in the background. Cook was the father of J. Guy Cook and grandfather of William Cook, both former editors of the *Green River Republican*. The man walking away is dentist William Keown.

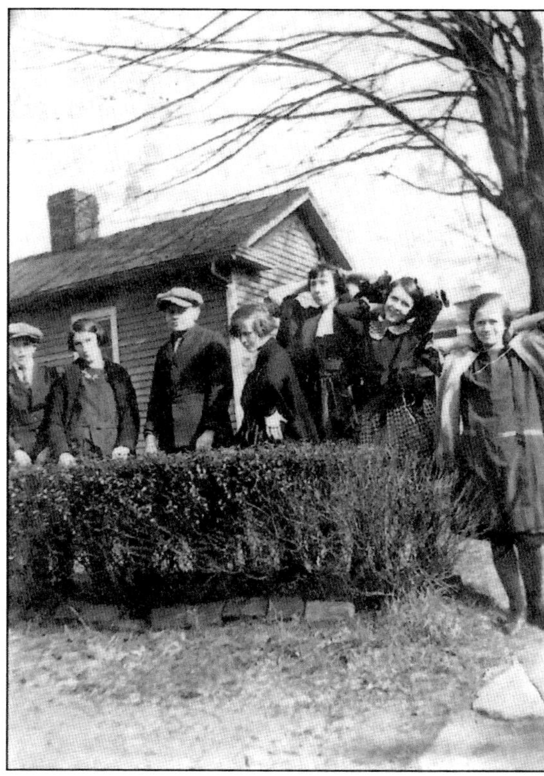

A group of young Morgantown folks posed for this photograph around 1923. The only individuals identified are best friends Myrl Embry (in the center, with her hand on her hip) and Mildred Forsythe (far right).

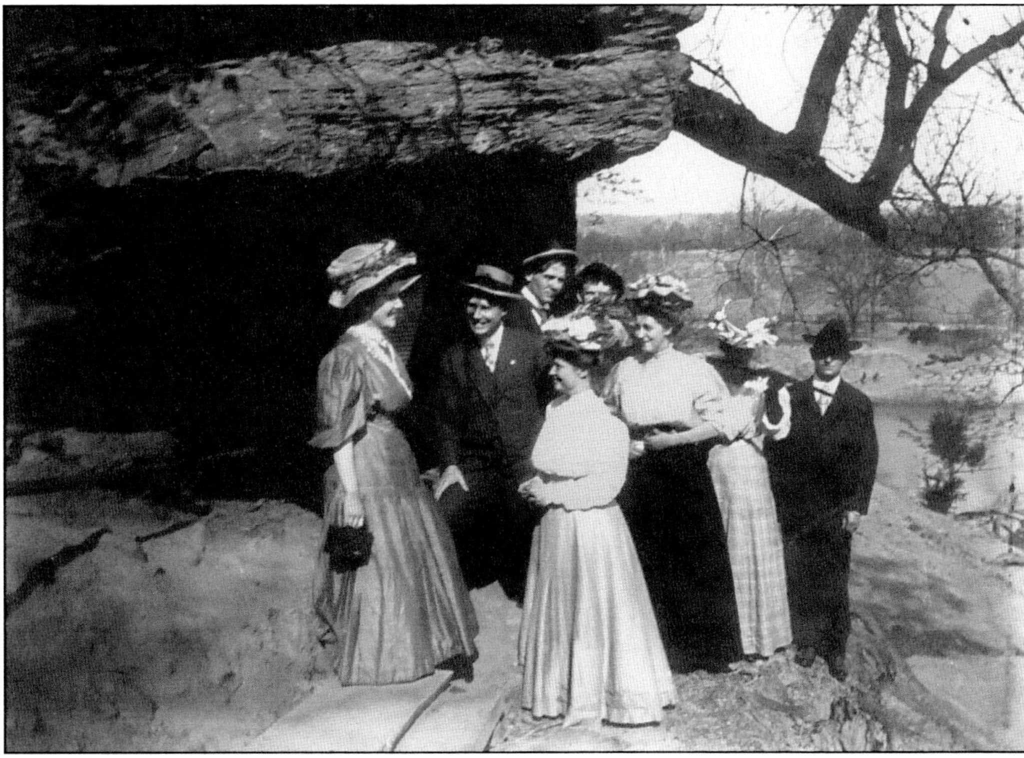

This c. 1900 image shows a stylish group of young people strolling along the bluffs at the Morgantown landing. The Green River is visible just behind the group. At the time, a carved sandstone walkway was laid along the edge of the road from Morgantown down to the boat landing. Note the fine hats worn by the young women.

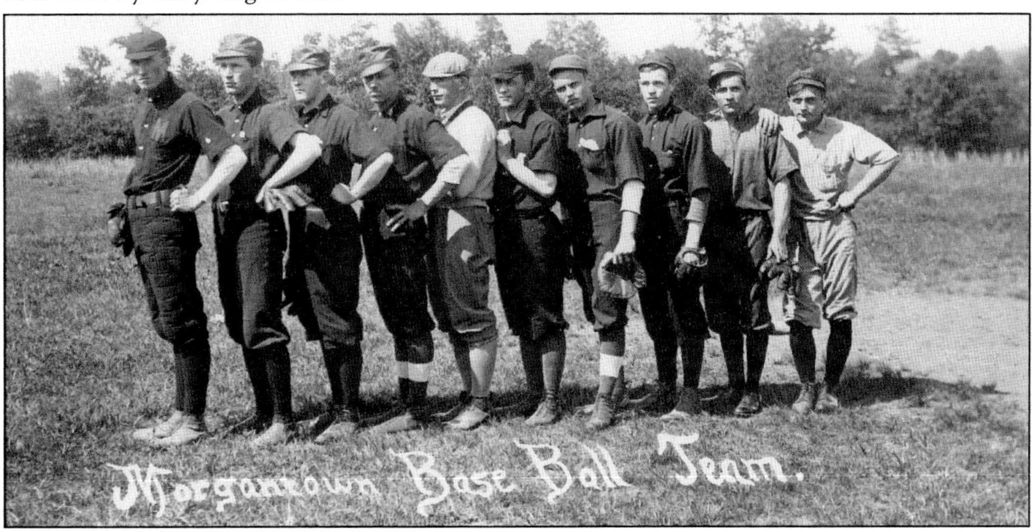

Baseball has long been a beloved sport in Morgantown. This early 1900s Morgantown team included, from left to right, Bud Taylor, Frank Lane, Clyde Helm, William Kuykendall, Eldred Daugherty, George Taylor, George Leach, Clay Forsythe, Lofton Morehead, and Enid Howard. Until the early 1980s, when community involvement waned, there were several baseball teams throughout the county.

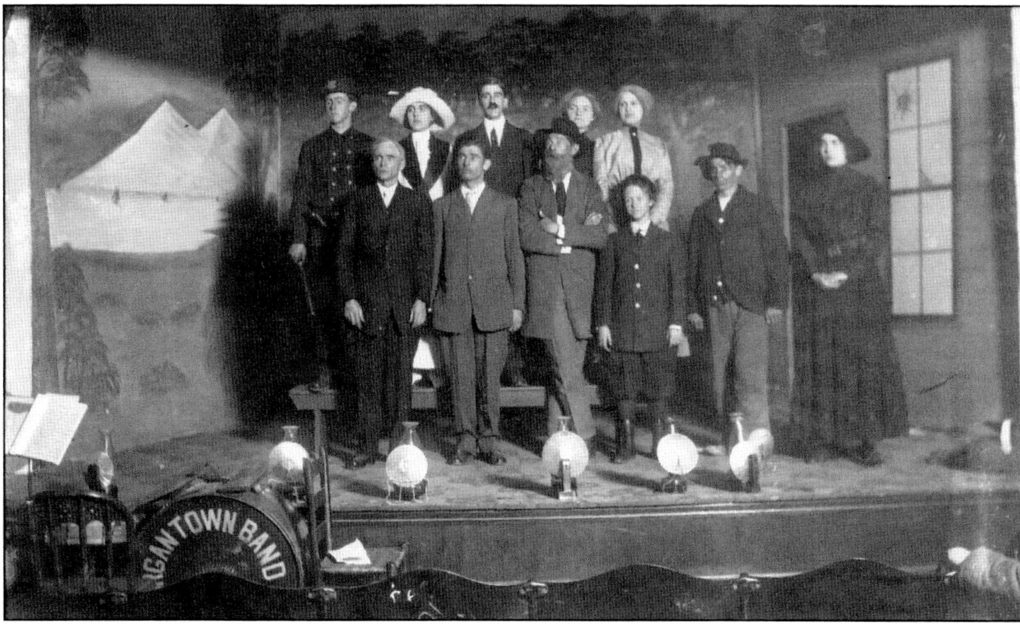

The cast poses on stage during a performance at the Tilford Theater on Ohio Street. The theater featured live music provided by the Morgantown Band. The only identified cast member is William Kuykendall, who is in the center of the back row. The location of the Tilford Theater later became the Roy Phelps car lot.

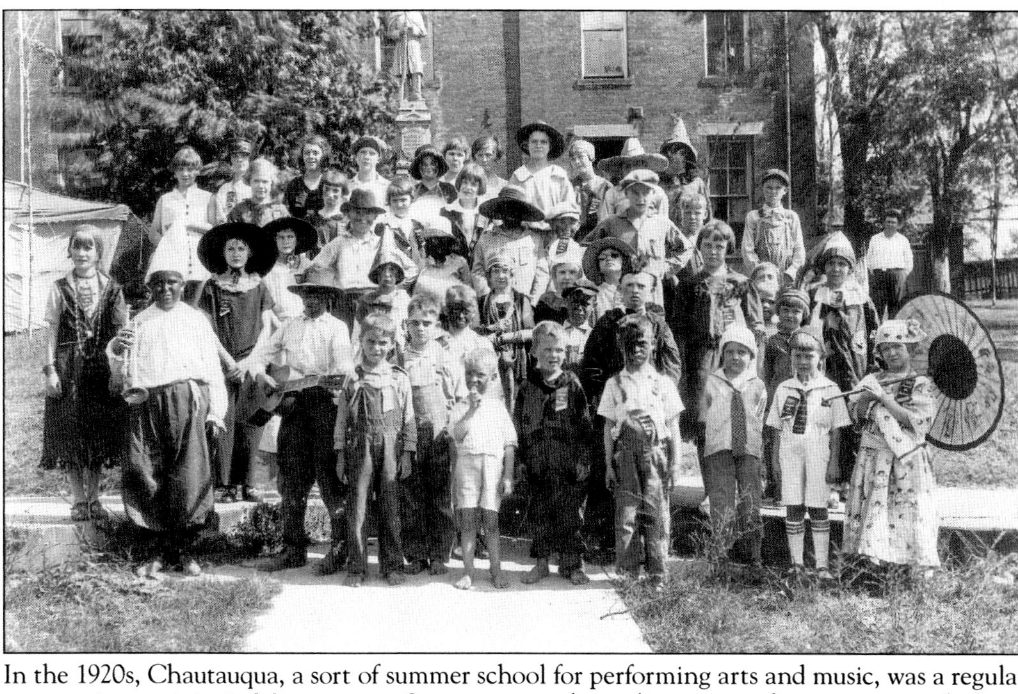

In the 1920s, Chautauqua, a sort of summer school for performing arts and music, was a regular summertime activity in Morgantown. State-sponsored traveling teams of instructors taught local children of all ages, producing plays and other performances. The only individual identified in this photograph is Joe Forsythe, who is fifth from the right in the first row.

In 1925, members of Cook's Band included Joe H. Rust, C.N. Cook, George Dabbs, Piner Long, Frank Power, J.M. Derrington, W.H. Kuykendall, J.C. Hill, W.N. Ashby, R.H. Burton, and Troy Daughtery. The "for hire" band played at festivals, nightclubs, and various events.

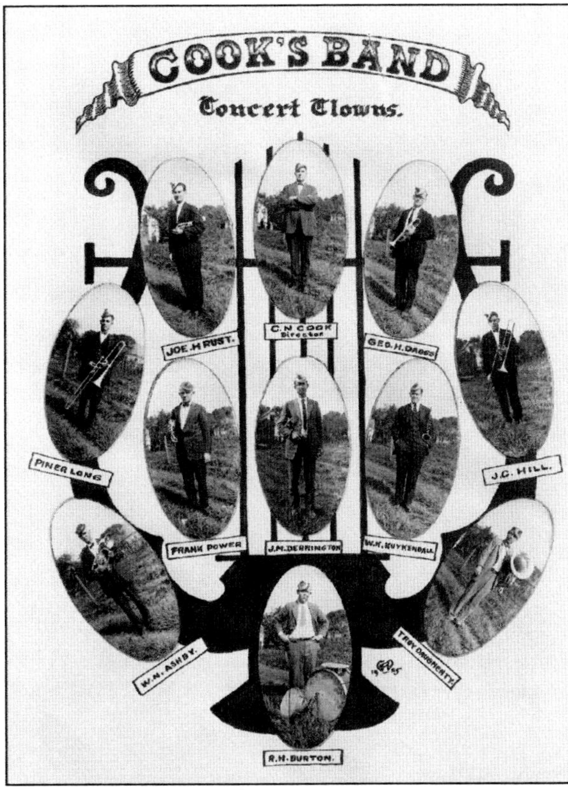

This June 30, 1920, photograph shows a meeting of the Woman's Missionary Union. The WMU was founded in 1888 and is the largest Protestant organization for women in the world. It also remains the largest body of organized laity. The women would meet to learn about and raise funds for Christian missions. Here, they stand on the steps of the First Baptist Church.

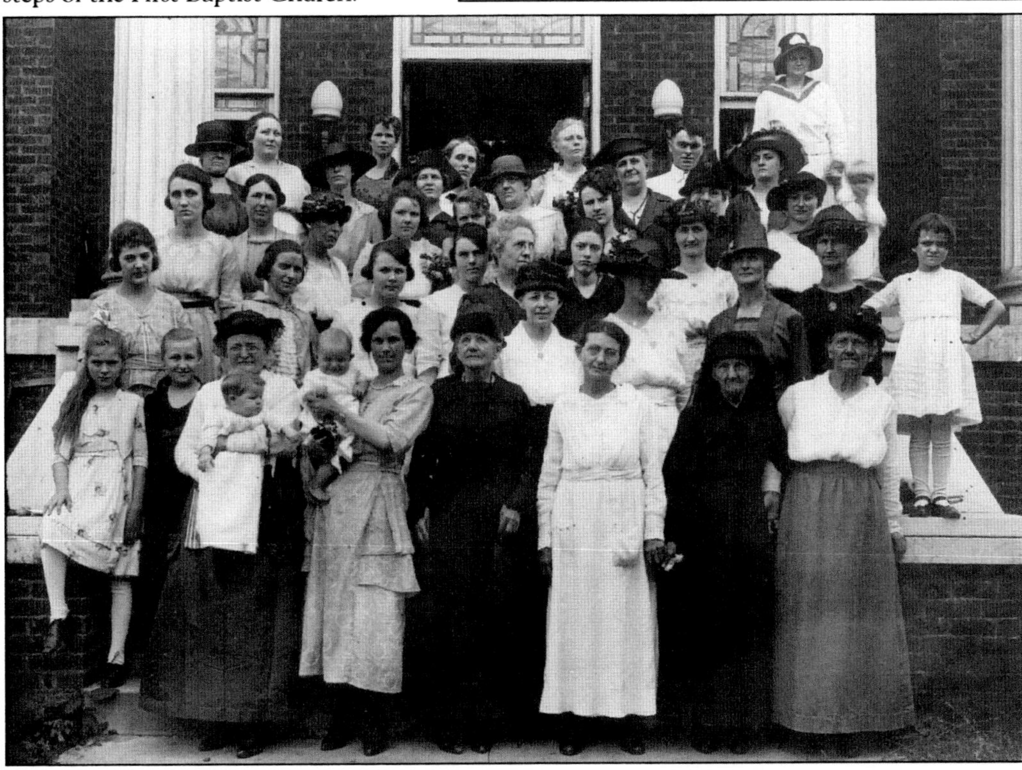

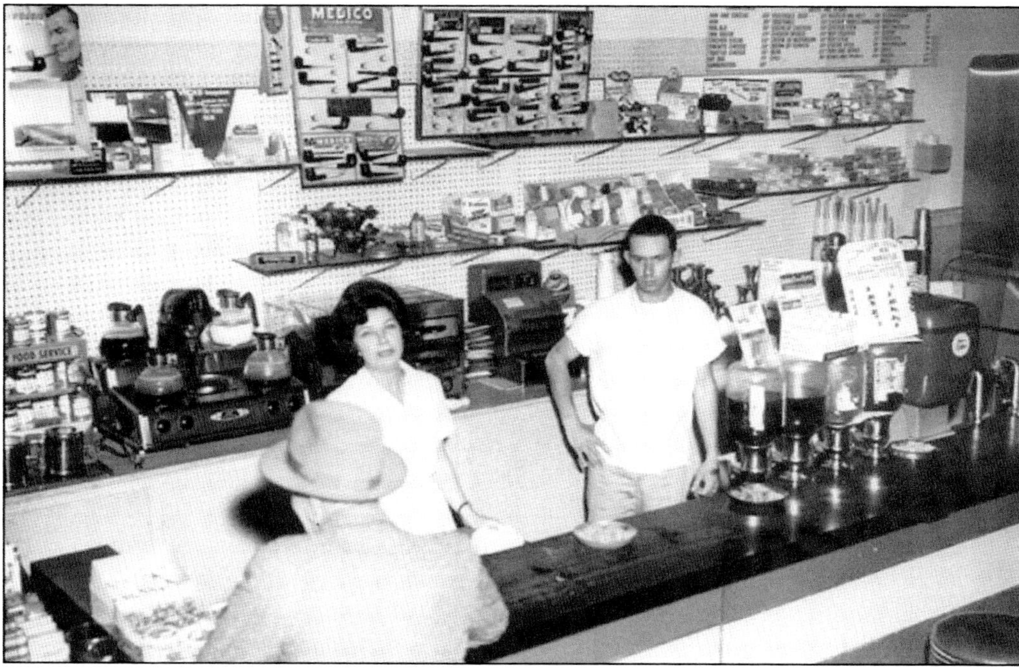

Ernestine Morris (left) and Jerry Hatcher (right) were the "soda jerks" at the Butler County Drug Company in the late 1950s. As indicated by the five-pot coffeemaker and warmer, coffee was a big item at the snack bar. A banana split or a milk shake—flavored from the syrup bottles to the right of Hatcher—were also favorite items.

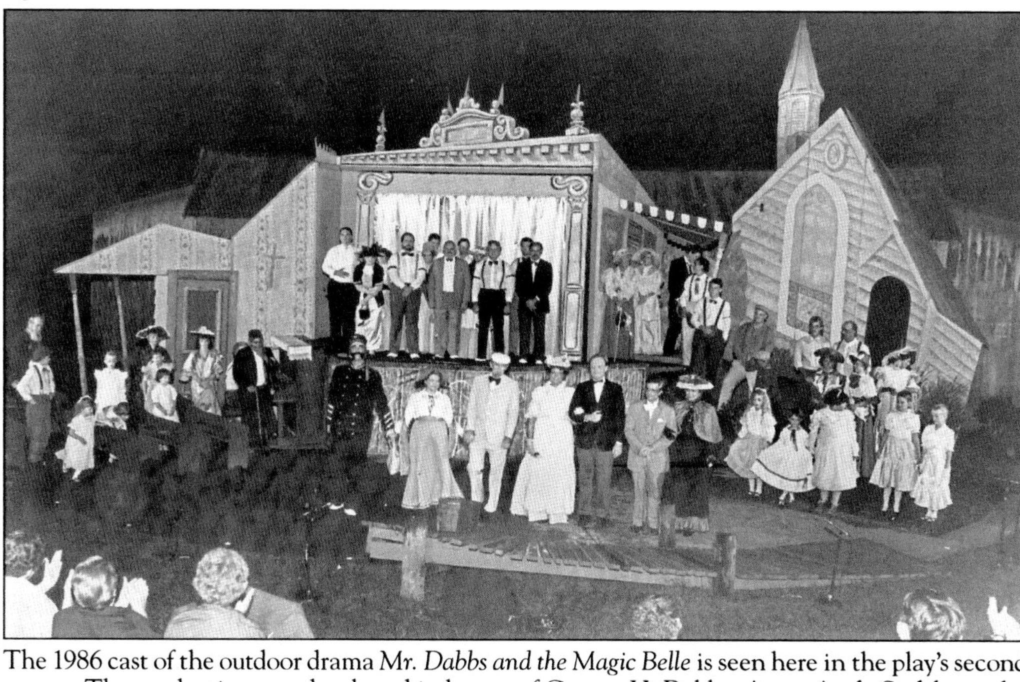

The 1986 cast of the outdoor drama *Mr. Dabbs and the Magic Belle* is seen here in the play's second season. The production was developed in honor of George H. Dabbs. Actor Andy Stahl was the production's first director, and Ken Jenkins, who later acted on the television series *Scrubs*, wrote the script for the play, which ran for 10 seasons.

William S. Taylor was born in a log cabin about five miles from Morgantown on October 10, 1853. His parents were Sylvester and Mary G. (Moore) Taylor, and he was a teacher, farmer, lawyer, and local politician before becoming governor of Kentucky. In 1882, he was elected Butler County clerk, and in 1886, he became the Butler County judge. In 1895, Kentucky voters elected him attorney general, which opened the door for his statewide political aspirations. He was inaugurated as governor in 1899 after a bitter and disputed election against state senator William Goebel. On January 30, 1900, Goebel was shot and killed near the "Old Capitol" building. Taylor served only 50 days as governor and left Kentucky under threat of indictment for alleged involvement with the assassination of Goebel. He spent the rest of his life in Indiana. His Morgantown home is shown below.

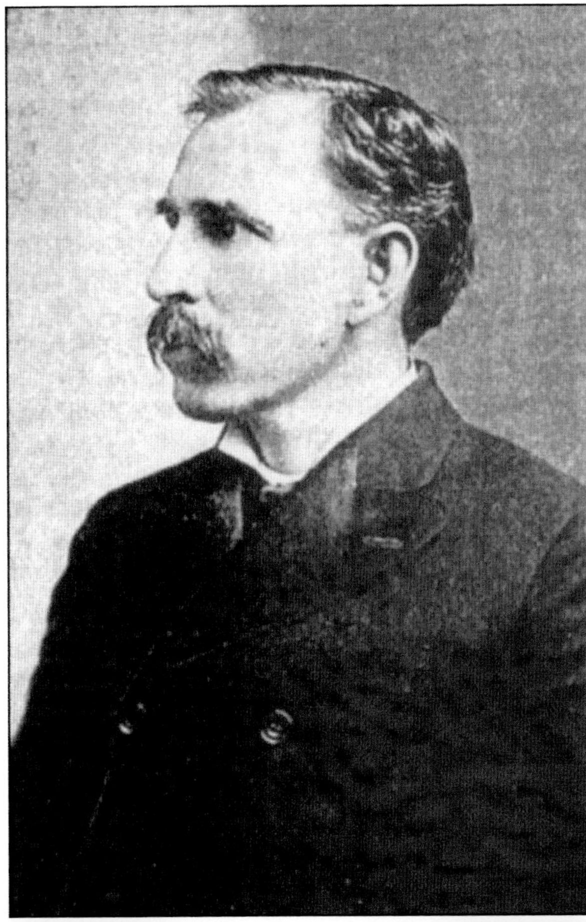

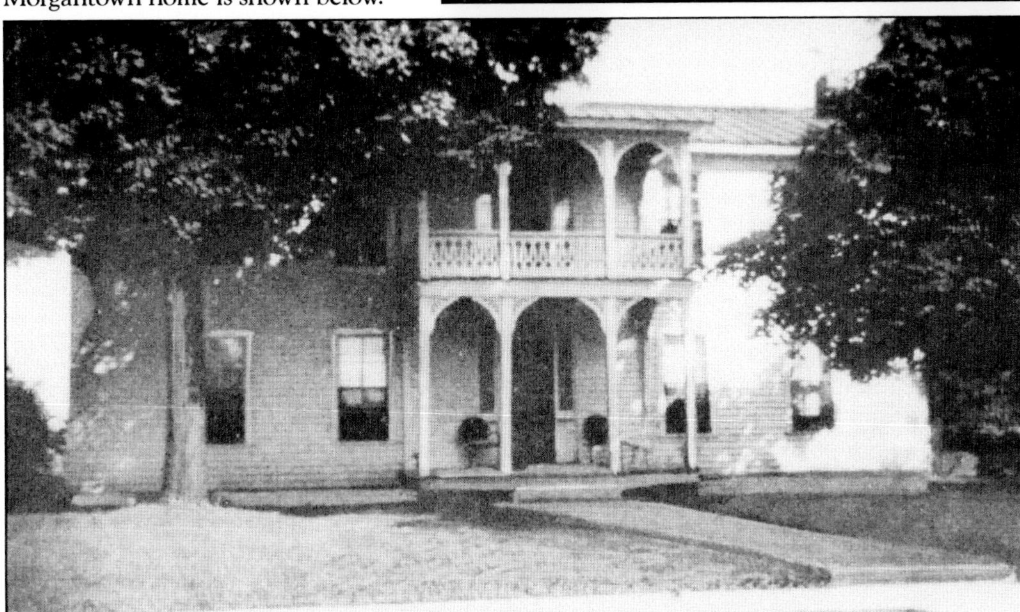

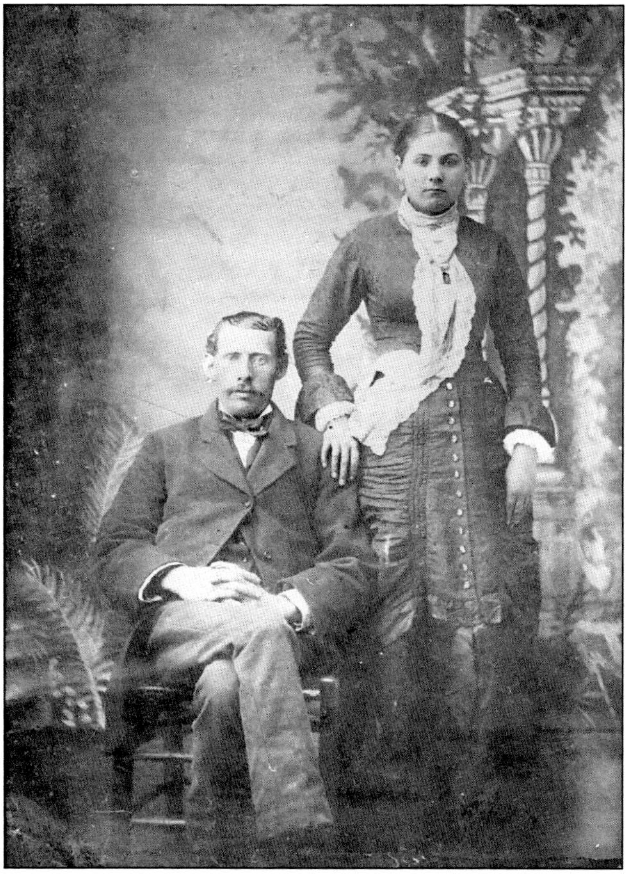

This faded tintype portrait is of James and Rebecca Cole, who owned and operated the Pine Lawn Hotel in Morgantown. A December 1946 *Green River Republican* article about a fire at the hotel stated that the Coles had previously sold the hotel to G.D. Beck. The article declared that the hotel had a reputation as one of the area's finest in the riverboat days.

It is not known if these men were really riverboat gamblers or just posing with their cards, drinks, and guns. The studio location is unknown and very plain, with an unpainted backdrop and rough wooden floors. This tintype is associated with the Burchfield family.

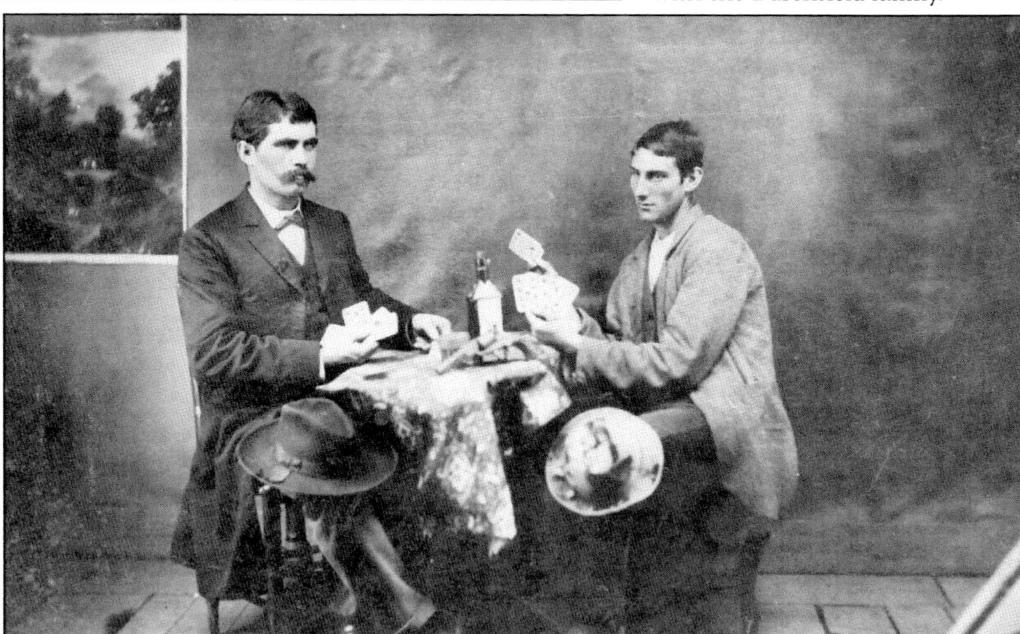

Seven

Rochester

Some historians have referred to the area around the confluence of the Muddy and Green Rivers as "the Mouth" and Big Falls. The earliest documented names are Skilesville, on the Muhlenberg County side; McCrearysville, on the Ohio County side; and Suffolk, which platted and organized in 1802 but sold only a few lots before failing. In 1839, William and Ross McDowell; their sister, Ann Redding, the wife of George Redding; and three children of Samuel J. and Nancy Rochester McDowell came to the area. They named it for Lord Rochester of England, an ancestor of Nancy's.

The town soon became a busy river port after the opening of Lock and Dam No. 3 in 1838 and the subsequent beginning of the steamboat trade. The post office was established in 1843 with William McDowell as postmaster. During the Civil War, Col. Pierce Hawkins established Camp Underwood, a recruiting station for the 11th Kentucky Infantry, on the river just above town.

From those small beginnings, Rochester became the largest town in Butler County in 1870, with a population of 228. By the late 1800s, the town was referred to by riverboat people as the "Queen of the Green." The town steadily grew and reached its peak population of 439 in 1910. The town suffered three catastrophic fires—first in 1913, when Meyer's drugstore and two other businesses were destroyed; in 1930, another fire destroyed three businesses; and in 1942, the most devastating fire occurred, destroying the Rochester Mill, the Wood Hotel, and three other businesses.

With the discontinuance of the riverboat trade after the burning of the steamer *Evansville* in 1931 and the lack of a major highway or railroad, Rochester experienced a steady decline in businesses and population over the years. Only a bait shop and a bed and breakfast remain, and by 2000, Rochester's population was 186.

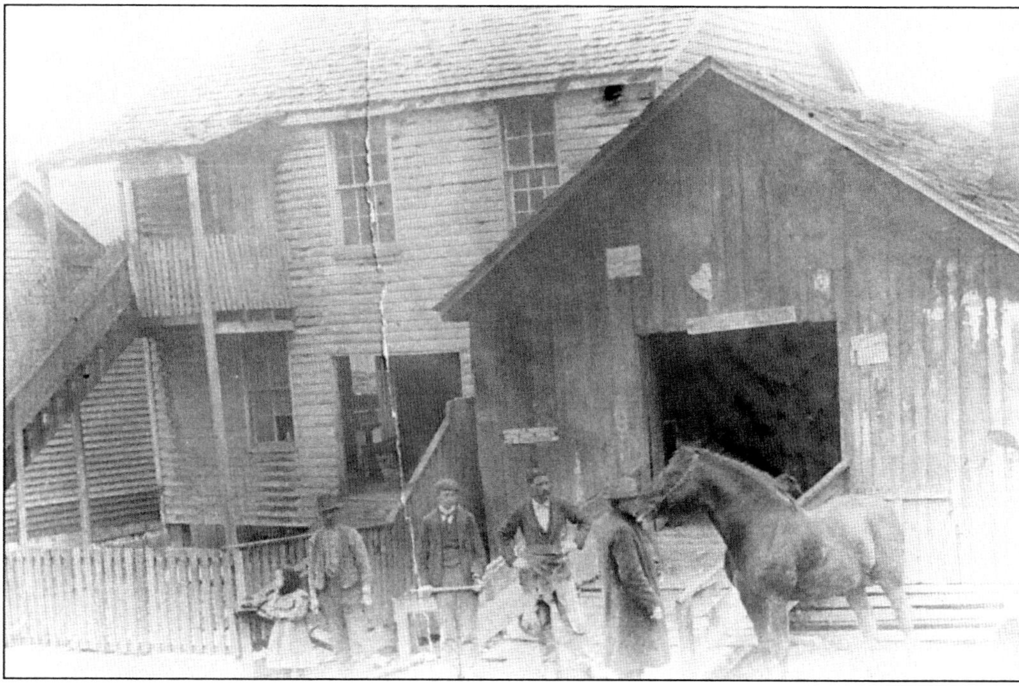

The only known locations of livery stables in Rochester were next to the corner of Ferry Street and on the alley running behind today's volunteer fire department building. There were two known livery stable operators, England and Hayes, who each owned a stable.

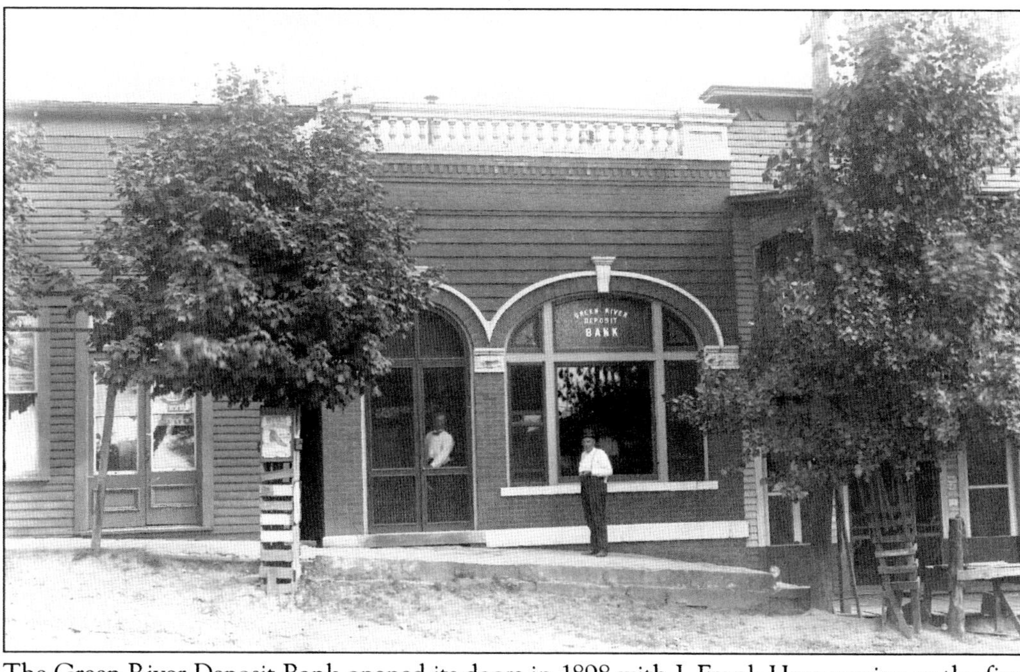

The Green River Deposit Bank opened its doors in 1898 with J. Frank Hays serving as the first president. Also instrumental in its organization were Jake Wilson, Bailey Wooten, Wallace Brown, George Shultz, and John Bowles. The business achieved the distinction of operating in its original building—later as a branch office—for more than 100 years before closing in April 2005.

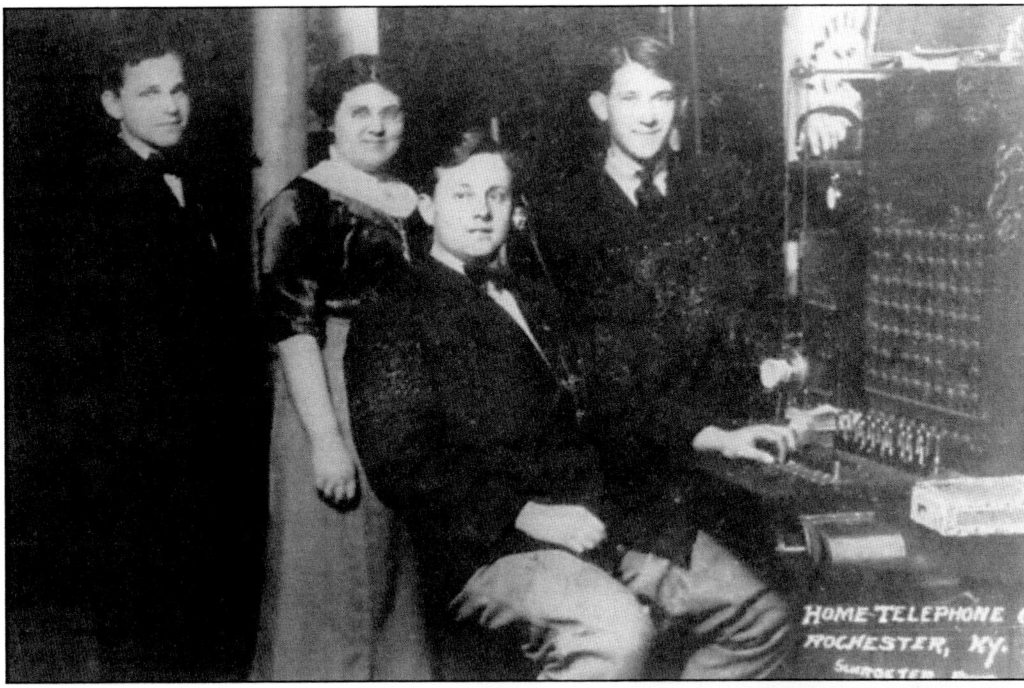

The 1909 Home Telephone Company switchboard and operators are pictured above. The company's office was located in Rochester, near Hay's Blue Front store. It also served the Provo and Huntsville areas. The operators are, from left to right, Evans Hunt, Isa Carey Taylor, Johnnie Evans, and William Walker.

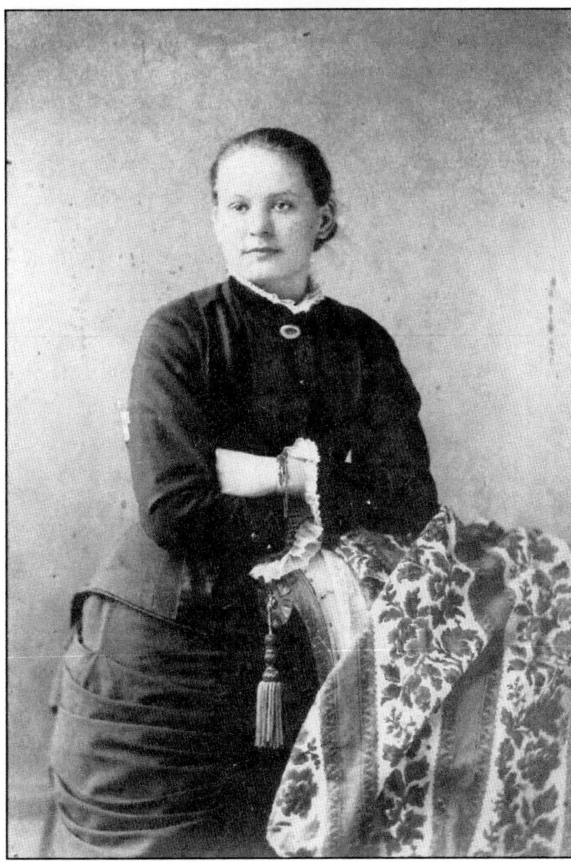

This portrait is stamped "Pomeroy, 16 W. Main Street, Rochester, Kentucky." This cabinet card is the only known evidence of the business. Schroeter Floating Studio is the only other documented photographer that operated out of Rochester.

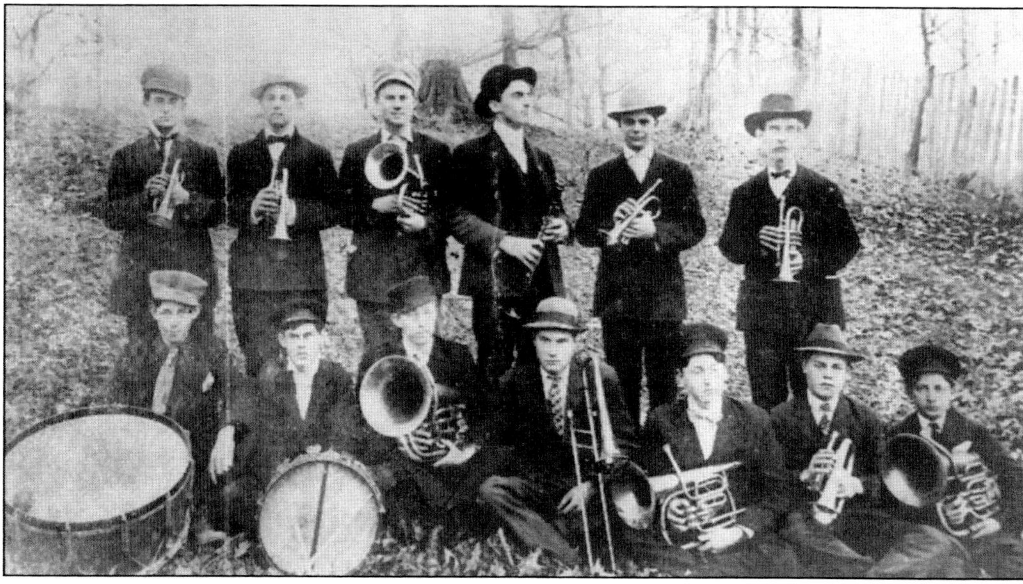

The Rochester Band posed for this outdoor photograph in 1910. The members included, from left to right, (seated) Ivan Walker, Oliver Westerfield, Albert Strother, Theron Dorris, Carl Davenport, Cody Yates, and Hugh Willis; (standing) Guy Manley, Johnny Evans, John Westerfield, Professor Lawrence, Thixton Smith, and Caleb Willis.

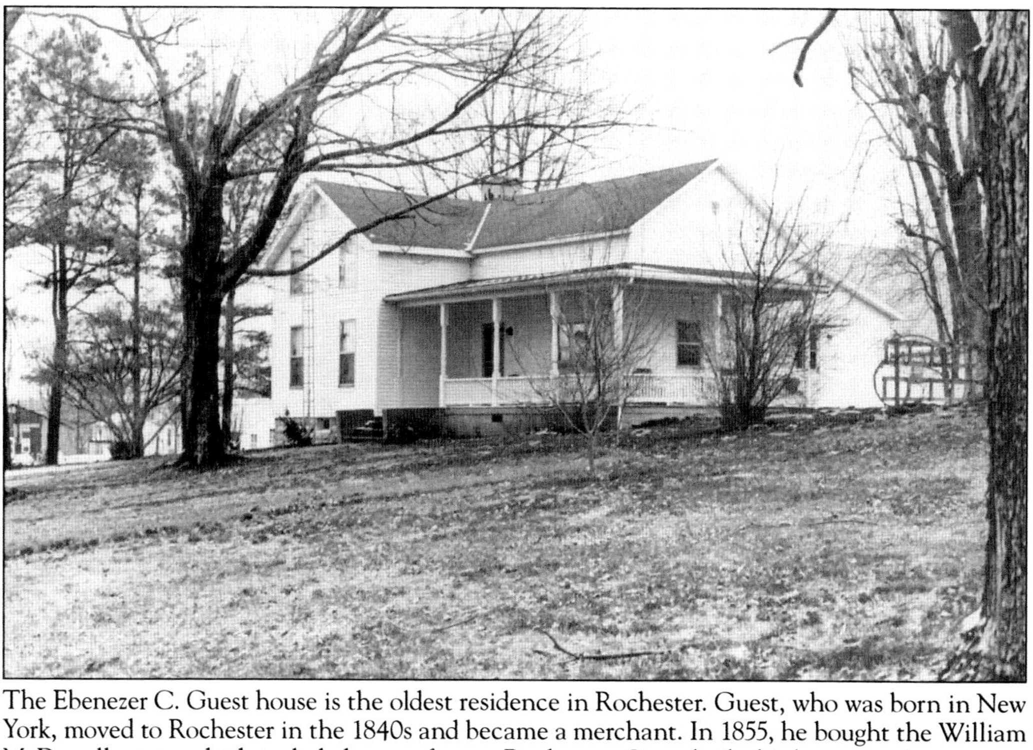

The Ebenezer C. Guest house is the oldest residence in Rochester. Guest, who was born in New York, moved to Rochester in the 1840s and became a merchant. In 1855, he bought the William McDowell estate, which included most of upper Rochester; Guest built this house on the property in 1863. It was designated a Kentucky Landmark in the 1980s.

Local carpenter Phillip Manley constructed this building for the members of the Rochester Christian Church in 1900. The congregation was organized in 1872, when they purchased their original meetinghouse across the street. The church bell was salvaged from the steamer *Bridges*, which sank near Rochester. This building was designated a Kentucky Landmark in the 1980s, but the church is no longer active.

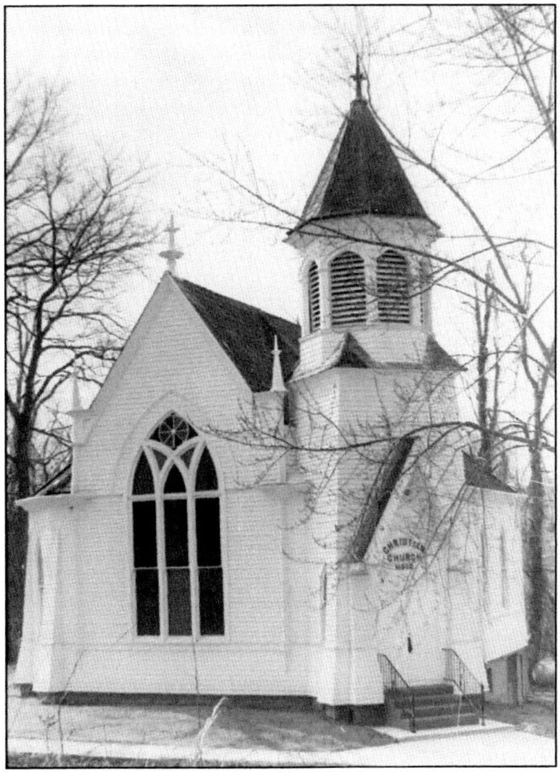

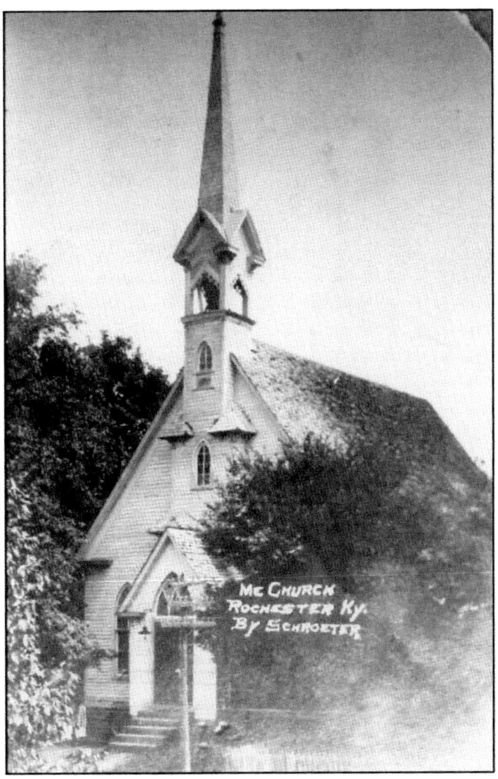

The Rochester Methodist Episcopal Church was established around 1850, when this building was erected. In 1924, this building burned down after a gas lamp exploded, and it was replaced with the present-day brick structure, which is now called the United Methodist Church. The congregation is still active after 162 years.

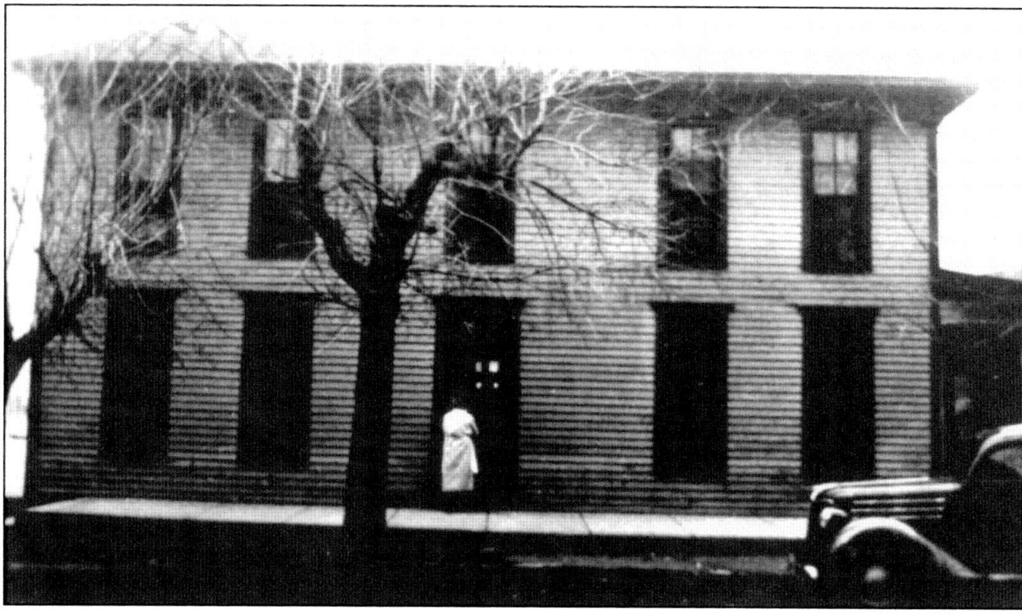

The Cole Hotel, built in the 1880s, was one of two hotels operating in Rochester around 1900. Jeff Cole owned it, and Phronia Wood owned the other hotel in town; the residents dubbed them the "Coal house" (a play on words) and the "Wood house." There was one other hotel in the town's early years—the Rochester Hotel, on Water Street near the Mud River.

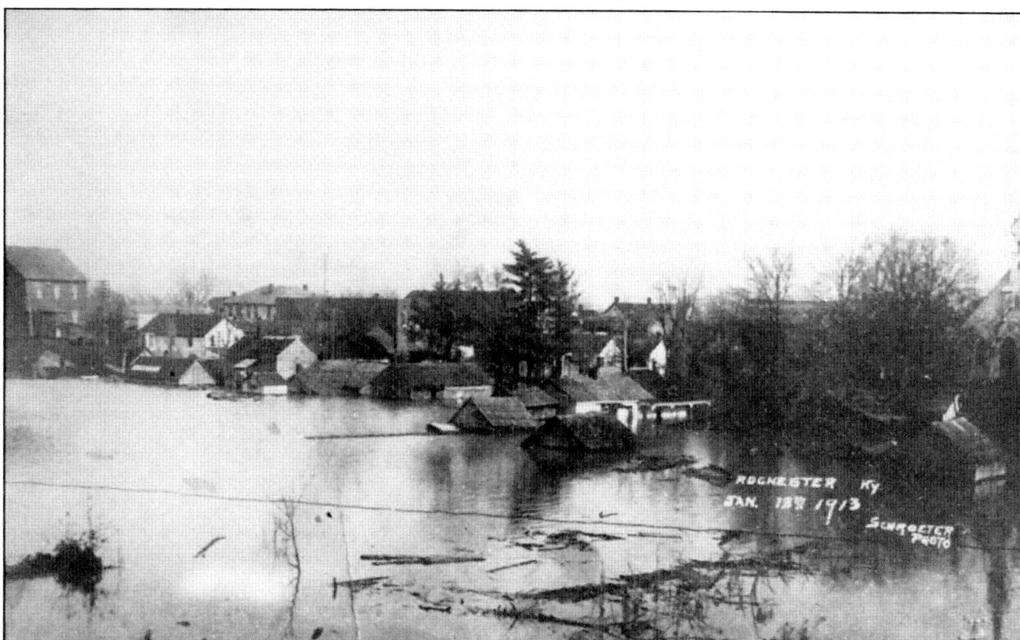

Rochester suffered two major recorded floods, first in 1913 and again in 1937. This Schroeter photograph shows the water's elevation on January 13, 1913, after the first flood. The tall building at far left is the Rochester Ice and Milling Company, which was located on the corner of Russellville and Main Streets.

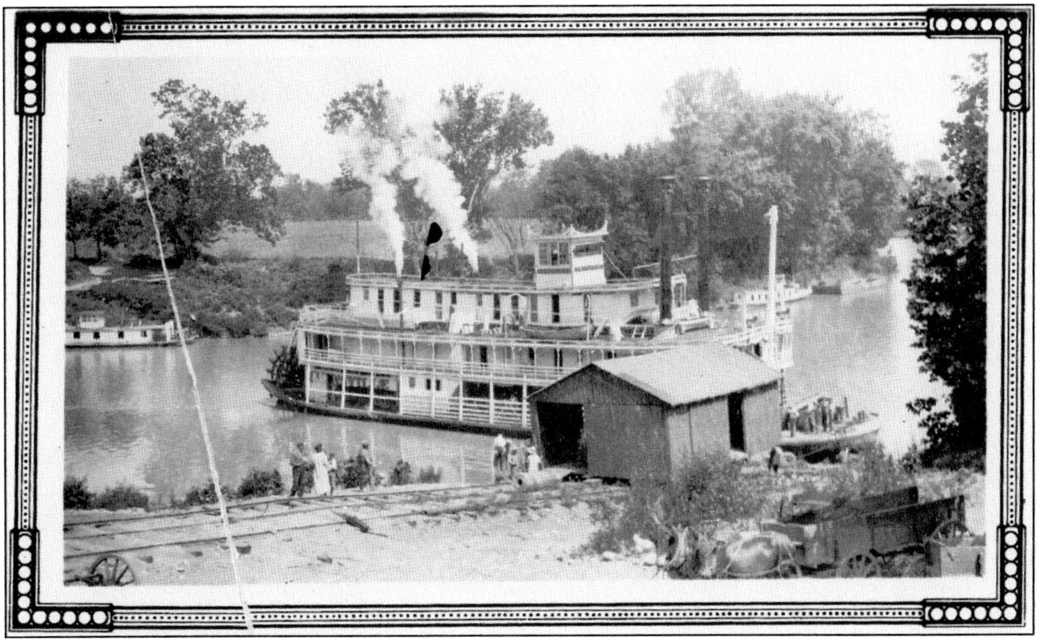

The steamer *Evansville* is docked at the Morgantown landing. The dock house was pulled up and down the riverbank on rails according to the river elevation. The Morgantown landing was at mile 143.3 on the Green River. Charles W. Hill was the wharfmaster. The locally owned towboat *Morgantown* is tied up on the north bank across the river.

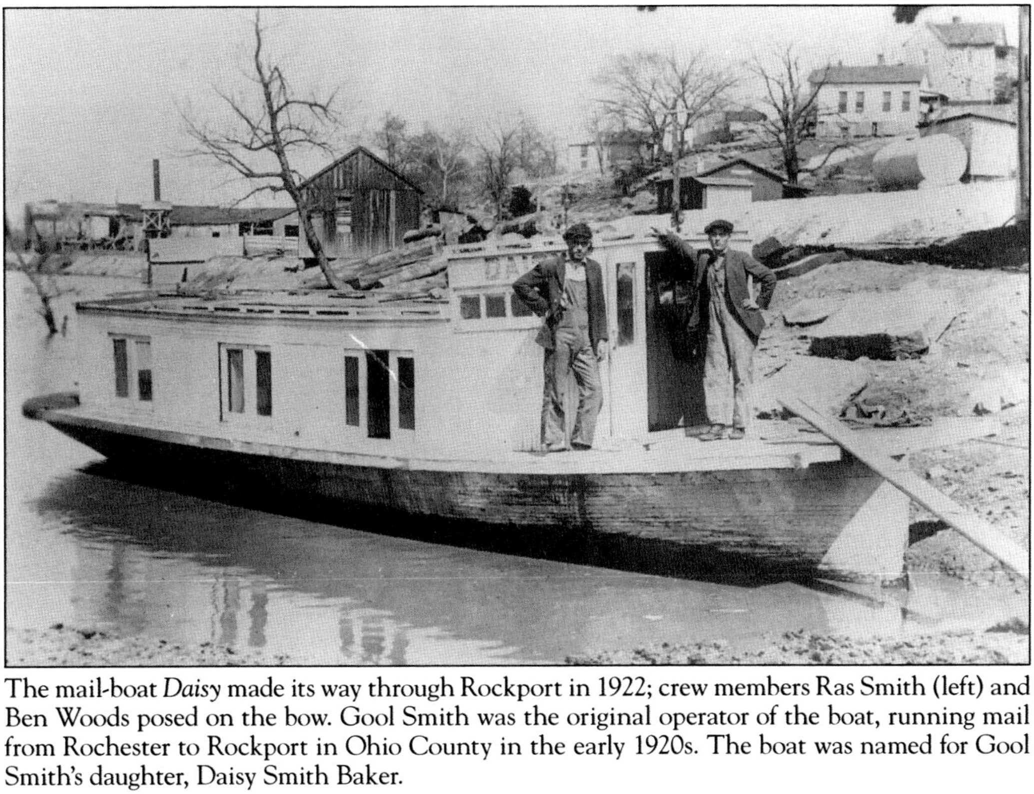

The mail-boat *Daisy* made its way through Rockport in 1922; crew members Ras Smith (left) and Ben Woods posed on the bow. Gool Smith was the original operator of the boat, running mail from Rochester to Rockport in Ohio County in the early 1920s. The boat was named for Gool Smith's daughter, Daisy Smith Baker.

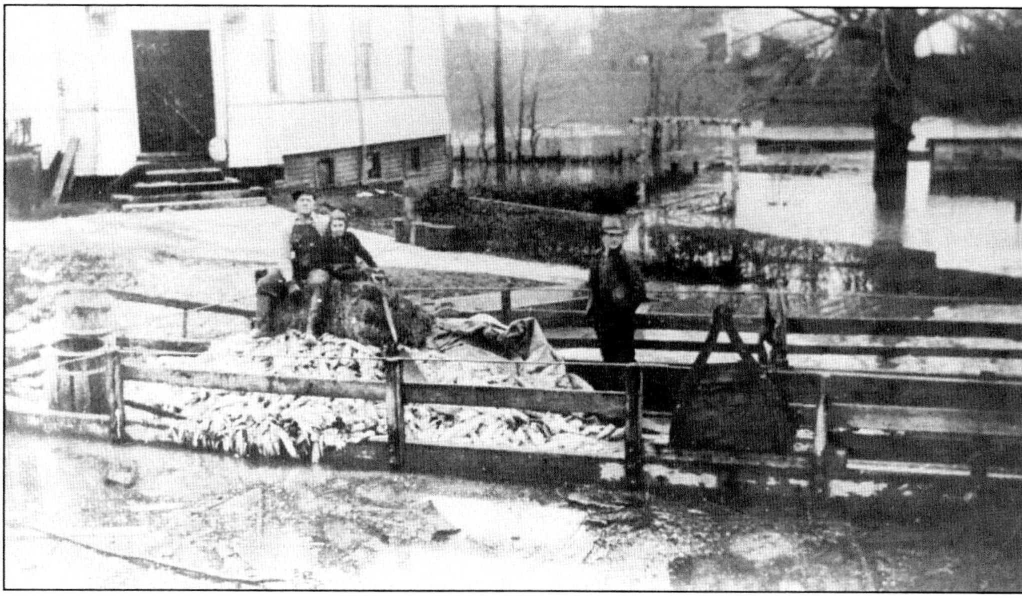

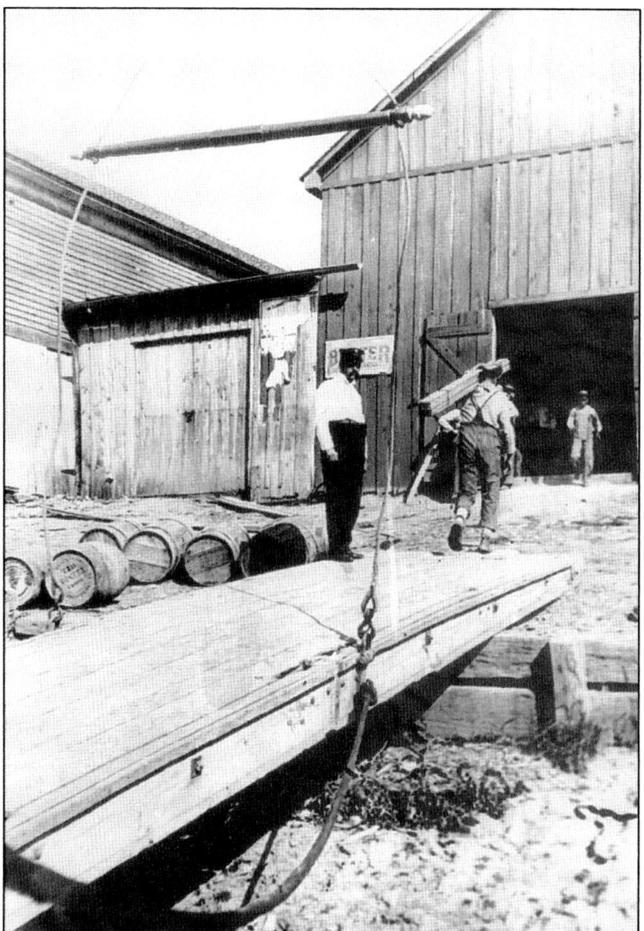

During the 1937 flood, water reached the highest recorded levels in Rochester. Here, the ferryboat is loaded with corn and hay in front of the Rochester Christian Church on Russellville Street. The image provides an idea of the flood's magnitude. Surveying the damage are, from left to right, Carroll Brown, Jean Wester, and Henry Smith.

Capt. Charles Sturgeon (left) observes roustabouts unloading freight from his packet boat *Bowling Green* into the Rochester warehouse. Sturgeon piloted all three boats named *Bowling Green*. The location of the Rochester warehouse is now home to Jenkins Bait Shop.

These handsome young Rochester residents were photographed in 1905 or 1906. They are, from left to right, (first row) Bunnie Wood, Hazel Westerfield, ? Schroeter, and ? Hunt; (second row) Ernest Tipton, Mildred Craig, Earl Holder, and Carson McPherson; (third row) Georgia Willis, Thixton Smith, Viola Bowles, Cook Downing, Sadie Evans, and E. Schroeter; (fourth row) Savil J. Manley, Sylvia Brown, Evans Hunt, and Blanche Willis.

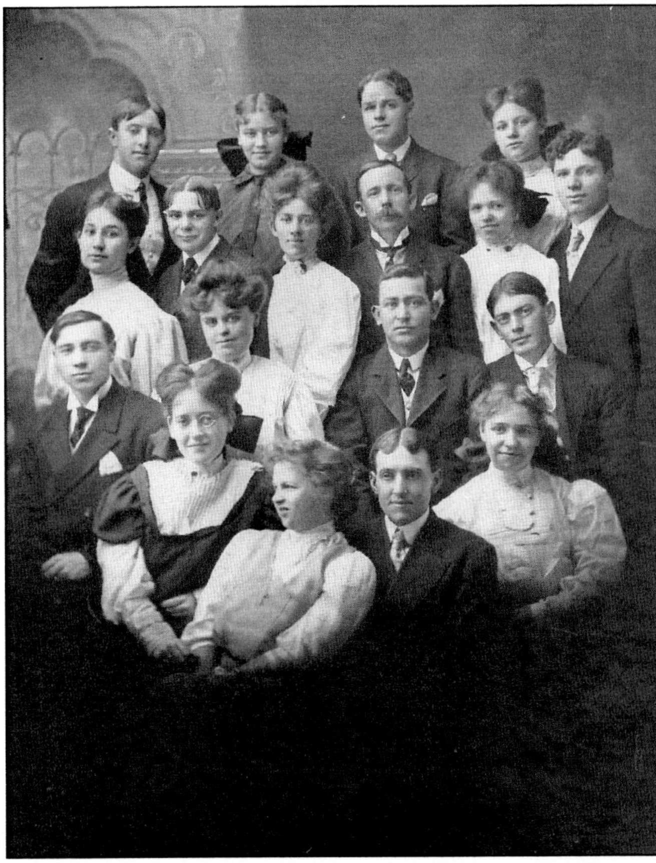

This building was originally Barbee's Store, but later housed Baker's Grocer, operated by Thurman and Urith Baker; the Bakers got the contract for the post office in 1953. This building burned down in the late 1970s and was replaced by a mobile structure.

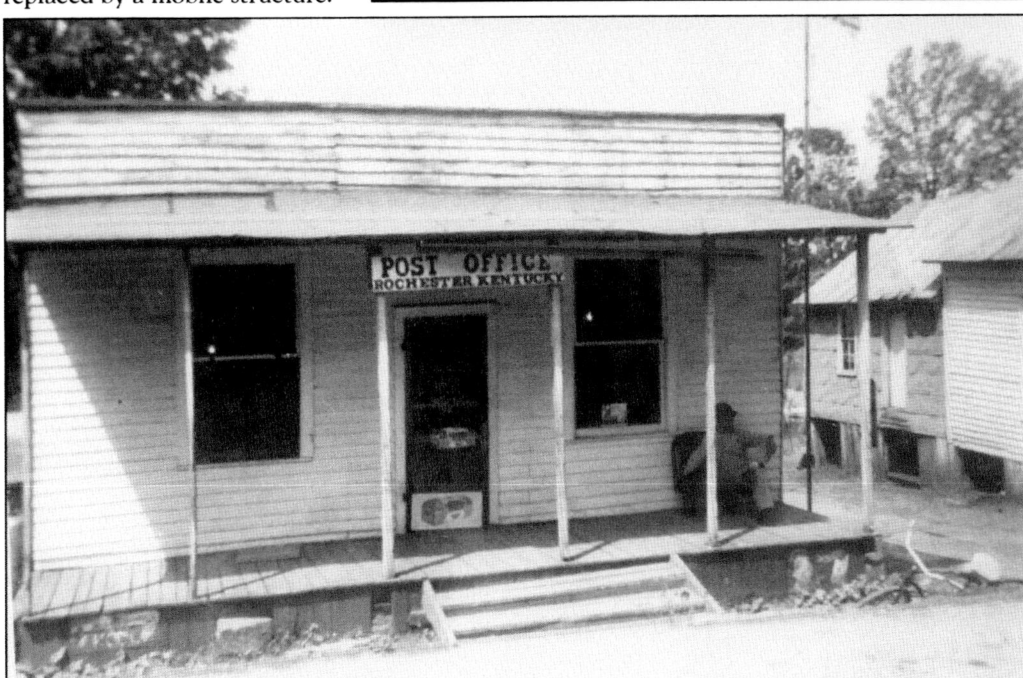

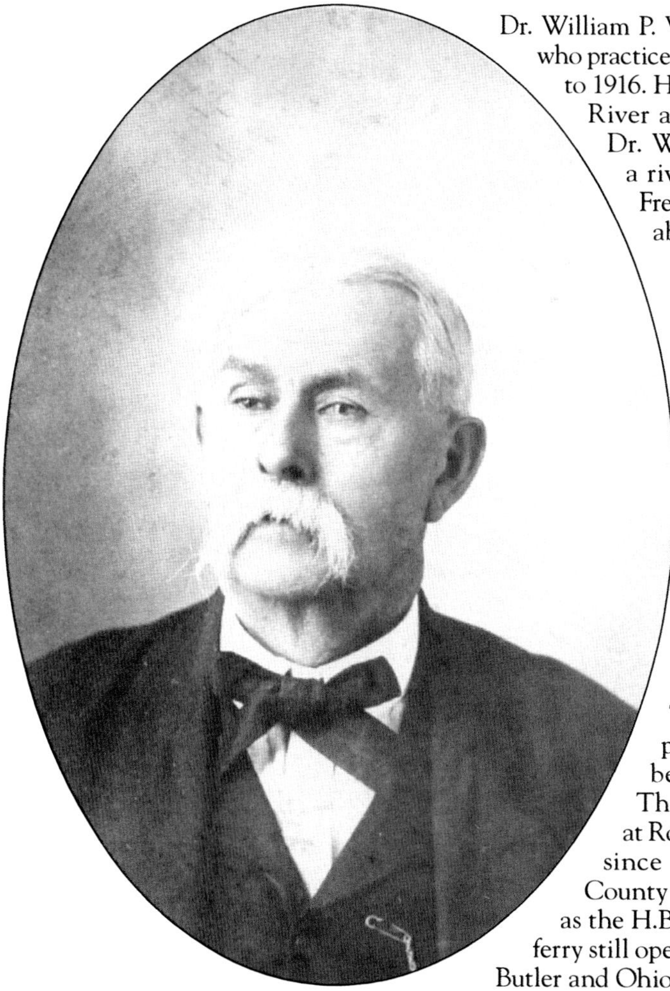

Dr. William P. Westerfield was an area physician who practiced medicine in Rochester from 1861 to 1916. He lived on the banks of the Green River at the end of Russellville Street. Dr. Westerfield's son, Oliver, became a riverboat pilot, and his other son, Fred, was killed in a riverboat accident about five miles below Rochester.

This wagon, horse, and family prepare to cross the river by ferry before the days of automobiles. There were at least two other ferries at Rochester, but this one has survived since 1802, eight years before Butler County was formed, when it was known as the H.B. Wiggins ferry. A county-owned ferry still operates at this site, located between Butler and Ohio Counties.

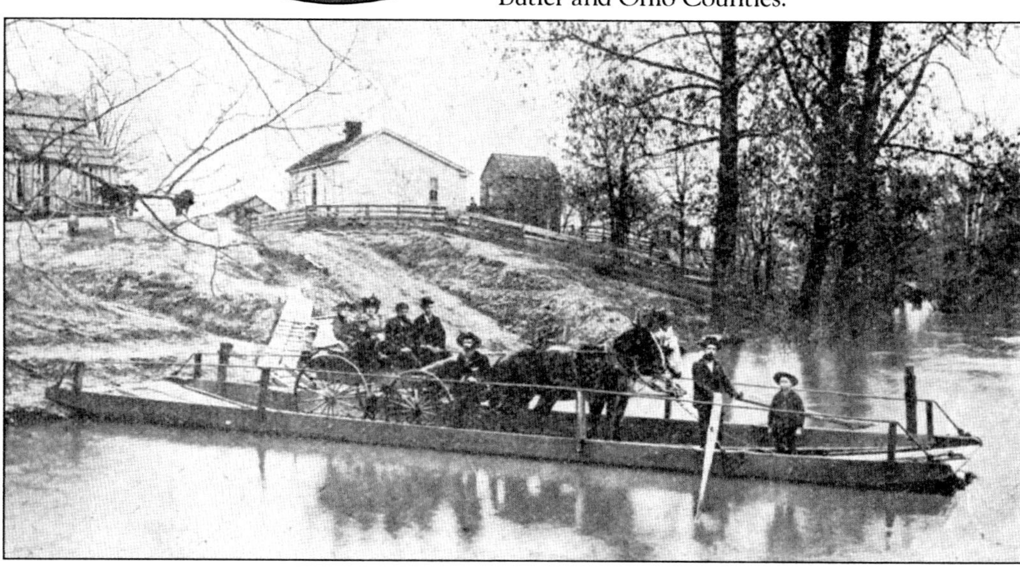

Eight

WOODBURY

In the 1790s, the James and Thomas Wand families and a Young family carved out homesteads in the area that would become Woodbury. In November 1806, Thomas Wand constructed a milldam about two-thirds of the way across the Green River. Other settlers did not move into the area until construction of the slackwater navigation system began in 1837, which included the building of Lock and Dam No. 4 at Woodbury. Willie Smith operated a cooper's shop, making barrels, hogsheads, and kegs, and James Carson opened a saddle shop. On April 5, 1847, the Lock No. 4 post office opened; a month later, the name was changed to the Wood Berry post office. The origin of the name is unknown, but a town was laid out and lots were sold beginning in 1852. In February 1854, the town of Woodbury was officially incorporated by an act of the Kentucky legislature.

The town quickly grew after the opening of the steamboat trade in 1841. In 1860, it was Butler County's largest town, with a total population of 175, including 12 African Americans. During this period, the town included a gristmill, a carding mill, an ax-handle factory, tobacco barns, a bank, two hotels, six general stores, and a blacksmith shop. In 1912, the US Army Corps of Engineers established a Green and Barren River Maintenance Headquarters in Woodbury. Woodbury thrived until 1927, when the Corps moved its headquarters to Paducah. The town has experienced a steady decline since; in 2000, the population was 87.

Two Woodbury natives, Thomas Hines and Andrew Hamilton, led the two most famous prison breaks of the Civil War. Additionally, of the nine Kentucky men to achieve the rank of admiral in the US Navy, two were born in Woodbury—Adm. Claude Bloch and Rear Adm. Wellington Hines.

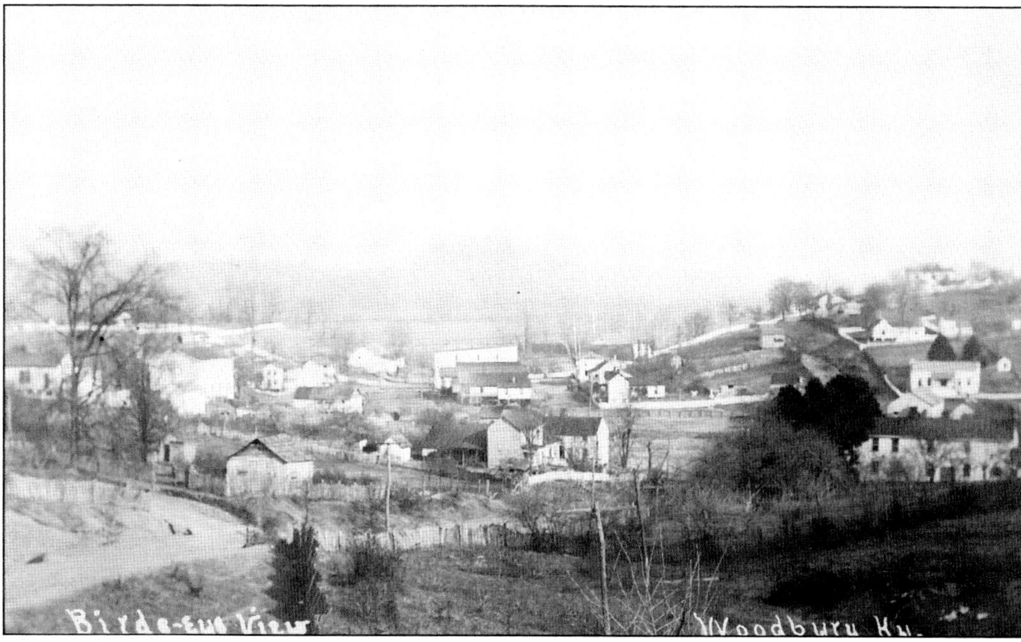

This bird's-eye view of Woodbury demonstrates the quaint quality of the early village nestled between the hills surrounding it on three sides and the river at the far end of the valley. This image, taken from atop Schoolhouse Hill, captures most of the early town.

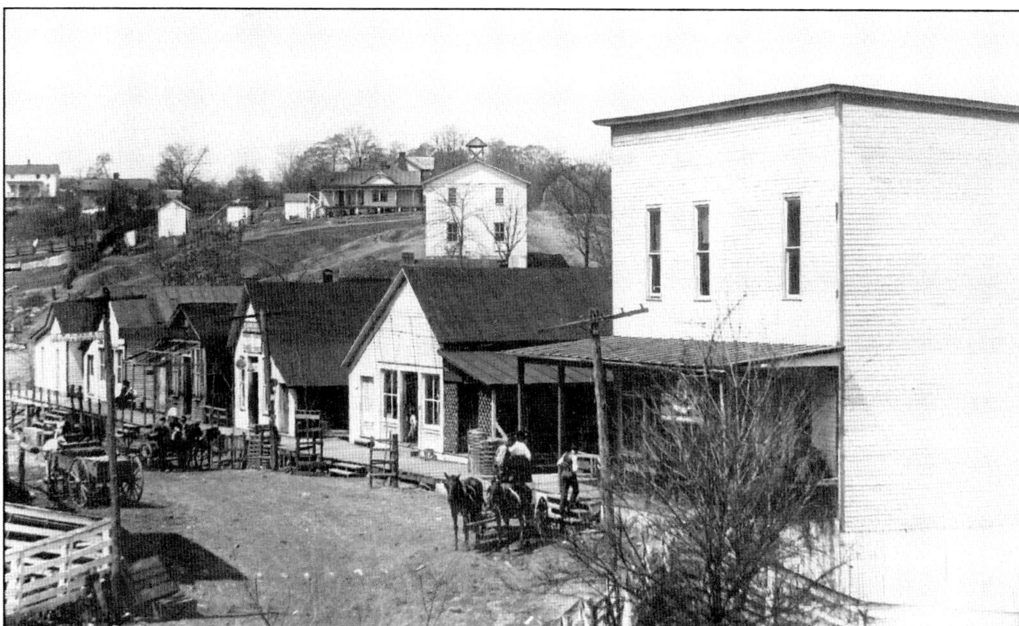

This postcard provides a good view of the businesses along the northeastern side of Main Street. The two-story building in the forefront is believed to be Brown's Cash Store. The white fencing at lower left surrounds the lock and dam property. The two-story church on the hill was built in 1853 as Union Church and is now United Methodist Church; since 1854, the second floor of the church has housed the Masonic Lodge.

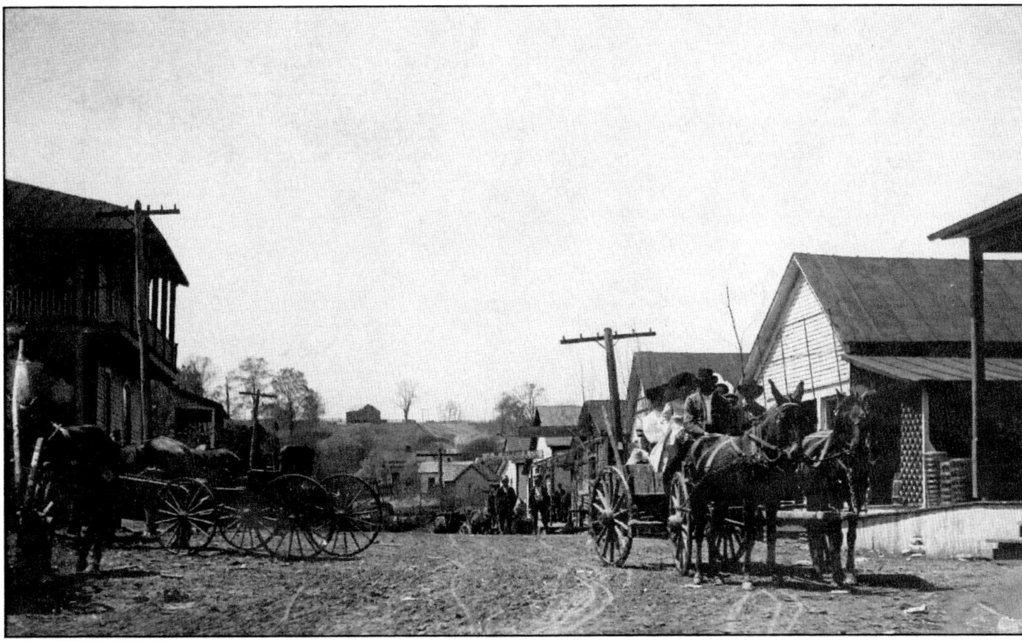

Woodbury appears to be a busy place in this 1890 photograph of Main Street. Notice that there was already a telephone system. The two-story building at left is the Woodbury Deposit Bank.

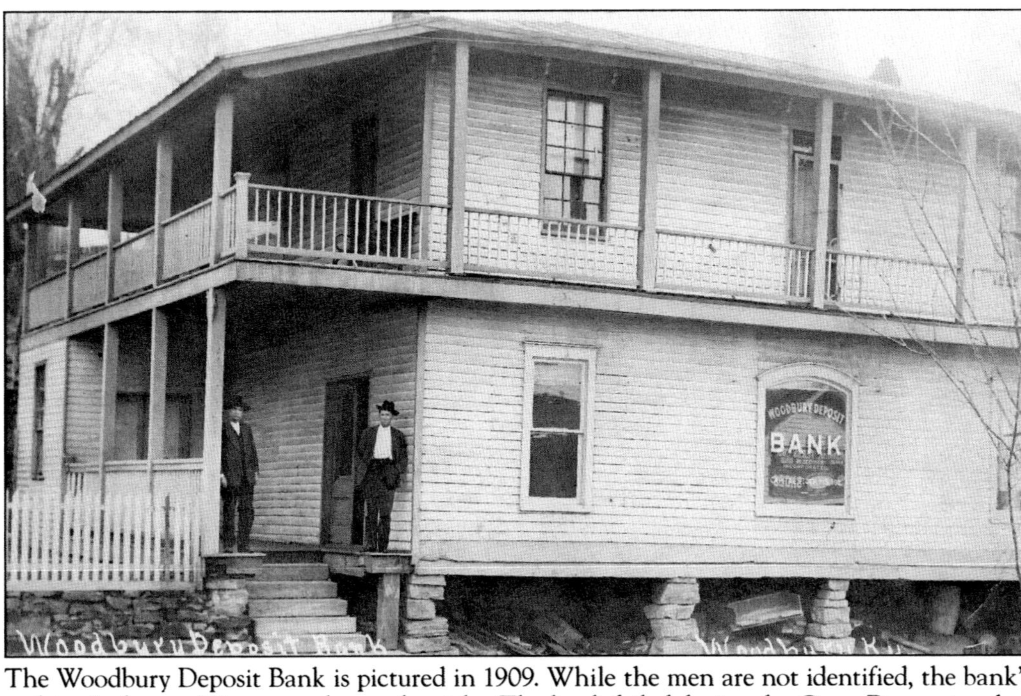

The Woodbury Deposit Bank is pictured in 1909. While the men are not identified, the bank's cashier, Lafayette Hines, may be on the right. The bank failed during the Great Depression, but thanks to the work of Hines, no one lost money. The Adolphus Bloch family, including future US Navy admiral Claude Bloch, lived above the bank.

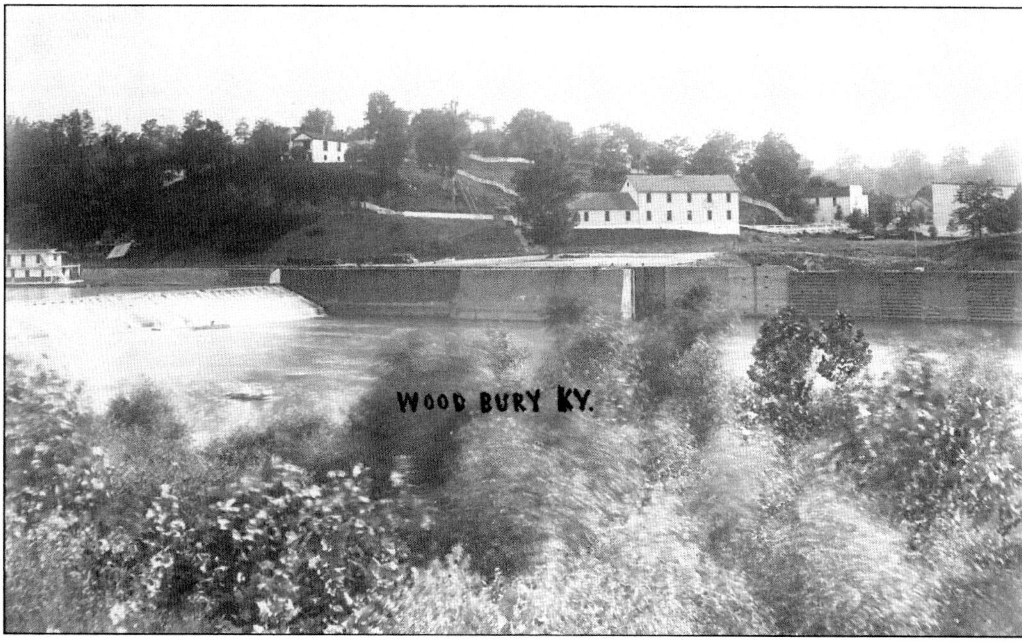

This photograph above provides a view from the north side of the Green River looking across to the US Army Corps of Engineers' Lock and Dam No. 4. The warehouse is just above the locks. Tied up outside the upper lock guide wall is the Corps's shanty boat, which was used for office space before the brick office building and superintendent's home were completed in 1913. The photograph below was taken from the top of the hill, where the Green River Museum is now located. The roofline of the government warehouse is visible at the bottom of the image, under the bluff. Two steamers are also visible—one preparing to enter the lock's upper guide wall and the other tied outside.

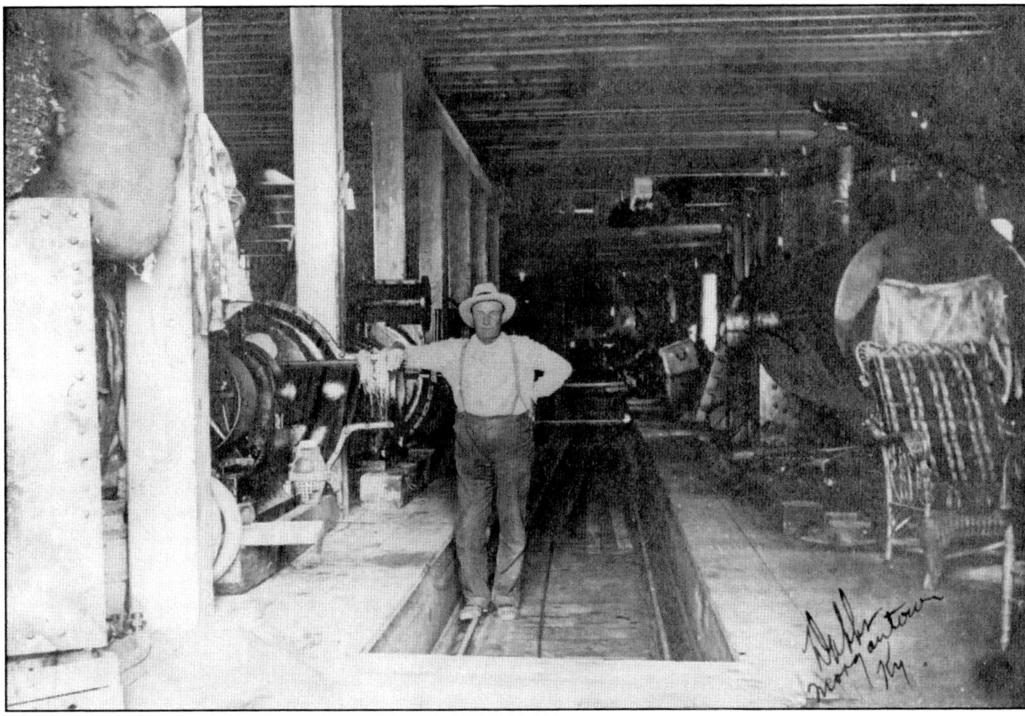

This rare photograph shows the interior of the US Army Corps of Engineers' warehouse and machine shop. The small railroad track in the center (where the man is standing) ran down to the locks to facilitate the unloading of boats and the hauling of freight back to the warehouse.

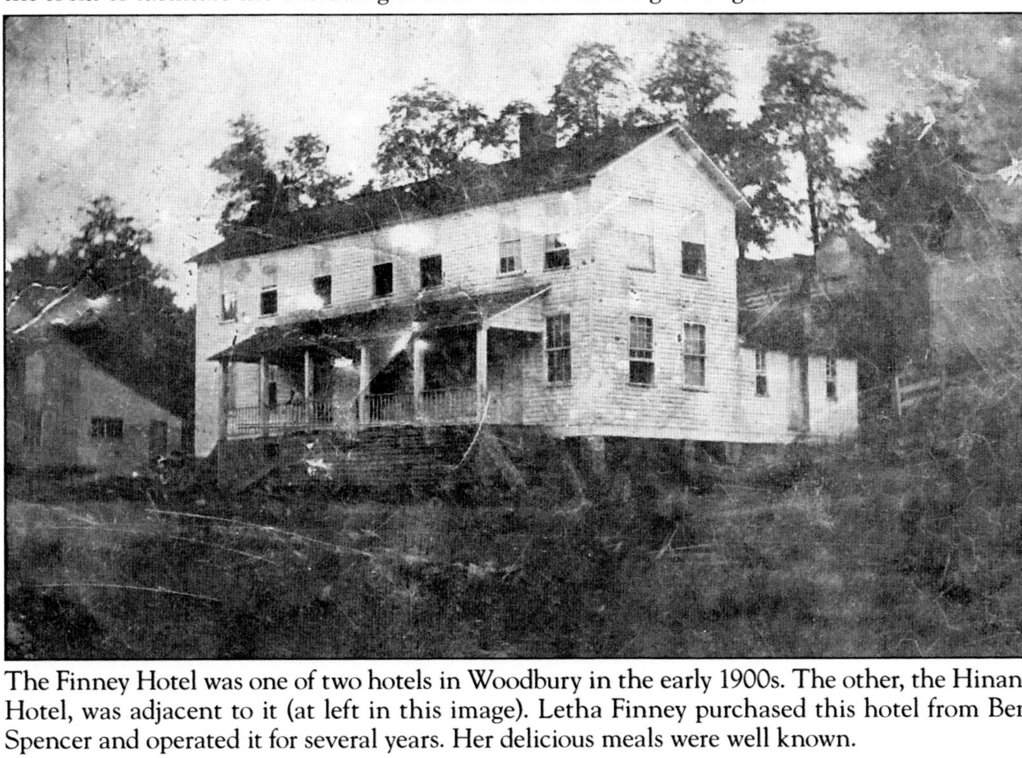

The Finney Hotel was one of two hotels in Woodbury in the early 1900s. The other, the Hinant Hotel, was adjacent to it (at left in this image). Letha Finney purchased this hotel from Ben Spencer and operated it for several years. Her delicious meals were well known.

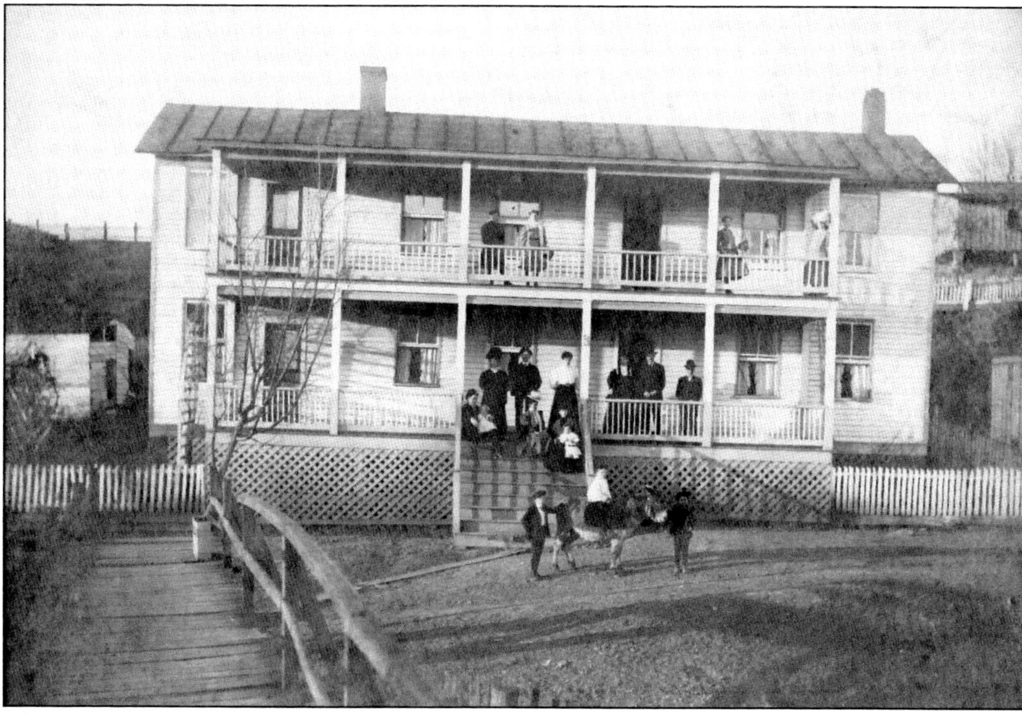

The Hinant Hotel, owned by John and Elizabeth Hinant, still stands today, although it is now vacant and boarded up. This establishment was once the most popular in Woodbury and featured a boardwalk from the main street to the hotel.

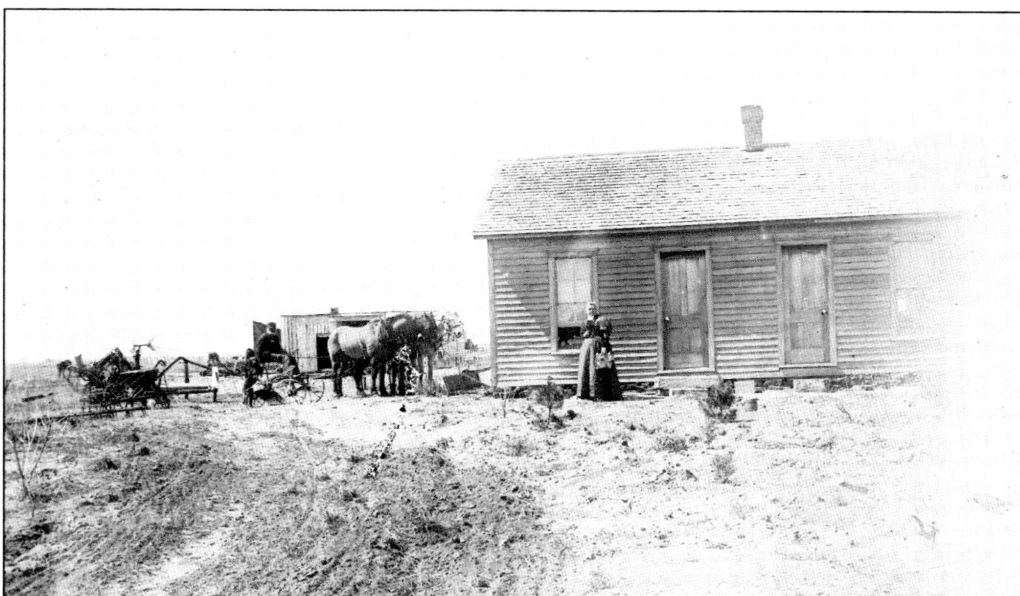

Burlie Burchfield sits on his John Deere "Sulky" plow with his son, Burlie Jr., behind the plow and his wife, Sally Hinant Burchfield, standing in front of their old home place. They ran a well-equipped modern farm at the time, as evidenced by the McCormick reaper to the left.

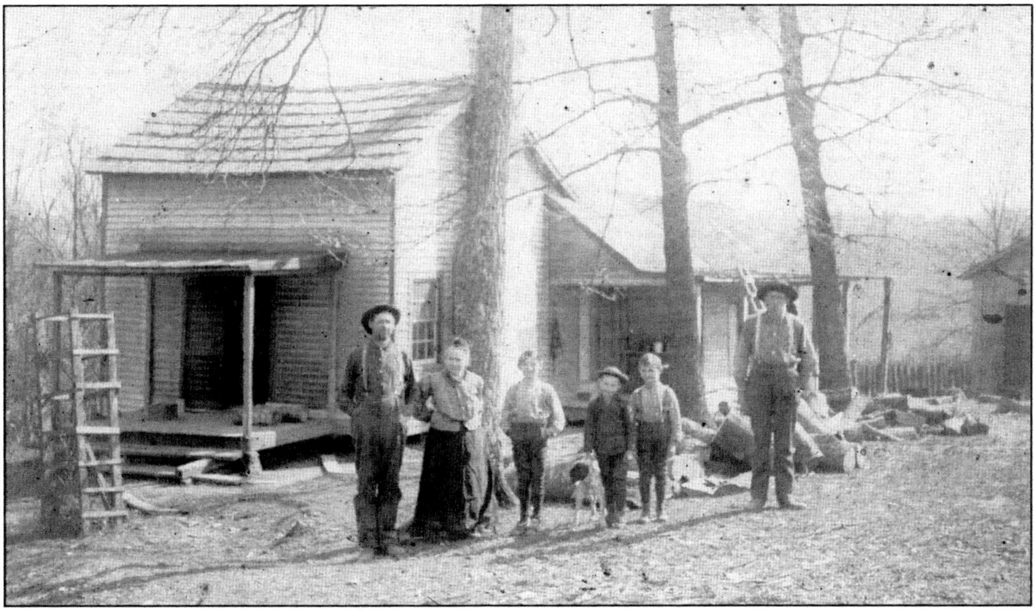

An unidentified Woodbury family posed for this photograph around 1900. Note that the small, shotgun-style home is too narrow for windows in the front—typical at the time. This picture, which is from the Burchfield collection, most likely features Burchfield relatives.

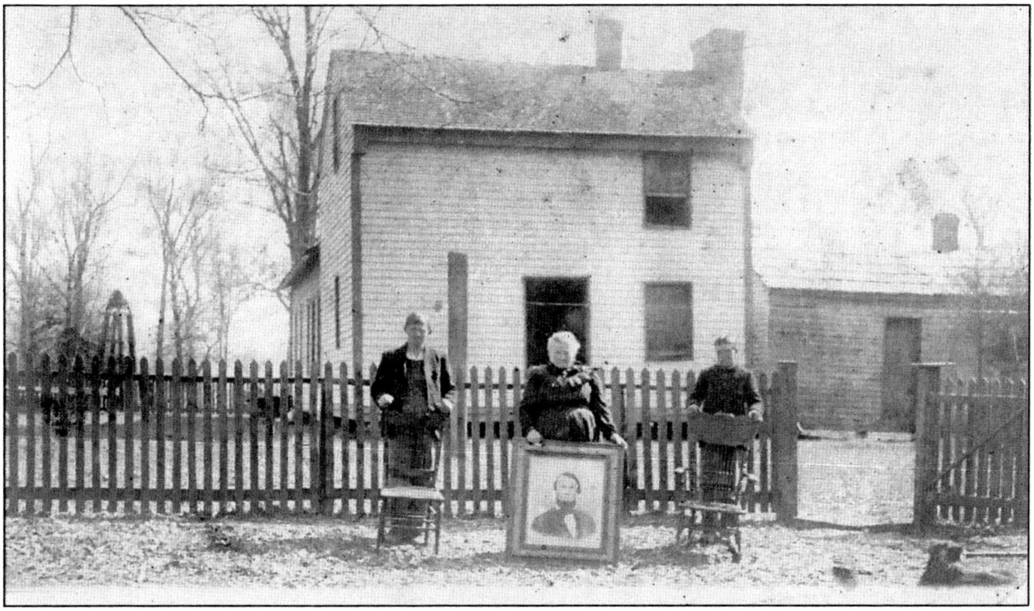

These people, who may also be related to the Burchfield family, pose with two empty chairs and a large portrait, perhaps in remembrance of recently lost family members.

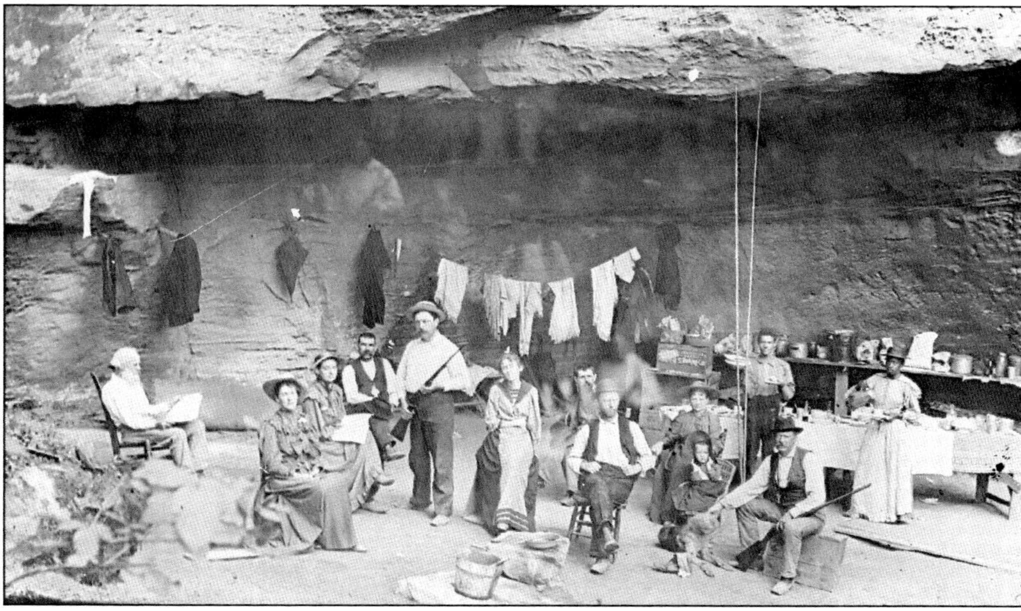

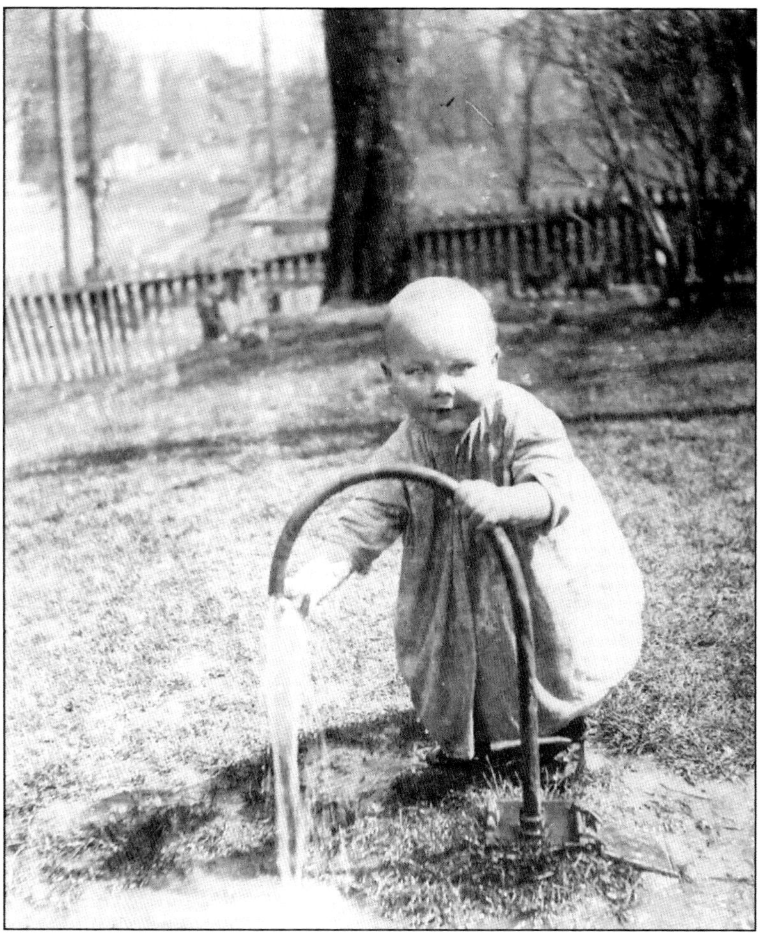

This group enjoys an extended hunting and camping adventure just below the dam in Woodbury, on the left bank exiting the lock. The man seated with the rifle at far right is Will Wright, and the photographer was recorded as William Wortman.

In this 1912 image, a young Burchfield relative retrieves water from a hose, most likely at the US Army Corps of Engineers grounds in Woodbury, as it was the only place in Butler County (besides Morgantown) with running water at the time.

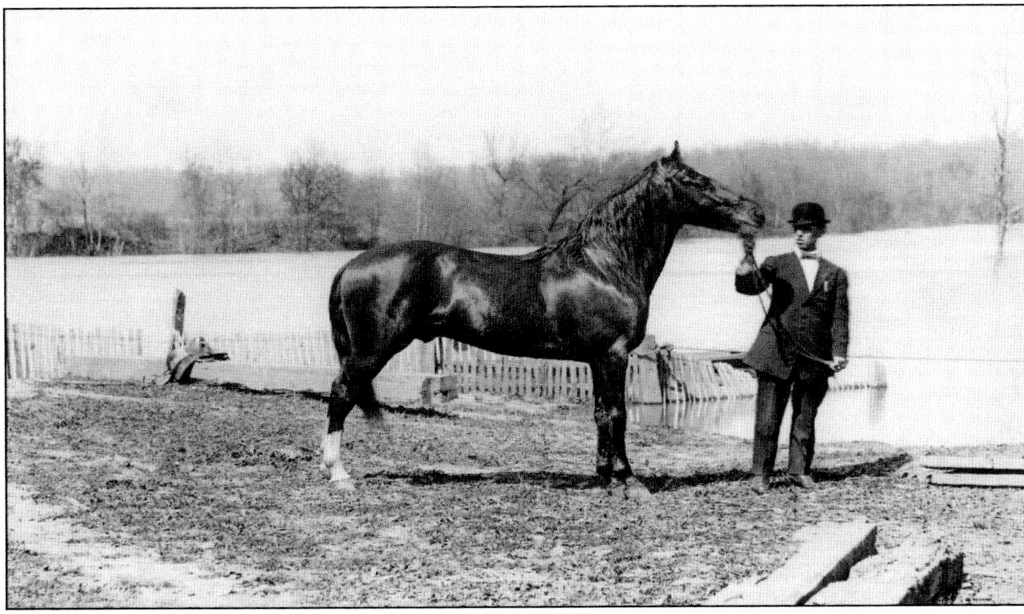

According to the 1912 *Register of the American Saddle-Horse Breeders' Association*, this horse, Frisco Dare, was owned by Dr. Elwood Wand, who sometimes used horses to visit his patients. The register stated that Frisco Dare was a bay stallion born in Beaver Dam, Kentucky, in 1907. The man in the picture is unidentified.

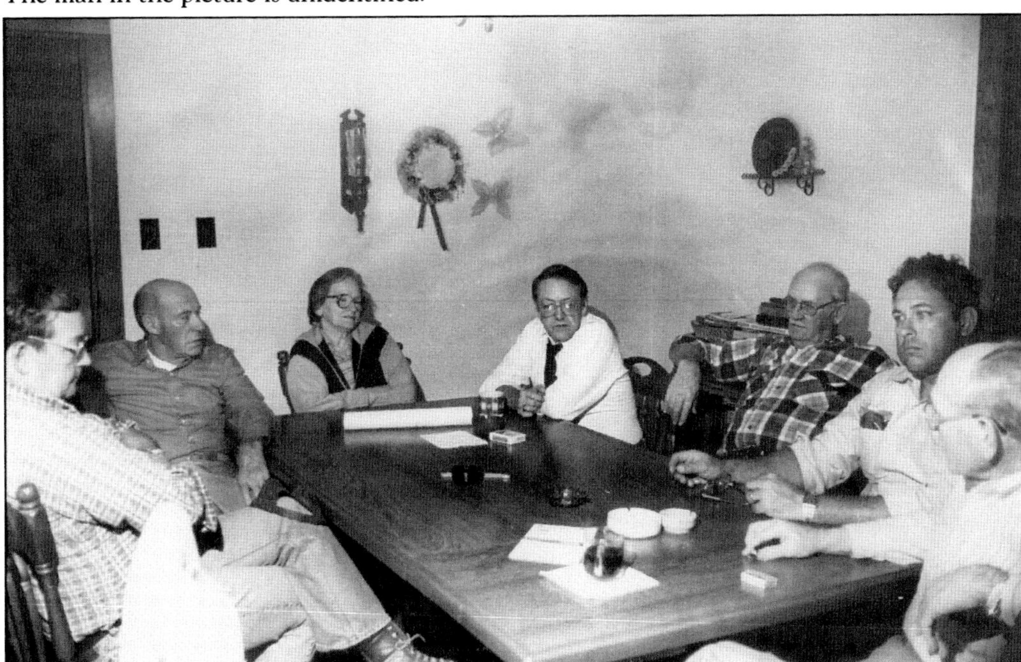

Woodbury was originally incorporated in 1854, and its government functioned into the 1940s before becoming inactive. In the 1980s, this group of citizens decided to reactivate the government. They are, clockwise from left, David Dotson, Euda House, Joyce Neighbors, William Lawrence, Emory Morris, Russell Towe, and Maurice Hines. The charter was reactivated by Gov. Martha Layne Collins in January 1986, and Lawrence was appointed mayor.

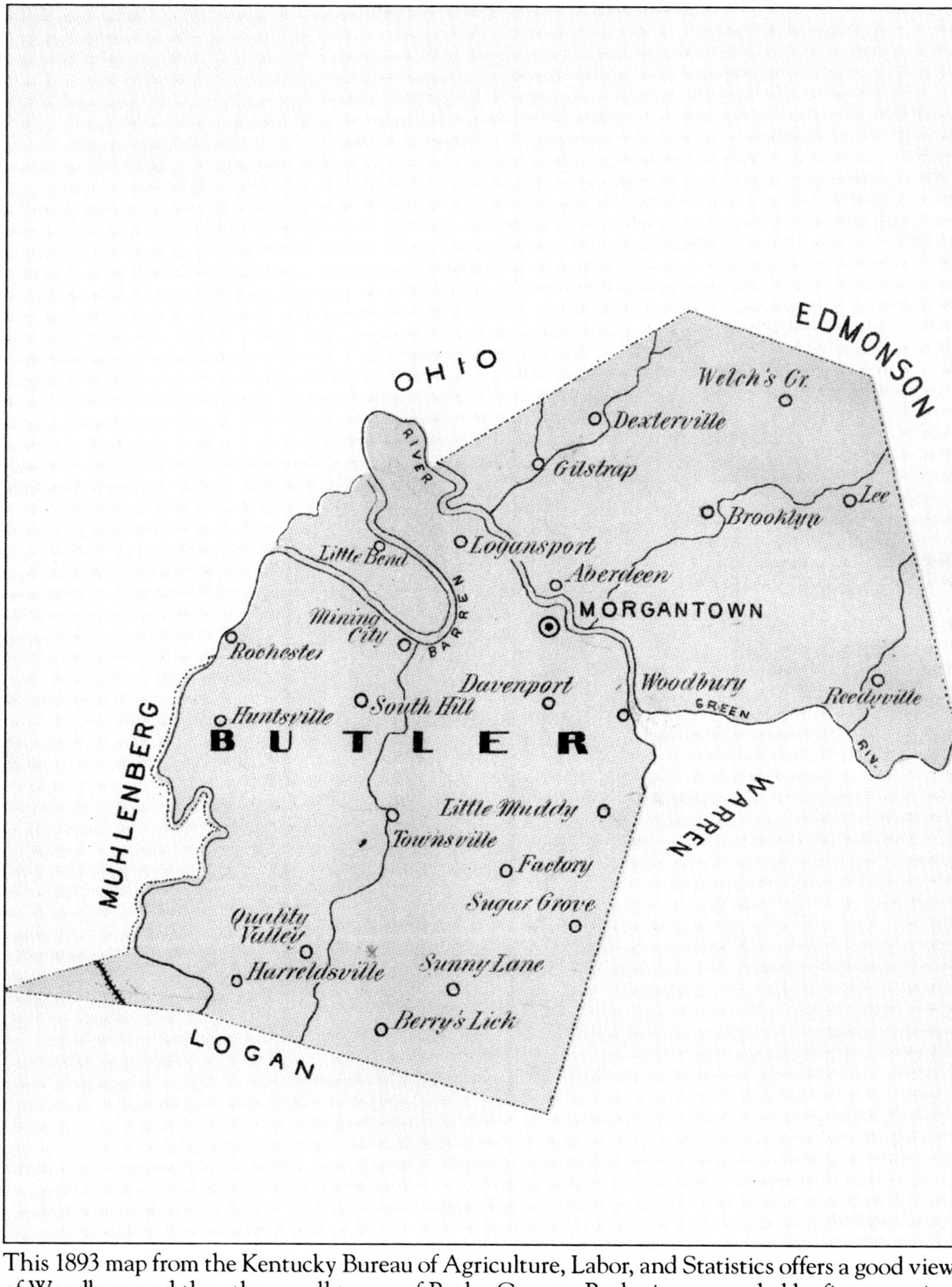

This 1893 map from the Kentucky Bureau of Agriculture, Labor, and Statistics offers a good view of Woodbury and the other small towns of Butler County. Butler is surrounded by five counties, including its parent counties, Logan and Ohio. Although the Green River is most often associated with the county, the Barren River joins the Green at Woodbury. The report also noted that there were no railroads in Butler County, and the land was selling at an average of about $7 to $8 per acre. The report also lists "the lands hilly, timber mostly cut, [but there remains] some splendid bottom lands along Barren River."

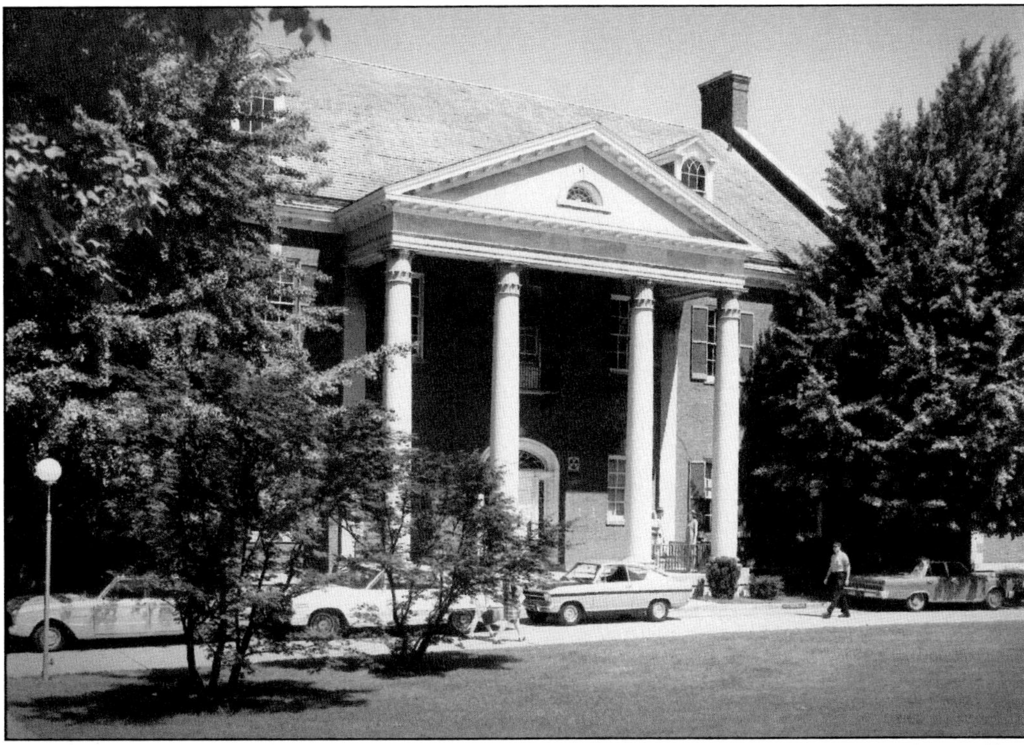

The Kentucky Library & Museum at Western Kentucky University was conceived to collect and preserve Kentucky's historical materials. Although the focus has expanded, the mission has remained unchanged. Everyone is welcome to explore the rare holdings of the library, which includes one of the finest available collections of family and Civil War research materials.

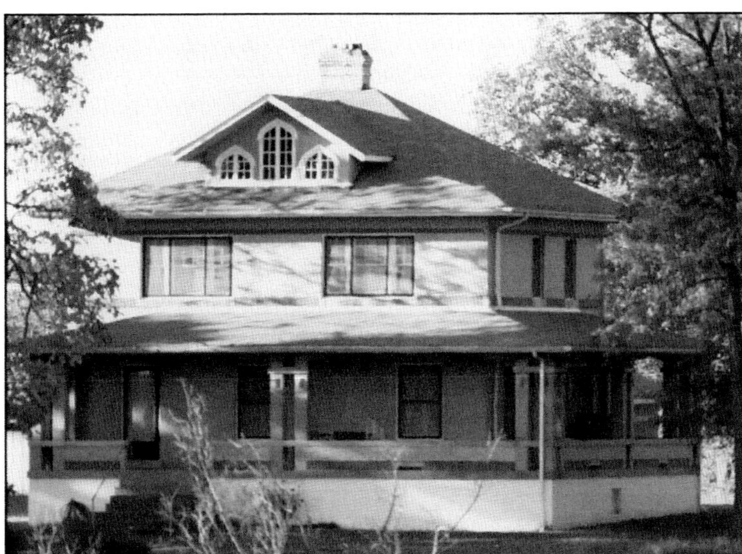

The Green River Museum exists to preserve and protect the history of Butler County and is housed in the historic structures that were originally the government's headquarters for Green River navigation. This house features exhibits detailing life in Butler County in the past century.

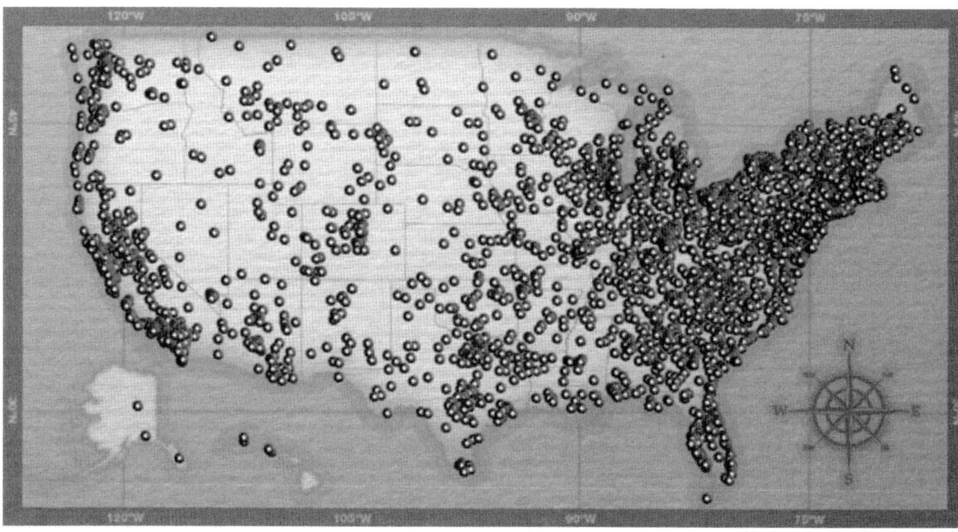